NAMESAKE

NAMESAKE

REFLECTIONS ON A WARRIOR WOMAN

N. S. NUSEIBEH

OLIVE
BRANCH
PRESS

An imprint of Interlink Publishing Group, Inc.
Northampton, Massachusetts

First American edition published in 2024 by

Olive Branch Press
An imprint of Interlink Publishing Group
46 Crosby Street
Northampton, Massachusetts, 01060
www.interlinkbooks.com

Published in Great Britain by Canongate Books, Edinburgh

Library of Congress Cataloging-in-Publication Data available
ISBN 978-1-62371-687-5

Printed and bound in the United States of America

There is a little girl in West London whose first name is Nusayba;
apparently, she keeps ending up on her classroom blackboard's "Naughty List."
Since Nusayba is her namesake as much as mine, this book is for her;
and for my fiercely brilliant niece;
and for anyone who needs a warrior woman to stand beside them.

"To survive by loving each other means to love our ancestors too. To know their pain, struggles, and joys. It means to love our collective memory, who we are, where we come from."

—Susan Abulhawa, *Against the Loveless World*

"None of the Arab countries I know has proper state archives, public record offices or official libraries any more than any of them has a decent control over their monuments or antiquities, the history of their cities or individual works of architecture—mosques, palaces, schools. What I have is a sense of a sprawling, teeming history off the page, out of sight and hearing, beyond reach, largely unrecoverable. Our history is mostly written by foreigners—visiting scholars, intelligence agents—agents we rely on personal and disorganized collective memory, gossip almost, and the embrace of a family or knowable community to carry us forward in time."

— Edward Said, "In Memory of Tahia"

"This book is intended to be a narrative of recollection, gliding toward the areas where memory breaks down, dates get mixed up, and events softly blur together, as in the dreams from which we draw our strength."

— Fatema Mernissi, *Women and Islam*

CONTENTS

Preface 11

Author's Note 13

Map of Arabia, Seventh Century CE 14

Timeline of Events in Islam in the Seventh Century CE 15

Introduction 17

Bettinjan 25

Warrior, Worrier 39

House Guests 57

The Seder 65

Ummah/Ma 83

The Road to Damascus 105

Good Girls, Nasty Women 123

Tied Tongues 141

Superwoman 153

Bint 165

Endnotes 183

Further reading 215

Permission credits 219

Acknowledgements 221

PREFACE

The following essays were written and finalized before the events that unfolded during and after October 7, 2023. As I write these words, days before this book goes to print, I have no idea how long this war will last, whether Gaza will still exist by the time of publication. There is no point writing down the number of children killed; that number will have been dwarfed by the time you read this. I hope, therefore, that you will forgive those portions of the text that are now out of date, and the glaring absence of reference to these most recent atrocities.

My intention with this book was to bring certain narratives—Muslim, Arab and Palestinian ones—into the cultural consciousness of those outside the Arab world; to explore, as per Cathy Park Hong, the minor feelings inherent in living those narratives. I wanted to write for others who know these same narratives well, and also to show those who don't how much we actually have in common. I hoped, in this way, to bring us all closer to each other. Maybe, on some level, I also hoped to humanize myself in the eyes of those who cannot see the human in the Muslim, the Arab, the Palestinian. To make myself worthy of dignity, of statehood, of life. Look at me, I write in these essays, I'm not so different from you. And wouldn't you want freedom?

It is clear to me now that this is futile.

Instead, reader, whoever you are, I simply hope that whenever you open this book, you think of Gaza.

AUTHOR'S NOTE

The stories about Nusayba that I retell in these essays are drawn mainly from the hadith—the canon of traditions about the Prophet Muhammad and his companions—as well as from Ibn Ishaq's definitive *Life of Muhammad*. Though I have let my imagination add some spice for flavor, the meat of the stories is unchanged, and the dialogue is quoted as it appears in the traditions.

MAP OF ARABIA,
SEVENTH CENTURY CE

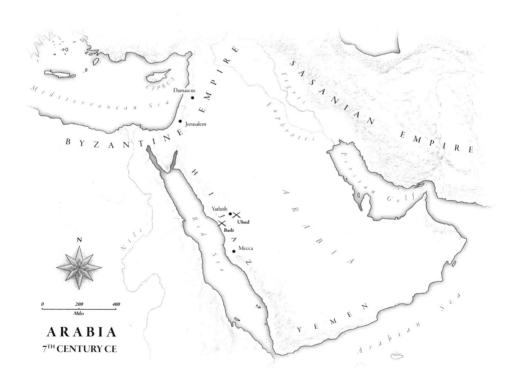

TIMELINE OF EVENTS IN ISLAM IN THE SEVENTH CENTURY CE

610   The first revelation of the Quran in the cave at Hira

622   Muhammad's migration to Yathrib

624   Battle of Badr

625   Battle of Uhud

627   Battle of the Trench

629   Muhammad's pilgrimage back to Mecca

630   Conquest of Mecca; Battle of Hunayn

632   Death of Muhammad; Abu Bakr chosen as caliph

637   Conquest of Jerusalem

644   Uthman becomes third caliph

656   Ali becomes fourth caliph

661   Death of Ali; succeeded by Mu'awiyah

INTRODUCTION

It is 1999, and I am in my grandmother's house on Nablus Road in Jerusalem, a road which happens to go along the 1949 Armistice Line, also known as the Green Line, dividing East from West. My grandmother sits in her spot on the gray embroidered sofa beside my great-aunt, both frowning at me imperiously as the former lectures me about the importance of fasting. She hasn't asked whether I'm fasting this year—she assumes that I am, and I don't mention that I have just enjoyed a bottle of iced tea on my way over, having walked to her house from my primary school by way of the grocery store—but she takes the opportunity to remind me how serious she is about it while *The Bold and the Beautiful* is on an ad break. She *is* serious. She will continue to fast every year until her health starts to fail her, and even then, will only break her fast in order to take small sips of water. After she passes away, over a decade later, our dedication to the seriousness of Ramadan will slacken; we still wait impatiently for the cannon to sound in order to eat our first proper meal of the day, but now only my father will go without food or drink from sunrise to sunset. The rest of us will smugly sip our morning coffee, and then, at our iftar, enjoy the special foods that are reserved for Ramadan: eggs and basterma, the spicy lamb bacon; syrup-soaked atayef, nut-filled pancakes; colorful juices from dried fruit meant to "keep the system moving." At the end of Ramadan, we will go through all the rituals of the Feast: the men of the extended family, all in suits, will go from one house to another being served cardamom-rich coffee or treacly orange juice and sugared almonds by the women waiting there. We will eat a lamb stuffed with saffron-flavored rice studded with roasted pine nuts, dollops of cool yogurt on the side, followed by round, crumbly, pistachio-filled biscuits for dessert, dipped into a sugary, thick white cream.

Now, though—during the ad break—our Ramadan breakfast is still a few hours away. After my grandmother finishes her lecture, my great-aunt, who visits every few days, gives me a hard look. "Are you English or are you Arab?" she asks me in Arabic, glaring, her bun impossibly high on her head. "I'm a Palestinian Muslim Arab from the Nuseibeh family," I tell her, my answer well rehearsed from the thousand and one times we have been through this ritual. "Descended from Nusayba bint Ka'ab al Khazrajia."[1]

"Bravo!" she says, clapping delightedly.

If you are Muslim, chances are you will be familiar with Nusayba bint Ka'ab (نسيبة بنت كعب), sometimes known as Um 'Umarah. You will know her story—that she was one of the first women to convert to Islam in seventh-century Arabia, that she became one of the companions of the Prophet Muhammad, and that she is, in particular, famous for losing an arm while defending him in one of multiple battles. She has, in Islam, almost folkloric status; many Muslim girls are named Nusayba (نسيبة) for that reason. In my case, though, the myth runs even deeper: that the Nuseibeh (نسيبة) family is directly descended from her, making her, in family lore at least, our ancestor and our namesake. Little has been written about her, a lot is contradictory, and whether she even really existed is up for debate—yet she remains an important proto-feminist figure, cited in the works of famous scholars and feminists like Leila Ahmed, Nawal El Saadawi and Abdelwahab Bouhdiba. As such, Nusayba is easy for me to imagine, as I sit curled up here on my bed, in a slightly cold room in Oxford, thirteen hundred or so years later: a stout, muscled woman atop a horse, licking sweat from her lips as she strings a bow one-handed.

I did not set out to write a book about Jerusalem. In fact, I intentionally chose a subject matter—my Arab warrior ancestor—that I felt would be broader, less controversial, more fiction than fact. But it turns out that it is impossible to write about early Islam without reference to Jerusalem, and impossible for me, as a Palestinian, to explore the personal without reference to the political. Being Palestinian, especially one born and raised in East Jerusalem, is difficult in ways that very few have taken the time to imagine, and to think about a Muslim warrior ancestor is to invoke questions that have clear bearing on the "conflict": questions about what bravery looks like, about community, anger, loyalty and the glorification of violence. About what it is to be a warrior, to be religious, to be a Muslim woman, an Arab feminist. Although these questions do, I hope, have larger resonances, these are all subjects that have direct meaning and consequence to a Palestinian. And so I found that every essay I wrote ended up being, at its heart, about my much-disputed, much-coveted home.

That said, it is the warrior woman that sparked it all. Nusayba bint Ka'ab al Khazrajia, early convert, fierce protector of the Prophet, gender-bending rule breaker. Unfazed by pain or men. Prior to writing this book, Nusayba felt, to me, like a character from a children's story. Kan ya makan fi 'adim il zaman, my father would always begin, and then he would tell me a tale of a witch and a princess. *There was and there was not, in the depths of the past . . .* And sometimes I would find myself daydreaming, in amongst the princesses and the witches, of this ancient warrior woman, my family's namesake, our ancestor, who both was and was not. She developed a spectral presence on the edges of my thoughts: a fun fact I would bring out during drinking games; a skipped heartbeat at the mention of Arabia. At one point, soon after leaving Jerusalem to study at a university in the UK, she became, also, a rope I could grab if I felt my identity—as Muslim, as Arab, as Palestinian—slipping, or being forced, away. I may not be (Arab/Muslim/good/brave) enough, I would think, but somewhere deep inside me there is, perhaps, the kernel of someone who is.

I conceived of this book in the context of a cultural climate increasingly focused on both identity politics and legacy, two issues that, as a Palestinian, have been front and center for me for a very long time. In Britain and the US, though, I found myself struggling. I do not fit expectations of Arabness, Muslimness or Palestinianness. Half-English, I am light-skinned, fair-haired, American-accented (thank you, Hollywood), agnostic, mild-mannered, people-pleasing, quiet, shy, apologetic, studious. I am enormously privileged in myriad ways—hey, a famous ancestor will do that for a person—and also, simultaneously, have lived without many of the comforts, rights and freedoms that my peers in the UK or the US take for granted. My own stories of identity and legacy seemed too unwieldy for the wider cultural conversation taking place, my lived experiences stubbornly refusing to match the cultural narratives with which I seemed, constantly, to be presented.

There also seemed to be strange blind spots in people's efforts at revisiting their histories. In discussions of colonialism, it was rare for my fellow Brits to acknowledge, or even recognize, the British Empire's role in Palestine. Feminist societies I joined at university often seemed disorientingly Orientalist, with images of women in hijabs used as shorthand for gender oppression. (Members of these societies would frown and nod, or shake their heads in dismay; one earnest-faced attendee would inevitably say something solemn-toned along the lines of, "Girls, it's our *duty* to help these women.") Even where they were more intersectional, there still seemed to me an absence of Arab perspectives; I never heard mention of Nawal El Saadawi or Mona Eltahawy. Most of all, it struck me that, in conversations about and by Muslims outside the Arab world (such as in Britain, where, as Suhaiymah Manzoor-Khan has shown, anti-Islamism[2] is rampant and systemic[3]), there was very little room for the Muslimness I embody; that is, as a type of "cultural heritage inscribed within family traditions and behaviours,"[4] as Aziz Al-Azmeh puts it. The kind of neutral, secular connection to religion I see Christian and Jewish friends and writers wearing easily and without question, referencing Jewish or Christian tradition without being labeled "*religious*,"[5] let alone fanatical or extreme. Perhaps linked to this, there appeared to be little to no knowledge of Islamic culture or history and no awareness of how that culture and history are inseparable from European and American cultures and histories—indeed, how much of our histories are one and the same. Most of the time any connection is denied entirely. In the absence of this understanding, I saw a gulf between my worlds, and so I reached for Nusayba.

I cannot do justice in these essays to the richness of life in those early days of Islam, nor is it my intention. If your appetite for this history is whetted, then I will feel I have done something right—there are readings (listed at the end of this book) that can get you started. Instead, what I hope to show through these essays is how *interconnected* all of our concerns are, across time, across space. How close the Arabia of the seventh century is to the London of the twenty-first century. I write, in this collection, about issues that interest and affect many of us: about boundaries and anxiety, the appeal and impossibility of anger, violence and superheroes. About the inescapably gendered nature of food, about how our duty to remember is often at odds with the need to move on. About the ambivalence that can be felt around motherhood; the sanctity and power of language; and the complexity of Arab Muslim feminism.

There is a tradition in sociology of stating one's "positionality," highlighting the ways in which one's own perspectives and biases may have limited and influenced the interpretation and conducting of the research. This is important in academia because most social science is in some way empirical, making some truth-claims about cause and effect. Without awareness of the ways in which we, the researchers, shape the narratives of those truth-claims, we risk adopting an omniscience we don't possess, and this in turn affects our collective understanding of a phenomenon. It's inevitable that our views will be restricted by the various experiences and identities that define us. Sociological research accepts this. The important thing, though, is that we acknowledge these limitations, so that our work may be understood in context.

This book is not a piece of sociological research—far from it—and I'm not making any truth-claims about cause and effect. Instead, these essays are rooted in the personal because I believe the personal is the only perspective I can honestly offer. But I am aware of the responsibility of being given a platform and, in researching these essays, my own blind spots also became apparent. I'm no religious scholar or historian. Growing up, I had never really thought about Nusayba as a three-dimensional person, knew little about life in the seventh century or the beginnings of Islam. Prior to writing, I was not aware of the complications surrounding the "truth" of the source texts,[6] the hadiths, and indeed I hadn't read many at all. There is therefore an awful lot I can't speak to—experiences of religious Islam, for instance, and what Nusayba means for those who *believe*. Unlike many Muslims (including my siblings), I don't come from a place of having studied the Quran at school or at a mosque. Instead, I read and studied alone, curled up against mold-covered walls in student rooms in Oxford. My writing is therefore necessarily informed by this secular perspective, as well as by the various privileges that allowed me to be at Oxford in the first place.

So no doubt it will be felt that, in many ways, I am not the person to write about anything to do with Islam, or Arabness or Palestinianness—what do I know? Who am I to represent any of these groups? To these readers I say: I emphatically do *not* represent anyone apart from myself (and perhaps, to some extent, my family, and to them I have apologized profusely). It is a function of the way the publishing world works that it feels like a zero-sum game (in the sense that if my book gets published, another Muslim Palestinian writer will not), what Elaine Castillo calls the "false narrative of scarcity that a lot of writers of colour feel."[7] I hope and trust that publishing is changing, and that even if this was the case in the past, it will not be in the future. It must not be. We need a plurality of opinions and experiences precisely *because* none of us can or should represent more than our own selves. The more voices are platformed, the more opportunities for connection we are likely to find—let it be loud, cacophonous even, with our different points of view.

Rather than speaking *for* anyone, I hope instead to be speaking *with* and *to* whomever keeps reading past these few pages, and to find, in this process, a sense of communality. Maybe there are others who have unwieldy identities, wish they were braver, or feel they are not enough. A lot of us probably feel disconnected, in some way, from our homes; feel shame about who we have been made to think we are. As Pragya Agarwal writes, "It is also easy to assume that our story is mundane, not of value or interest to anyone. [. . .] When we are inside them, they often just seem ordinary. Our struggles seem hackneyed, our wanderings so conservative and cautious, our triumphs so commonplace."[8] But bring our stories together, and suddenly we may find we've been fighting together on more battlefields than we realize.

Arabs are a people of lineages, sons of so-and-so, daughters of so-and-so. As Edward Said has argued, we lack written histories, and so instead our histories are passed on through blood, the connections between our ancestors and ourselves traceable like a delicately woven daisy chain. The word "human being" itself, in Arabic, refers to lineage: bani Adam, sons of Adam. Nusayba's stories have been passed down from one Nuseibeh to another, were recounted by her sons to their sons and their daughters after that. In Arabic we get renamed after we have children; we become *Um-* and *Abu-* the child's name, *mother of* and *father of*, a recognition that each identity is poured into the next like tipping beakers in a chemistry experiment.

Jerusalem is full of families who claim interesting origins; most believe themselves to be directly descended from the Prophet. Other Palestinians from outside Jerusalem can trace their lineage back to the Ghassanids in the fourth century CE.[9] But ancestry is a funny thing, not really meaningful outside the selfhood narratives it gives rise to, at best a pass-the-parcel of specific genetic information, a layer unwrapped with every descendent. How much can we really claim an inheritance from our forebears? As Heba Zaphiriou-Zarifi points out, "identities have a multiplicity of beginnings; moreover, they are a becoming."[10] We make ourselves with our stories, more than we are made by our genes.

Genealogically speaking, we are, in any case, much more interconnected than we might think. Research suggests that humanity's most recent common ancestor may have lived as recently as 55 CE, only six centuries before Nusayba. "No person has forebears from just one ethnic background or region of the world," writes Scott Hershberger. "Your genealogical connections to the entire globe mean that not too long ago your ancestors were involved in every event in world history."[11] Go back to a not-so-distant past, and our family trees all end up being not only from the same garden but of the same type in the same grove.

Much in the way that some might examine the stars and find guidance in the sign of the Taurus, I look towards Nusayba as an ancestor not in the literal sense of believing that she was truly *real*, somehow making me a special vessel of her bloodline, but instead as a roughly sketched figure from whom I might draw some strength, some clarity, some direction. And because I believe that she exists and persists through story rather than genetics, she is available to anyone—her connection to me arguably no stronger than to any other child who grew up hearing the tale of the warrior woman. "If you are interested in what your ancestors have contributed to the present time, you have to look at the population of all the people that coexist with you," says Susanna Manrubia. "All of them carry the genes of your ancestors because we share the [same] ancestors."[12]

Insomuch as she existed, my ancestor is your ancestor, and so her stories are your stories, too.

BETTINJAN

On a hazy September afternoon, I go with my family to the West Bank village of Battir. Slow and winding, the drive takes us southward through the dramatic valleys near Bethlehem, past hills with freshly turned earth the color of cinnamon, the clear landscape occasionally punctuated by the sea-gray of olive trees. Beyond, in the distance, I see the slopes of deep green mountains, the texture of the bushes like a head of short, tight curls, but as we enter Battir, nature is temporarily replaced by a languishing urbanity: every other house is half-built, neat piles of ceramic slabs stand tall beside messy heaps of rubble, misspelled graffiti covers a low-rise cement wall. Half-dead banana trees and 1980s-era cars gather dust on worn-down half-pavements. We don't spend long driving, we reach our destination quickly: we have come here, as we always do, to eat.

The West Bank village of Battir is famous for its eggplants, which are small and sweet and silky. My grandmother would cook these, when the season would come round, roasted in a thick tomato sauce, each small, midnight-purple eggplant stuffed with meat and pine nuts and spices. This was my favorite meal when young: bettinjan battiri. I have tried, many times, to make this dish myself, but without the eggplants from Battir, it feels impossible. Maybe without my grandmother, and a steamy kitchen, and a large rubber-duck-yellow plastic container of oil pressed from her olive trees, it just *is* impossible. I keep trying, though, to approximate it, and sometimes, when I manage to fry the meat with just the right amount of nutmeg-to-cumin-to-allspice mixture, and I've not added too many onions and the evening light in Oxford is just the right shade of milky twilight, I can, for a moment at least, suddenly be in Jerusalem, two decades ago. Food's magic is here, in this, in the way that it brings you back: the tastes a product of the ingredients, the ingredients a product of the specific textures of the earth and air in which they are grown. Fundamentally local, of a particular place.

Food is central to Arab families in general, and my family in particular. It is through food that we gather, that we celebrate, that we communicate. It ritualizes the days: in the morning, my father will pop out to busy Salah'eddin Street to buy ka'ek, oblong bread covered in sesame seeds; freshly made hummos, scooped from a large metal vat into a white plastic dish to takeaway; spicy black bean fool, lemony and sprinkled with green chili peppers; and fresh, hot falafel that will steam and grease the paper bag it's packed into. My mother and I, meanwhile, will go to the kitchen to prepare the rest of the breakfast; she will boil white cheese, taking it out when it is half-melted, stretchy and scalding, and I will make a tomato salad with lemon juice and olive oil, slice small, crunchy cucumbers, and pick mint from the garden to make a big pot of sweet mint tea. Za'atar and olive oil and spicy, bitter green olives and labaneh will be taken to the table, each in a little colorful dish. Sometimes we will also add pickled cauliflower, which comes, for some inexplicable reason, in a neon shade of pink, as well as raw onion, sliced into quarters. The spread, once it's all laid out, looks almost absurd; it's enough to feed an army. And we eat it like an army, too; we get through it all, messily dunking bread into one dip and then another, trailing crumbs and oil and coriander across the table. We are, in many ways, a quiet family, but we bring a raucousness to our eating. Often, in place of conversation, there will be the crunch of the onions and the tearing of bread and the delicate crackle of a baked egg shell being crushed gently against a blue china plate.

In the evenings, we will have shawi in the garden; my brothers will stand outside beside the round black barbecue, lighting the coal, chatting and smoking cigarettes, maybe sipping a Taybeh beer out of a brown glass bottle. When they stand together it is apparent that they are siblings; they have the same hint of lankiness in the shoulders. My mother and I will, in the meantime, work in the kitchen: we'll squash mincemeat into balls, spread it onto bread for 'arayes, chop up the trusty tomato and cucumber and onion and mint again to make an Arabic salad. We will push cubes of lamb onto fierce metal skewers, pile these high onto an orange dish that has been around since the

1970s; my brothers will then carefully grill these until perfectly tender, often continuing to stand and rotate the skewers while the rest of us begin to dig in to the food. Hummos will also reappear (it's not a stereotype, we do eat a lot of it), as will a white plastic bag of kmaj, thick pita bread that will come hot and squishy from an oven in Jericho's city center. The meat will be brought to the table as it's readied, searing and a little charred; it will be pulled off using the pita like a glove; each tender piece dipped into the creamy hummos, salty fat melting into tart tahini, balanced with a bite of light, lemony salad. The scents of smoke and mint and orange-blossom and beer will mix in the air as we pile our plates high with food. Again, it is messy, it is chaotic. It is what makes home feel like home; an overabundance of familiar flavors.

A few months before writing this essay, I interviewed a Syrian woman as part of a research project on refugees in Oxford. In the din of a Caffè Nero, she leaned her small body forward to hear me, her long hair brushing the slightly sticky table, as I asked her questions about her life and work in the UK. The conversation began in English, professional and a little distant, a knot of tension in my gut as I played the role of British academic; when we began wrapping up, though, I thanked her in Arabic. With the shift in language, we found ourselves turning, almost immediately, to food. The tenor of the conversation changed, suddenly nostalgic, wistful. As the barista called out broken-voiced orders of cheese toasties and caramel lattes, we reminisced about the texture of the bread we longed for—doughy and thick and stretchy—and talked about where we might find almost-good-enough substitutes for specific ingredients. I told her I would be going home to Jerusalem in a few weeks' time and I promised to bring her back some proper za'atar and sumac; she squeezed my hand and said I *had* to come over, any time, for some tabeekh: home cooking. Food is the way we hold on to and pass on culture, creating and recreating particular flavors that are brought by parents and grandparents from distant lands; maintaining an identity through recipes and rituals that get repeated across generations. As such it is perhaps particularly important for those who feel far from home, or for whom home has been taken away, as well as whose ethnicities are mixed. Maybe this is partly why food plays such an important role in Arabic literature, particularly for Arabs writing from the diaspora. It takes center stage in Abu-Jaber's *Crescent,* in Hala Alyan's *Salt Houses,* in Renée Ahdieh's YA novel *The Wrath & the Dawn.*

The writers of these books spend time on lush, detailed descriptions of meals that their characters eat and prepare; often these are the scenes that most vividly evoke a much longed-for and faraway homeland.

Perhaps these writers focus on the culinary also because food is an effective gateway for others, a means *into* a culture that would otherwise remain distanced and foreign. No wonder there is a growing canon of English-language Palestinian cookbooks, whether by visitors who have fallen in love with the flavors of the region, such as *Zaitoun*—meaning olives—by Yasmin Khan, or by Palestinians who grew up in the diaspora, such as Laila El-Haddad's *The Gaza Kitchen*, or by Jerusalemites like me, such as Reem Kassis, who wrote the brilliant *The Palestinian Table*. All these texts urgently remind readers in the West that the flavors of olive oil and sumac and chickpea and coriander are connected to a specific people. Food softens and connects us. When I make batata mahshi—potatoes hollowed out, fried until golden, stuffed with meat and pine nuts and simmered in beef stock, served with rice and a cooling yogurt—and British friends try this for the first time, they taste an essentially Palestinian combination of crunch and allspice and salt and potato and garlicky mince, a dish that we would have at 1 P.M.—on the dot!—on Saturdays at my grandmother's large Formica-covered dining table. If I share a recipe for mujadarrah—a traditional dish of slightly cinnamony lentils, rice and caramelized onions—I bring foreign friends an essentially Arab experience, a meal that has been eaten by Arabs since the thirteenth century, that my sister-in-law would cook up on a weeknight because it was easy and cheap.

And perhaps this is partly the reason Palestinian food is particularly important to me. It seems a gentle way of presenting my Arabness—and specifically, my Palestinianness, which so often is taken as political, or threatening—and making it quite literally palatable. It makes, as Laila El-Haddad puts it, "the issue of Palestine approachable. It's a way to humanize it. Everybody likes food."[13] Food—and feeding—is central to the way we come together, to a sense of companionship. (And this, of course, is no coincidence, the word itself coming from the Latin word companion; from *com*, meaning "with, together," and *panis,* meaning "bread," but also coming from the root *pa*—"to feed.") Feeding, breaking bread, togetherness—these all underlie everything from camaraderie to that building-block of capitalism, the company. They sustain society.

No wonder the idea of food as a reward is built into Islam, also. The Quran's descriptions of paradise are heavily sensory, a foodie's fantasy: heaven is filled with "rivers of water unaltered, rivers of milk the taste of which never changes" as well as "rivers of wine delicious to those who drink" and even "purified honey, in which they will have from all fruits" (47:15). Those in heaven can ask for any kind of fruit (44:55), and they will be given "what their souls desire" (43:71). At the end of a Ramadan day, you eat a large, celebratory breakfast; there's a big stuffed-lamb-filled reward to end the fasting month. Indeed, when I think about the fasting month, I think less of the gnawing in my stomach (I still fast occasionally, mostly in solidarity with my father) and more about atayef—thick pancakes, fried until golden, smothered in sugar-syrup and folded in half over candied walnuts or melted white cheese—and breads seeded with habet el baraka that will be dipped into eggs fried onto a layer of basterma. I think of thick, sweet juices and thin, sesame-seed barazek. I think of my father, pacing outside the front door, waiting for the cannon to be fired, signaling the end of the fasting day; I think of my grandmother and her maid in the kitchen, hunched over simmering pots, trying to tell whether salt should be added by smell alone.

There was and there was not, in the depths of the past, a woman filled with hunger. Nusayba bint Ka'ab al Khazrajia, the warrior woman, lived in a part of Arabia that was, and still is, infamously unyielding. Mecca was particularly rocky and dry; Yathrib,[14] the oasis roughly 250 miles north of Mecca where Nusayba lived, was only slightly better; Muhammad[15] reportedly described it as "a salty, swampy plain with palm-groves between tracts of rocks."[16] The town's main produce was dates, and—though it also cultivated some milk products, and some basic vegetables such as cucumbers and leeks, chicory, onions and garlic—the town relied on dates so completely that a shortage of these would mean a famine. There was very little wheat; generally, they had bread made of barley. She would have eaten meat only very rarely; mostly there was mutton. In very dire circumstances, there was camel. Compare this to the meals being eaten in nearby Damascus, Jerusalem, Alexandria and Antioch, where lavish feasts—consisting of stuffed vine leaves and grilled meats, beef cooked in spinach, honey-rich rice pudding and almond pastries—were being put on for Khusrau II, the monarch who had conquered the region.[17] Persia, under the reign of the Sasanids, was the center of this decadent, complex cuisine. Arabia, by contrast, was making the most of lean trimmings. No wonder abstaining from eating was common there, then, even before the advent of Ramadan. "Scarcity made a virtue of moderation," the hadith repeat more than once. "Two people's food is enough for three, and three enough for four."[18] For Nusayba and the other hungry followers in those early days, heaven would undoubtedly have looked like satiety.

Some sources suggest that in pre-Islamic Arabia, fasting would take place annually, during the spring season of Rajab; in Yathrib, where there lived some Jewish tribes, fasting would take place every year during Ashura, the Jewish day of Atonement. In fact, certain scholars have suggested the beginnings of Ramadan lie in Ashura:[19] when Muhammad moved to Yathrib and was surrounded by Jewish fellow monotheists, he asked that his followers fast on the same day as a sign of respect.[20] A year and a half later, a revelation came to distinguish Ramadan from Ashura;[21] Ramadan would be about commemorating the month in which the Quran was revealed to Muhammad. "Any one of you who is present that month should fast," the Quranic verse (2:185) states, "and anyone who is ill or on a journey should make up for the lost days by fasting on other days later. God wants ease for you, not hardship."

We know that Nusayba fasted even outside Ramadan because there is, oddly enough, a story about it. In amongst the tales of her sword-fighting and limb-losing, there is a story about food.[22] One day, Muhammad decides to pay Nusayba a visit, so he goes to her dwelling. There, she offers him a "vegetable dish" with a side of barley bread. T'faddal, I imagine her telling him, as she places a bowl on the table. He invites her to join him—come and eat, he tells her—but she refuses, telling him she is fasting. "When someone eats in the presence of someone who is fasting, the angels continue to bless him until he finishes his food," the Prophet responds, and proceeds to tuck in. Nusayba, meanwhile, simply sits beside him.

It is a strange, incongruous story, one that doesn't easily fit the narrative of a no-fucks-given warrior. For one thing, it is not clear why she should be fasting, when her own Prophet—the man who gives her the rules to her religion—is not. And it also seems a mistake, somehow, that our warrior woman should be cooking, feeding, not eating. When we picture warriors, we picture them ravenous, filled with appetite, a knight in a suit of armor tearing off a chicken leg with his bare hands. And yet here she seems to have no desire to eat at all.

This, I think, points to an aspect of food culture that often gets ignored when we talk about its importance for preserving cultural identity; namely, that food—though central to the way we maintain and pass on culture, particularly Arabic and Muslim culture—is, at the same time, inescapably, tediously, complicated by gender. I want Nusayba—with her unbridled bravery, with her warrior spirit—to offer a way out of paradox. Instead, she embodies it: she cooks, she feeds, she fasts. A man is enlarged by the fruits of her labor, while she is made smaller. That old familiar story.

My favorite dinner parties happen in New York, at a small, warmly lit apartment with windows half-blocked by the leaves of two plane trees. While acoustic music gently mellows the background, the guests, eclectic in both age and profession (though I am the only student), mingle around a long table made of solid oak, taking bites of expensive French cheese cut by tart fresh grapes. The hostess, a writer, wears a simple black dress, no apron in sight. For the first hour or so, she will be slightly apart, behind the kitchen counter that runs parallel to the dining table in the intimate open-plan space. Head cocked, she will make jokes, effortlessly chopping herbs, casually placing the artful finishing touches on her meals (which, despite being simple, are always elegant, never boring). When she finally serves up the homemade bread, the corn chowder, the aromatic apple pie, the pasta with fresh basil and crushed tomatoes and creamy mozzarella, she is nonchalant, casual. You know, I hate the co-op, but they do have the best ingredients, she says in response to the exclamations of thanks and admiration. She pours red wine into a guest's near-empty glass. Eat, eat, she says.

In my shared house in Oxford, I try to emulate her. I cook for my roommates and wear a black dress, put on jazzy music. But I get too stressed, overwhelmed by the small space, the not-quite-right ingredients, the various dietary requirements. I try to look effortless, fix on a smile, but find myself flushed and sweaty, covered in sauce spatter, as I bring out the meal. T'fadallu, I say, thinking of Nusayba as I sit down and start loading up their plates.

So how much do we owe you? a roommate asks, passing around a bowl of yogurt. The music has been switched off in favor of the TV; instead of the gentle buzz of conversation, there are the undulating sounds of a football match.

Owe? I say, confused and embarrassed. No, no, I tell them. Just, you know—eat, eat.

⟡

Food isn't just about ritual and place; feeding and eating in Arab culture are both essential to the way we demonstrate love. Food is prepared in excess. You must have more than enough to offer to family and guests, and often you have to eat more than you want, more than is comfortable, to show how much you care. My grandmother would dish up plate after plate for me if I was eating lunch at her house, the expectation being that I would keep going until the food had lodged itself like a golf ball in my esophagus. She would be offended if I had one helping only; she would sometimes clap if I ate three. Eating and feeding are so deeply embedded in the collective (and collectivist) culture that an individual's relationship to food is never considered. There is, seemingly, no room for vegetarianism, for sustainable eating, for orthorexia or anorexia or bulimia. (Often, people who don't eat meat are served chicken. What's the issue? It's not meat!) Disordered eating is generally considered a Western problem; something that happens "over there," but doesn't affect the Middle East. But, of course, this is not true: eating disorders exist everywhere, including the Arab world. Some studies even suggest that the prevalence in some Arab countries—from the UAE to the Palestinian territories—is higher than in the West.[23] And eating—or not eating—in problematic ways is particularly tricky to manage in the context of a culturally mandated eating culture.

It also doesn't help that Arabs have a compulsion towards bluntness when it comes to physical appearance: once, when a cousin came to visit from the UK, my aunts, meeting her for the first time over a giant lunch, barely pressed their foundation-covered faces to hers before adding, Yah allah, it's such a pity you're huge, habibti! Mashallah, your face is so lovely! (My cousin didn't touch her food all day.) It is a cultural obsession, to talk about other people's bodies in this way, to comment particularly on weight, and particularly on women's weight. When, after a period of illness, I became somewhat emaciated, people commented on that too. Habibti, shu da'faneh—you're skinnier than I was on my wedding day!—a heavy-set stranger in my grandmother's sitting room might tell me through a cloud of Chanel N°5. It creates a strange relationship with food, this attention to the body, particularly when coupled with the idea that eating and feeding are expressions of love, each grain of rice piled onto a plate a gentle sweet nothing to be consumed.

But disordered eating is often about much more than wanting to fit into a particular jean size; much of the time, it is about control, or punishment, or shame. Particularly for women, not-eating can be a way—the only way—of asserting autonomy where otherwise it is being denied, of claiming power over the self. Oddly enough, this is also what I am told, repeatedly, during Ramadan: fasting is about feeling with the needy, yes, but it is also about learning to use one's willpower, disciplining the body for the sake of a "higher purpose," what Christians often refer to as *askesis*. Scholars have long noted the similarities between spiritual fasting (known as *inedia*, taken from the Latin) and the starvation of those suffering from anorexia. Take the ascetics of the Christian fifth century: Marcella, the Roman noble, who founded a famous circle of female ascetics so extreme that one member, a young girl called Blesilla, died from the prolonged fasting.[24] Or, later, the infamous Saint Catherine of Siena in the fourteenth century, who was canonized after starving for her faith, one of many women between 1200 and 1500 who were glorified and sanctified as a result of *inedia*.

It is clear from this that even before the contemporary obsession with small bodies became ubiquitous, we valued self-denial, glamorized it even. Ascetic starvation, as it is known, or "starving for spiritual or cultural principles," as Mervat Nasser[25] explains, can be understood as "a form of body negation—a voluntary act that deliberately denies the body its basic need for nourishment." The aim, she explains, is "to liberate the soul from the somatic and material preoccupations of the body in the hope that it will finally reach spiritual purity."[26] During Ramadan, it is not only food that is meant to be eschewed, but cigarettes and sex also. And this same discourse—of fasting as a negation of need—also emerges in contemporary descriptions of anorexia,

33

in which we so often "turn skeletons into goddesses and look to them as if they might teach us how not to need,"[27] as Marya Hornbacher puts it, in her memoir of living with anorexia.

This negation of need is, in many ways, a particularly female issue: our narratives of sin begin, after all, with Eve's appetite (though not, it should be noted, in Islam). Historically, female appetite has always been regarded with suspicion; even today, it is transgressive—take Gillian Flynn's eponymous "cool girl," for instance, who "jams hot dogs and hamburgers into her mouth like she's hosting the world's biggest culinary gang bang."[28] Part of what makes her cool is that she eats with abandon, without the anxiety or shame that often sours meals for other women. But even those of us without eating disorders have rarely felt the freedom that many men do when eating a burger. We women are meant to be small, both materially and otherwise, taking up as little space as possible with our bodies and our needs. As Sandra Lee Bartky has argued, the "ideal body of femininity" is slender and weak rather than big and muscular: "massiveness, power or abundance in a woman's body is met with distaste."[29]

This distaste is what underlies the discourse around food, and thus shapes how we relate to it. So, though starvation is physically incapacitating, we have been sold the idea that to not-eat is to be strong; though emotionally draining, we buy that to not-need is to be invincible. Hence, for the mythical Chinese warrior Fa Mu Lan in Maxine Hong Kingston's *The Woman Warrior*, hunger is the key to a "transformative imaginative power." Maxine the narrator suggests that, maybe, "if I could not-eat, perhaps I could make myself a warrior like the swordsman who drives me."[30]

And it is easy to see why we are drawn in by this idea that not-eating, not-needing, is good: without any power at all, not-needing can feel an awful lot *like* power. Sometimes the only control one has is over oneself. Perhaps this is why my own warrior woman, Nusayba, fasts. Maybe this is how she, too, makes herself a warrior.

Despite my having lived on and off in the UK for the best part of a decade, I still see eating as a way of showing gratitude, I take seconds even when I'm not hungry, even when my host is British and would rather have the leftovers for tomorrow. The urge is instinctive and hard to control. I eat too much, and it is exhilarating and natural, and then I am filled with regret and embarrassment, despite the fact that for much of my life I have been, objectively, quite small. (Food is love, but food is shame, but food is love, but food is shame.) Whether eating too much or eating too little, we find ourselves trapped by what Natalie Jovanovski refers to as "food feminities,"[31] the gendered discourses that create our relationships to food. And it isn't just eating, of course—cooking, too, is gendered, embedded with the seeds of the domestic. In Abu-Jaber's food memoir, *The Language of Baklava,* it is her father who links her to Arabic culinary culture, but more often than not, these spaces are occupied by mothers and grandmothers, maternal figures who stand tirelessly over a stove, patiently cutting and spicing and stirring and cleaning, as though this is part of them, as though it were as natural as the eating itself. This is part of the story of the gendering of food, the fact that the act of cooking is thus naturalized, that it becomes so deeply ingrained that it forms part of our identity, sometimes even physically, by way of burn marks and scars from an absent-minded skin-slice. Centuries of reinforcement and forced domesticity can be felt in our bones, and it has served men well, the fact that we seem so often born to boil a broth. That picture of male warriors ravenously tearing at chicken breasts is incomplete; pull on that tab there above the side-door and out will pop the shape of a woman, preparing the meal.

This has been part of the feminist project, of course, to highlight the way that female labor has—almost always, almost everywhere—enabled male venture. And it is not just cooking but specifically *feeding* that is feminized: anatomically, a man might point out, we women are made for it, after all (though this of course ignores the many women, trans and cis, for whom lactation isn't possible). Though men might cook as part of a profession or as a hobby, women more often make food *for* people—"cooks," rather than "chefs." (This is not true for all men, of course. Despite the fact that my mother and I will, as described earlier, often do the preparation of meals, or parts of meals, my brothers are in fact excellent cooks, and they frequently feed me and their own families, much to my benefit.) Nonetheless the narrative that frames the way we relate to cooking positions kitchens as a feminine space, and we still internalize this, even in 2020, even in places we think of as nontraditional.[32] And, of course, as a backlash to the mainstreaming of feminism, there has been the growing "tradwife" (as in, traditional wife) trend in the West. Who can forget Kaley Cuoco, of *Big Bang Theory* fame, telling reporters she wasn't a feminist because she enjoyed cooking for, and serving, her husband? Meanwhile, the Arab world continues to assert its cultural identity in part through these traditional gender roles, distinguishing itself from the "West" by encouraging women to keep rolling rice into vine leaves.

I love cooking because I love to nurture, and to be creative, and to foster togetherness. I love companionship, and I love feeding close friends, bringing them flavors from Jerusalem—a lentil soup, made tart with lemon, into which fried cubes of pitta bread are scattered, or a green molokhia stew, made from a wild herb not found in Europe. It brings me joy, knowing I have made someone's day a little tastier. And I love the intricacy of Arabic food especially, the way it often takes hours, with multiple steps, to prepare. But I am forced to admit that, though I am no Kaley Cuoco, I, too, am drawn in by something suspect in the making of food. Sometimes it seems as though the more I learn to cook—the more recipes become muscle memory—the more myself I become. I feel most Arab in the kitchen. In fact I feel most Arab when I am slowly hollowing-out those potatoes with my mother or sister-in-law in front of the TV, as though my ethnic identity is made stronger by my gender identity, by the force of more women doing culinary work—though in truth this is romanticized and not particularly real. My grandmother barely did the cooking herself; she had a cook whom she would watch over (not that that meant she didn't take ownership of the meal). But the story of woman-as-feeder, of *Arab* woman-as-feeder, is so powerful that it overrides the reality. "As elderly Palestinians commonly reside with their children (often the eldest son), three generations of women often work together in cooking and processing food, and the many hours spent in the kitchen provide for the passage of both culinary and other forms of wisdom from one generation to another," writes the Institute for Middle East Understanding.[33] And I cannot ignore that there is some part of me that loves cooking precisely *because* it also feels deeply normative, non-transgressive. By playing the doubled script of Western woman and Arab woman, I can move—or rather be moved, effort-lessly—along a familiar and well-worn course. Playing this part is so deeply embedded that it is easy, and easy is, well, nice, sometimes.

Of course, there may be more to the story—perhaps Nusayba fasts because she couldn't fast during Ramadan, maybe she isn't hungry, or maybe she fasts because there isn't quite enough food, and she wants Muhammad to have her portion, which would be in keeping with her self-sacrificial instinct to fight for him. Sacrifice, after all, is "not destruction, nor is it an act of giving up, or giving away, it is giving: a giving of oneself, and from oneself, entirely, without any expectation of return," as Heba Zaphiriou-Zarifi explains.[34] In this way, sacrifice is not so different from feeding, from nourishing another. Maybe, actually, it's OK that she sits in this domestic space, a feeder, as well as being a warrior. Maybe this contradiction is precisely what makes her human.

Still, though, I can't help but feel frustrated that Nusayba has left me with the paradox unsolved, still torn between my desire to step out of prescribed gender roles, reject the forced-feminine, and the need to maintain that collective, cultural identity—that scent of the past and of home, of slightly burnt bettinjan and the tang of tomatoes.

I find a recipe for Thurid, a dish that is meant to have been Muhammad's favorite, from the tenth century. It is sparse, but I find the ingredients—fatty meat, chickpeas, whole onions, bread—and attempt to piece it together. I boil up the meat and chickpeas and water into a stew; I tear pieces of bread into "a wide bowl big enough for ten people" and pour melted butter over the top. I sprinkle some sugar on the bread, and then ladle the stew over the whole thing, and arrange the meat on the side. The overall impression is of a watery beige-gray paste; it looks, frankly, deeply unappetizing. I imagine Nusayba standing beside me as I cook; several inches shorter than me, because people were smaller back then, but nonetheless an imposing presence. I offer her a spoonful to taste; she sniffs it suspiciously.

I'm sure it's very different to how it's supposed to be, I say, apologetically. But would you like to try?

Um, I don't think so, she says, prodding the gloopy mixture with a finger. But I am a little hungry.

What about this? I ask, going to the fridge and pulling out a small white bowl wrapped with cellophane. I empty the contents into a saucepan and heat it up: the remains of my beitinjan battiri-inspired dish made a day previously.

Tesco eggplants roasted in the oven, resting on a sauce made of Sainsbury's tinned tomatoes, filled with Quorn mince and onions and pine nuts. Not quite my grandmother's, admittedly, but I'd eaten it the night before, with rice and yogurt, while reading about Khusrau II's feasts, and it hadn't tasted too bad.

What is it? Nusayba asks, peering at the simmering red stew.

Home, I tell her.

WARRIOR, WORRIER

WORRY AS ACCESSORY

Christians have rosaries; Muslims have worry beads. My father—an on-and-off smoker who, during the off years, needed a place for his fingers to fidget—has always had many, many worry beads. They were everywhere, these worry beads: strewn on mosaic-tiled tables; balanced on top of piles of yellowed, jacketless books; forgotten, beside a set of car keys; dropped and left in the corner of the kitchen, beside the drooping plant that needed watering. Necklaces of large, round red baubles; small delicate spheres of black stone on a small thin string; white plastic pellets dirtied by years of thumbs rhythmically moving each bead along its thread. As a child I'd find them and adorn myself, wrap beads around my tiny wrists, draw multiple strings around my little neck, place them as a coronet atop my head. *You are hereby crowned King of all the land*, I would say to myself solemnly, having reached the princess without waking the evil queen by craftily hopping from one sofa to another. Worry beads were my favorite accessory, I'd walk around in them all day, pleased and proud, their heavy weight pulling me down.

WORRY AS HAVING-IT-COMING

In many ways, my life has been a series of fortunate near-misses. I am not yet born when soldiers come into our house and take my father away. I am already inside the car when, at age six, my mother is shoved to the ground outside a McDonald's, and a man runs away into the darkness with her bag. I am late to school the day a bomb goes off outside its gates, so I am happily drumming my fingers on the black plastic of the passenger-side glove compartment of my mother's car, chatting about a television show, when a human head lands beside my classmate, traumatizing her so significantly that she stays silent for the entirety of the academic year. The café I sometimes stop in to have hot chocolate explodes on a day I didn't have a sweet tooth. I have my head turned when, out with my friends one night as a young teen, we are surrounded and attacked; in the two minutes it takes for me to process what is happening, my friend is already knocked out, spreadeagled on the ground, blood running down his face, while I remain safely unscathed. I am on holiday when our Beit Hanina house is broken into and robbed, and asleep in Jerusalem when my grandmother wakes to find a knifed assailant in her room. I am in Scotland when a Palestinian boy is kidnapped and riots break out outside my brother's house in Shu'fat, safely in the warm glow of an Edinburgh pub when I receive my brother's pictures of burning tires and armored trucks. Tragedies have hit the rest of my family—my grandfather had his leg shot off by the Stern gang, my grandmother was a refugee, my father was imprisoned, two aunts have buried their own children, having lost them to a car accident and cancer—but I have been, somehow, inexcusably, spared. Disaster feels due.

So: I worry about my family. I worry about my friends. I worry that I have not used my short time on earth wisely, that I have spent too much of it reading thrillers instead of philosophy, or cooking pasta instead of experimenting with new recipes. I worry that I have not used properly eco-friendly products, that I have just been taken in by branding, and that I have failed to recycle properly and upcycle enough. I worry after uncomfortable interactions—awkward hellos with acquaintances I don't know well—and also after wonderful evenings spent with close friends (Did I talk too much, hog all the attention? Should I not have brought up her ex?). I worry about losing my home, losing my family, losing my country. I worry about the planet that is quickly disintegrating, about the ways my future loved ones will be affected, and the ways in which I fail to address it in any meaningful way. I worry that I've said something wrong or that my work is no good or that I have not shown enough kindness to the people that I love. I worry so much that it consumes other emotions; sadness, loneliness, joy, excitement, even anger gets swallowed whole by worry. My brother forgets we made plans and fails to show up or message me, but how can I be upset with him? What if he gets hit by a car and anger is the last emotion we share? My worry swallows me whole, too.

WARRIOR AS FREEDOM FROM WORRY

There was and there was not, in the depths of the past, a woman I imagine was entirely free from worry. I see Nusayba bint Ka'ab al Khazrajia, my ancestor the warrior woman, on the battlefield at the Battle of Uhud, pressing her palms down on a fellow Muslim's wound, feeling his blood seeping out between her fingers, turning sticky, crusting under her already-crusted fingernails. Another soldier, lying nearby, asks her for some water; she finds her shin, her small water bag, and holds it firmly to his cracked lips, but the physics of it don't work: he sputter-coughs it out, liquid-tracks left on his otherwise dusty face.

In the distance, under the shadow of the mountain, she sees the soldiers retreating and Muhammad standing alone, the enemy drawing nearer. The archers have left their post on the little hill between them and the Meccan enemies. Her heart begins to thud, and her hand reaches for a forgotten sword, lying in the sand beside her. In this moment, is she anxious? Does she worry that she is about to break the rules—that she will be leaving the campsite? That she might die? Accounts of this moment emphasize her decisiveness: an important job was not being done, and so she would be the one to do it. She would be the protector of her Prophet. Determination: that's what she felt. She hitches her skirts up, tying them around her waist, and "when the wind turned against us, I started to fight with the Messenger of God, to defend him with the sword and the bow and arrows until I was heavily wounded,"[35] is how she later described it to a grandson. Thirteen injuries she sustains that day, but she continues to fight. To begin with, she doesn't even have a shield, and is making do with only her weapons. Muhammad, seeing this, orders a fleeing, frightened male fighter to hand over his own shield to her: "Leave your shield for someone who really fights!" the Prophet calls to him with disgust. Moments later, another fighter, an enemy this time, comes charging towards Nusayba on horseback; she sees his sword, glinting in the sun, level with her head, and she raises her newly acquired shield just in time. The blow lands on the metal, vibrating through her wounded arm and upper body, an agonizing hum through her bones and into her molars, but she manages to grab the horse's reins and pull, hard, destabilizing the rider, who falls off with a clatter and a cloud of dust. She doesn't have time to take a breath: another Meccan is coming towards her, yelling: "Show me Muhammad! I would die if he lives!" and she just stands before him, undaunted. He comes at her with his sword, and though she lifts her shield she is not quite fast enough this time; she feels the cold steel slice deep into her arm, a wound that would take a year to heal. Despite this she tries, several times, to hit him back, but, protected by two coats of armor, he is unaffected. She stands firm. Blow after blow after blow, she stands firm. The Prophet turns to her in awe and says: "Who can handle what you have handled, Oh Um 'Umarah?"[36]

WORRY AS A MATTER OF (A) DEGREE

In my second year at Oxford studying for my doctorate, I make an appointment to meet my college counselor. I worry that I will be late but instead arrive five minutes early and then wait until our exact appointment time before knocking on the door.

You're early, she says briskly, as I nervously crane my head into the room. You're going to have to wait outside. We tell students *not* to be early.

So sorry, I say, worriedly, backing away. I glance at the clock on the wall, which indeed suggests that I am several minutes ahead of time. Maybe my iPhone is fast. But isn't it set automatically? How would I fix it? I step backwards as she closes the door, and then I stand in the dingily lit hallway and fret.

During the session, I sit on a dark green velvet armchair and tell her that I think I am too anxious. I am constantly worried, I say, picking at the worn material on the seat. I feel like I'm drowning in my worries.

Yes, she tells me, writing something in the yellow notepad beside her. That's a common problem here.

She asks me if I ever think of killing myself.

No, no, I lie, mortified.

Well, she says, after a while. It doesn't seem like your situation is too serious. I would suggest, instead of making another appointment with me, you try out our Mindfulness course? It's on discount for our students. It's here in college? It's good for students like you who get a bit too, you know—she taps her forehead a couple of times—caught up in their own heads.

I leave, despondent, and sign up for the course as soon as I get home, worrying that I'd somehow done the counselling session wrong.

WORRY AS RATIONAL RESPONSE

When I am seventeen, my schoolfriend L convinces me that we should spend New Year's Eve at a party in Ramallah. There's a boy she likes—her plans are always about the boys she likes—who is likely to be there, plus, she adds, what else would you be doing? Watching TV with your parents?

She has a point. OK, OK, I concede. Let's do it.

We get to the party just after ten, absurdly early because we have mis-judged how long it would take to get there via the northern road—a much longer, circuitous way to reach Ramallah than the main road, but which has the benefit of a slightly smaller checkpoint reserved for diplomats and, to some extent, Jerusalem residents. We had calculated that it would take us over forty minutes that way, plus maybe twenty for the checkpoint, and figured that if we left at 9:30 P.M., we'd get to the party by 11 P.M. or so. But L drives fast, it turns out, and the roads are deserted—no one is going into Ramallah on this particular evening, it seems. We make it in just over half an hour, arriving as the hosts are starting to put crisps into bowls.

An hour later, L finds me, a look of somber disappointment on her face. This party sucks, she says, glumly. Clearly, despite her efforts, L's boy is more interested in his other friends than in her. People are so *boring* when you're sober, she says. Yep, I say, this not having been a problem for me, having spent most of the party hovering awkwardly beside the crisps, sipping a single bottle of Taybeh beer. We give each other a look. Let's get out of here, she says.

We get into her car and begin the drive back along the main road, knowing that at this time the northern one would be closed. The center of town is busy with people standing in the streets, and a few fireworks have burst color into the sky, but the roads forking out from the main square are deserted. It feels eerily quiet as we reach the Qalandia checkpoint. No other cars are around. The streetlights are broken, so the only light is coming from the soldier's watchtower, and we can see him in there. He is alone, and swaying slightly, whistling a tune that is a tad off-key. L approaches the barrier and slows down as the soldier makes his way down from the watchtower. He is holding a bottle of something and takes a swig as he comes towards the car, eyeing us blearily, one hand on his long black M16. I suddenly feel all too aware of the red dress I'd put on for the party, a bit low-cut, a bit revealing.

As he nears us, I imagine having to do what passengers often have to do at this checkpoint: walk through the labyrinthine pedestrian barriers, through the metal gates and along the dark passageway, alone in my red dress with the soldier and his gun, and my heart begins to thud. I feel the anxiety seep into my spine, freezing it, stiffening my limbs so that I feel trapped in my useless body. I close my eyes, steeling myself, but before he's reached us, L shifts the gear from park into drive. I am *not* letting him make you get out of this car, she tells me firmly, hands gripping the steering wheel. Thanks, I say softly, my voice cracking a little, though I am not sure what she could do to stop him. I think then of Nusayba, and wonder where in her long line of descendants her bravery disappeared.

The soldier knocks on L's window, and she rolls it down, holding up her hawiya, as do I, to show that we have a right to leave the West Bank. Shalom, she says to him, as though she hasn't a care in the world. He leans forward slightly, and his face is made visible in a shaft of light: red and blotchy, slightly greasy, an uneven sprinkling of facial hair. He is definitely drunk, and only a couple of years older than me. I see his gaze move lazily from our IDs to us, to the neckline of my red dress, and feel a sudden swoop of cold fear go straight to my stomach, my cheeks flushing, but before he has had a chance to say anything, L has hit the accelerator. The car lurches forward abruptly, and we drive away, swerving the barrier and speeding on down towards Jerusalem. "Oh my GOD," she says, as we keep going, seemingly with no soldier behind us. "Fuck that guy."

Maybe there's been some mix-up, and L is really the one related to Nusayba. I could see her charging into battle, wielding a sword.

WORRY AS CLINICAL ANXIETY

We live, according to pop culture, in an age of anxiety. In fact, this was the title of the art exhibition due to open in Sharjah in March 2020—delayed due to the pandemic—which sought to "explore ways everyday devices, technology and digital networks altered the collective consciousness."[37] It is harder today than it would have been for Nusayba, to escape worry. There are too many tweets and posts and messages and alerts to remind us, every minute, of what we are missing, what we have misunderstood, what disaster is imminent. The threat, we are made to feel, is constant. If not wildfires that rage for months, it is cities submerged in water; if not a flood, then a war. Maybe we can't quite recognize it, or we don't know what to call it, this sense of ticking doom, but it lurks within many of us, ready to detonate. Nadiya Hussain, author and winner of *The Great British Bake Off*, in her documentary *Anxiety and Me*, puts it this way: "I had no name for it, but I knew something wasn't right."[38] She describes having a panic attack when her food delivery replaced coriander with parsley.

I start to write this essay while the world is gripped by the virus, an event that has cleaved modern history into a Before and After. It's a bad time for worry. My family is far away and dispersed, some in countries that seem safer, some in countries that seem worse. My roommate's lung condition is deemed a high-risk factor. I see disease everywhere. I barely leave the house. I have my own anxiety attack when, during a virtual work presentation, I get a surprise delivery and I carry the bag I am given into the house and then don't wash my hands straight away. I am sure I will die, I am sure I will bring death to others. On Twitter, ominous voices warn that "even if you think you're safe, all it takes is one mistake." Oh Um 'Umarah, I think. I don't feel I can handle this, I don't feel I can handle anything at all.

In seventh-century Arabia, a warrior woman charges forward to defend her Prophet. In twenty-first-century Britain, a worrier woman wakes up from her comfortable double bed in a sweat, heart beating so strongly she can barely breathe, body shaking as if charged. *Someone has died. Someone I love has died.* They haven't, but as I lie there in bed, I feel certain of this, and gripped by a nauseating terror, each thud of my heart pumping bile into my throat. Maybe my mother was hit by a car. Maybe my father has had a heart attack. My partner could have caught the virus, could right now be in the hospital, on a ventilator. My nephews, my niece, my brothers. My sisters-in-law. My best friend, in LA, maybe she's been attacked at a protest. I get so worked up that I throw up, and then start to cry. I text them all, and even though it is 3 A.M. and I'm unlikely to get an answer, I stare at my phone, waiting. Worrying, worrying, worrying.

WARRIOR AS ACTION-TAKER

Picture Nusayba's strong body straddling a horse, the desert night air cool against her sweating skin, muscles taut as she charges towards an attacker at the Battle of Hunayn in 630 CE. She plunges her sword between his armored plates and continues to ride forward. There are over ten thousand fellow warriors surrounding her, all armed, ready to fight the Bedouin tribe the Hawazins; many of these men are her brethren from her city, Yathrib, but there are also many more, now, from Mecca—Muhammad's hometown from which he had been exiled but where, recently, he has been accepted as religious and political ruler. Abu Sufyan, whose wife Hind the Liver-Eater had defiled the corpse of a Muslim fighter in an earlier battle, leads the army. But the Hawazins are also numerous, and had arrived earlier that night, had hidden in the valley, in crevices and inlets, ready to attack. As soon as Nusayba and the other Muslims had tried to set up camp, they had heard a whistle in the wind: thousands of arrows raining down on them. The Hawazins had then given the order: *charge*. So now it is bedlam.

Before she knows it, the Muslims, confused and overwhelmed, begin to flee. She stays where she is, though, gripping her sword. I imagine it is heavy. I imagine she is an uncomfortably feverish mixture of hot and cold, joints stiff and achy, her body, like any other at that time, having been through the many traumas our twenty-first-century world frees us of even imagining, her arms puckered in strips showing where earlier battles had left their marks. She lifts her arm and begins shaking the sword at her fellow fighters. "What is this habit of yours? Why do you keep fleeing?" she yells at them frustratedly, as a Hawazin man on a camel canters towards the Muslims just beyond her. She sees he is leading an entire brigade, and so—ignoring the other soldiers who are running away—she thinks fast, picks up her bow and strings the arrow, pulling it tight against the string, and then lets it loose to hit the animal, which falls on its back. She goes to the fallen Hawazin fighter and stands over him, breathing heavily, to take one of his swords. She is a fearsome sight to behold, strong and solid and sure. Powerful and mighty.

WORRY AS COLLECTIVE POWERLESSNESS

Palestinians, it has been shown, have the highest levels of anxiety in the Middle East and North Africa region.[39] Not surprising: we have been occupied by dispossession for generations. Precarity and instability, the very real presence of violence and death, the knowledge that our extermination is the stated end of the hegemonic government project. Even more than this, though, I suspect it is the absence of a conclusion that turns our thoughts into question marks, the never-ending no-solution-in-sight—how could we not have worry running thick and treacly through our veins? We have so little control, and it is interminable.

Growing up, unease hung in the air as thickly as the ever-present cigarette smoke. In my grandmother's house in the evenings, people would sit, tapping the ash from their Marlboros into heavy china ashtrays, ticking each worry bead into the next, and talk about loss and powerlessness and the pain they were enduring, while in the background the TV news presenter reeled off the names of the dead, and in response to this suffering the other smokers present would breathe out gray air and reply: May God hold you, may God have mercy on you. Most of the time this was not meant religiously—the phrase, so well used that its literal meaning was wrung out long ago, was now more reflex than plea—but I wonder if some did mean it literally. Faith seems a reasonable option for the powerless.

Despite its omnipresence during my upbringing, I didn't know anxiety could be more than just a feeling until I was in my twenties. An interview with Lena Dunham was the unexpected bearer of this new information: asked by Marc Maron about her day-to-day, she told him she suffered a lot from anxiety. "Anxiety?" I thought, rolling my eyes. How typically American, to pathologize a universal human state. But when later I asked my friends about this, and read about it online, I discovered—to my enormous surprise—that not everyone experiences their daily activities as though walking along a precipice. Not everyone has "the baseline feeling" of "having just finished a third coffee when someone texts: "we need to talk" and then doesn't call for hours, or at all," as Olivia Sudjic puts it.[40] Some people, even those who aren't warriors, rarely worry at all.

The issue was perhaps that anxiety was—and continues to be—such a common and appropriate state of being for many Palestinians (and indeed, many Arabs and Muslims more generally) that there is little sense of its also, in some cases at least, being an illness. This, of course, then limits the possibilities for support and recovery. And it doesn't help matters that, across the Arab and Muslim world, acceptance of mental health as a legitimate area for study and care has a long way to go, more often stigmatized than supported. "There's no way to talk about it in our community," explains one of the Muslim women Nadiya Hussain meets in her documentary. "It's always, pray to Allah." The unspeakable nature of anxiety-as-illness—of any mental health issue, really—suffuses it in shame.

So instead, Palestinians—and Arabs and Muslims more widely—are known to somatize their worries, the fear turned physical.[41] Headaches and backaches and gastrointestinal trouble. Shooting pains in the arms and legs. Exhaustion. We are all exhausted, all the time. Somatization has Freud to thank for its origins, and, in part because of these suspect roots, it is and always has been difficult to define. It sits in that strange liminal space between disciplines and institutions, not quite psychological, not quite physical; the word "soma" itself suggesting a dichotomy between body and mind to which not every culture or religion subscribes. In Arabic, the word "soma"—meaning the body as separate from the mind—is simply translated as jasad, meaning body, and so there is, in fact, no word for somatization in Arabic dictionaries. As Zakiya Al-Busaidi points out, "in the medical literature, the Arabic term used to indicate somatization is *tajseed*. When translated back to English, this word means 'embodiment' or 'embodying.'"[42] This is perhaps a more accurate description of somatization than any other: a literal embodying of our mental states.

WORRY AS DISEASE

I worry myself sick: this, it turns out, can be literal. A few months into the pandemic, despite a compulsive over-cautiousness, I catch COVID. The symptoms are strange and moveable, appearing in the stomach, in the lungs, in the head. The physical and psychological blur. Is my heart beating so fast, am I finding it hard to breathe, because I am anxious, or because of the virus? Is my exhaustion—my body so heavy I can barely open my eyes, my limbs useless bags of sand—a symptom of depression, or of a physical ailment? It feels impossible to tell. Though scans eventually reveal cyst-filled lungs and a swollen and malfunctioning heart, it still seems as though somehow these are merely physical manifestations of my mental ill-health. Of *course* my heart is swollen, I want to tell my doctors, it's been tightly squeezed for months without end! My feelings of worry, which became so acute during the pandemic, have simply wormed their way into my body more permanently and settled in for the long haul. I have embodied my mind's worry beads.

This is what happens, after all. Even sceptics of the mind-body connection can admit that, under stress and with worry, our hearts begin to pulse more strongly, that this in turn will make the blood push violently through our delicate veins; that this, if continuous, will lead to what is commonly referred to as high blood pressure, for which, in order to ensure that the force of this pressure does not cause strain and ultimately damage to the eyes and brain and kidneys, we will perhaps be given little orange pills to materially slow the heart down. During a panic attack I am often not aware of my mind, but instead become hypersensitive to the physical: my breath will feel thin and wispy, caught somewhere beyond my reach; my eyesight will blur, bringing with it a mild, whooshing vertigo; my hands will tremble and begin to sweat. I won't feel my feelings but I will feel my body; my body will tell me that I am scared, that I am anxious.

The term "psychosomatic" has connotations of fabrication or invention—and has been used to delegitimize many, very real, illnesses—but the boundary between the body and the mind is thinner than we'd like to think. Bessel van der Kolk has argued that trauma can quite literally reshape the brain, that constantly being alert to danger—and feeling helpless in the face of that danger—leads to the body being flooded by stress hormones, which in turn devastate the immune system and many of the body's organs.[43] Experiences like anti-Islamism "live under the skins of those of us it marks," writes Suhaiymah Manzoor-Khan. It "alters our physiologies, lives in our nervous systems, makes us hypervigilant and afraid."[44]

The late writer and thinker Dr. John E. Sarno argued that the brain deliberately but unconsciously directs blood away from certain parts of the body, thus creating pain and distracting us from our negative emotions. The pain feels real—it is, in fact, real—but the *cause* is the negative state of mind, such as anger or worry that we haven't dealt with.[45] Mental health is physical health is mental health. Things like back pain or migraines, especially, are increasingly understood to be "biopsychosocial" conditions,[46] much more likely to be suffered by people who have anxiety or who have lived through trauma. Thus, an epidemic of painful backs and throbbing heads across the war-torn Middle East. A worrier with a quite literally broken heart.

WARRIOR AS NUCLEUS REUNIENS

Not so long ago, researchers made a breakthrough in the study of the fight-or-flight response. Looking at mice, scientists at the Stanford University School of Medicine found that the determining factor was a set of two nerve clusters, or nuclei, located in the middle of the brain. Signals sent from one of the clusters, the xiphoid nucleus, went down a highway to the amygdala, inciting the freeze—panicked—response. Messages sent from the other cluster, the nucleus reuniens, traveled instead to the medial prefrontal cortex, and researchers found that stimulating this nucleus in the presence of a predator led to an extraordinary reaction from the mice. Rather than hide, like they normally would, they stood their ground. They shook their rumps and ran across the enclosed compartment. "You could hear their tails thumping against the side of the chamber. It's the mouse equivalent of beating your chest and saying, 'OK, let's fight!'" the lead scientist, Andrew Huberman, told reporters.[47]

Malfunctioning circuitry—too many signals sent to the xiphoid nucleus, not enough to the nucleus reuniens—might be the cause of constant anxiety, Huberman went on to explain. Simply reducing the signaling, or changing the balance of the two, might be the answer. A tweak of the brain's motherboard is perhaps all it would take to feel like Nusayba.

50

WORRY AS LACK OF FAITH

The day after the Battle of Uhud, Muhammad orders those who had fought to march towards the Meccans—a way to signal strength and solidarity, to show that the Muslims were persevering. Nusayba, her injuries still bleeding, readies herself, tying her skirt back up around her waist again. But she struggles to stand, the blood is too profuse, and she finds she cannot walk. She keeps trying, eventually weeping in frustration that she can't join the other fighters.[48] Here, in this moment—perhaps this is a sign of anxiety? Worry that she'll miss out? Worry that she won't be able to help? This is the first time she is powerless, is unable to take action.

Perhaps she is buoyed by her faith: she was, after all, a Muslim (musill-meh), meaning she who has surrendered, submitted. The root word also being related to peace (as in salaam), which makes sense, because surrender is freedom: from worry, from anxiety, from responsibility. If anxiety is a type of struggle—an effort to swim as forceful waves push you back and down, gulps and gasps as you try to keep your head above salty water, ocean all around you as far as you can see—surrender is breathing out and lying back, floating on a gently bobbing surface, letting the current carry you as it will, eyes on the blue sky above. There is peace in surrender.

In a later battle, at Yamama, Nusayba's hand is sliced clean off, but she goes on fighting undeterred, a true warrior, no anxiety in sight. The worriers among us, by contrast, will nick a finger and imagine the worst: infection, hospital, death. Where did I put the Band-Aids? Do I even have any? Why didn't I buy Band-Aids? A friend once explained that anxiety could be described like this: a future worry about a future you handling a future problem. How has your past you handled problems thus far? the friend asked. Not too badly, I suppose, I admitted. Then you should trust your future you to do the same, the friend told me confidently.

But we have very little faith, we worriers, in anything at all.

WARRIOR AS FAITHFUL FRIEND

That's not to say that belief in God is a panacea. Devout Muslims have written eloquently about the struggles of being both religious and mentally unwell; how, indeed, it can be *more* painful and lonely for those who believe, too often told that "a true Muslim would be content with what God had planned for them", and that their issue was simply "their faith is low."[49] But for Nusayba—an early convert—this belief was easy, active, thriving even, as Muhammad's followers grew in number and as the religion spread. He was there to guide her, to relay messages from God directly, to instruct on both the specific and general, to comfort and rally. He would have told her about Islam's idea of predestination, explaining that whatever happened out on the battlefield, it was mektoub. She would have been told, also, that in Islam, humans were born with the innate and natural predisposition for good,[50] no sense of "original sin," and so she would have felt no need for guilt or redemption; he would have told her to trust in herself. Her Prophet was not a distant figure she had to make herself believe in, but instead a close friend into whom she could wholeheartedly pour her faith.

If, as she pulled herself up onto a horse and galloped towards him, sword in hand, bow slung over her shoulder, she feared for the lives of her sons or her husband, these fears would surely have been lifted by the knowledge that it was in the hands of God, and that if he should take them on this day, she would see them again in heaven. She knew that, no matter her misgivings (if she had any at all), Muhammad had to live, that his enemies were her enemies, that God's messenger simply could not be killed. She believed she could save her Prophet; she believed she could fight, and win.

WORRY AS PERSONAL POWERLESSNESS

One of the exhibitors at Sharjah's *Age of Anxiety* exhibition was the exiled Iraqi artist Wafaa Bilal. His installation was a video of a previous live performance art piece from 2007 that took place in the USA. In that piece, Bilal transformed a room at a Chicago gallery into a small bedroom and locked himself in. Aimed at him were a webcam and a large, looming, threatening paint-gun, three times the size of anything else in the room, which could be triggered remotely by any visitor to the exhibit's website. For four weeks, Bilal lived in this room, the gun pointed at him, a living target. He was shot over 65,000 times.[51] He spent most of his days in such a heightened state of fear and anxiety—the paintball gun could hit him at any second, he was never prepared—that at times he "even lost [his] sense of reality." Despite this, Bilal explained, the performance helped him—was the only thing to help him, in fact—surmount the sense of powerlessness he felt around the escalating situation in Iraq. In other words, embodying his anxiety by creating this constant faux physical attack was in fact more bearable than the unending worry he was fighting out in the real world.

WORRY AS PERSONAL POWER

It's a mistake, I think, that "fearless" and "brave" are synonyms. In biomedical research, courage isn't the *absence* of fear or anxiety—it is, instead, action in the face of these emotions, making them, ironically enough, necessary prerequisites.[52] Put differently, there *is* no courage without fear, no daring without worry.

It's easy to see how this works in the cases of Nusayba and the mice: clear enemies, clear response. Pick up a spear, run around the chamber. Where there is the straightforward dichotomy of predator and prey, good and evil, there is, also, a straightforward adversary to be faced. The fear has reasonable, challengeable, cause. What happens, though, when the anxiety is faceless or unfaceable? Embodied rather than a separate body against whom to fight? A war happening far away, a decades-old occupation, a future ecological collapse? What does courage look like then? When I think of Nusayba, I think of the power in her vibrating arms as she keeps her shield steady against the many blows. Most of my inner battles, by contrast, are waged against the future. What power do I have against that? What shield can I grip? Maybe just by living, besieged by our anxieties, we worriers are braver than we might believe.

WORRIER, WARRIOR

Though often, these days, we are encouraged to be warriors of various kinds—chronic illness warriors, boardroom warriors, environmental warriors—with everyone from Demi Lovato to Lisa Guerrero espousing the virtues— I am not actually drawn towards warriordom. It's true that I do envy Nusayba's extremely active nucleus reuniens, and wish my own xiphoid nucleus would calm down a bit, but out of the context of tribes and horses, in the real world now of bombs and guns, I am not keen to be a fighter. Instead, I am interested in self-belief: in whatever made Nusayba feel that she could leave her post and pick up a sword in the first place, in the confidence she placed in her future self to succeed. In other words, I want to hear what the nucleus reuniens tells the mouse to get him to stand in the middle of the chamber, underneath the looming predator, assertively rattling his tail.

So: she was a warrior, I am a worrier, and between us are a couple of vowels and a few hundred years. I wonder, though, whether worriers and warriors have more in common than we might think. "Warrior" of course has its origins in war, originally from the French *guerre*. A brave fighter or soldier. But "worrier," too, has violent linguistic roots: from the Middle English *wir-ien* (c. 1300), "to slay, kill or injure by biting and shaking the throat," from the Old English *wyrgan*, "to strangle." Even "anxiety" itself has choking or strangling in its linguistic ancestry, and we can feel it as we say the word: the *x* following the *n* as a contraction, the *siety* a soft exhale as if the first half used up all the air. A violence turned inward rather than out, perhaps. We pull and rub and tear at ourselves until, like those worry beads, we have lost all color. Who's to say that worriers aren't constantly in battle (embattled as they are) with those aggressively anxious thoughts? We worriers have scars, too.

WARRIOR AS INNER PEACE

A few weeks after the counselling appointment, I walk into the Sunset Room, a large window-filled room in college where the first Mindfulness session is being held. The course is well attended. At least forty students sit on chairs arranged in a semi-circle in the large conference room; many more have spilled onto the floor and are sitting cross-legged, hunched over their iPhones. The screen at the front of the room reads MINDFULNESS in capital letters, white against a soft sky-blue. A woman sits serenely on a chair in front of the screen, smiling at us warmly as we enter and sit down. I am reminded of a cult induction scene in a film. After a few minutes, the woman, still smiling pleasantly, presses a button on her phone, emitting a soothing gong sound, made slightly tinny through the iPhone's small speakers.

Welcome, everyone, she says. She introduces the course and then gives us our first exercise. Close your eyes, she says. Put your hands out in front of you, palms up.

I do as commanded. I hear her footsteps start and stop as she presumably circles the room. They get louder; she reaches me and I sense something smooth and round, the size of a small bead, being placed into my hand.

Feel the object I just gave you, she tells us. Keep your eyes closed. Trust yourself. Surrender to the moment.

HOUSE GUESTS

It is a well-known stereotype amongst Palestinians that we Jerusalemites are uncharacteristically[53] unwelcoming. When a guest arrives, the old joke goes, the Jerusalemite says: Welcome, welcome. When did you say you were leaving? And wouldn't you be more comfortable in a hotel?

The summer before writing this essay, one of my closest friends came to stay with me, in the small house I was renting with five other people in Oxford. It was a last-minute and indefinite visit, sprung on both of us because of a work crisis of hers: a real test of my hosting ability. I was desperate to help her and house her: not only do I not get to see her very often—she lives across the world—but I knew how awful I'd feel in her place, how much it would mean to me to be offered a home. She showed up with two large suitcases and I readied myself. Welcome, welcome, I said to her, sternly shushing my inner Jerusalemite. Please, stay as long as you like.

As the days turned into weeks, she kept apologizing and I kept insisting—both to her and to myself—that I was delighted to have her around. But the truth is, it was hard. As a graduate student, it is assumed that my time is my own, or, more to the point, when a visitor comes, that my time is theirs. There are no set hours, there is no office to go into. Work space, friend space, me space, it's all the same: one rectangular wooden table in the cramped kitchen-cum-dining-cum-living room. I would make a cafetière in the morning and settle down in the seat directly in front of the oven (so close the oven door will barely open), leaving the better seat—by the doorway—for my friend. We'd sit there for hours and I would look at datasets I didn't understand and talk with her and plan our lunch and wash our mugs and

57

get emails from senior researchers who needed something written by me desperately urgently, and I would feel torn between all these sides of myself and all of my conflicting duties. I'd worry that, between the both of us, I was taking up too much of the communal space in the house, so I would try to make myself smaller, so that she could take up more room. I worried I was not giving her enough time, or comfort, or hospitality, and I worried that my housemates were getting frustrated by the imposition of an additional person in the house. I wanted to make her feel welcome, but I worried that my worry was too visible for that. The day she left, I burst into tears—yes, in part because I missed her. More so because I was relieved she'd gone. I could finally have my space again, my privacy.

There was and there was not, in the depths of the past, a woman with very few boundaries. Nusayba bint Ka'ab al Khazrajia, my supposed ancestor the warrior woman, lived at a time with very little privacy. In Arabia in the seventh century, people lived in tribes, in compounds or in tents, with multiple wives to one husband and, in the case of many of the nomadic Bedouin tribes, multiple husbands to one wife—husbands who would often casually drop in on this wife individually or as a group, a constant stream of sexually demanding visitors. The idea of private time, of private space, would have been laughable. (That said, the way a Bedouin woman would divorce a husband was to simply turn her tent around so that the entrance would face away from him when he came over.[54] I picture this like in a cartoon: a woman standing up to raise the structure and spin it round, a puff of smoke in the air, creating a threshold across which, it was clear, he was no longer welcome.)

When Muhammad was at his peak as a prophet, living in Yathrib, Nusayba's hometown, and with thousands of followers, his house was also the mosque: visitors and locals would come to pray with him, meet him, meet each other, put up tents and stay for days in his compound, using his personal space for social and religious purposes. This was a hangover from his early days as a leader, when he'd first arrived in Yathrib with only a few dozen followers and the local tribes—Nusayba's among them—to welcome him. Out of his compound he'd created a center for his teachings, and from that, a community.[55] All welcome into his faith and into his home. But that level of porousness was not, it seems, wholly sustainable once Muhammad became truly renowned. At that point, in 627 CE, after a particularly long wedding party of his, a conveniently timed divine revelation created a clear boundary between the private and the public—one translation of the Quranic verse puts it particularly strongly: "Believers, do not enter the homes of the Prophet without permission and if invited for a meal, do not come too early and linger until the meal is ready. But if you are invited, then enter on time. Once you have eaten, then go on your way, and do not stay for casual talk. Such behavior is truly annoying to the Prophet, yet he is too shy to ask you to leave." (33:53) Perhaps Muhammad was also, in his soul, a Jerusalemite.

That same verse is also where the idea of the hijab first appears; in fact, this verse is commonly known as "the verse of the hijab." The next sentence of the verse above is: "and when you ask [his wives] for something, ask them from behind a hijab. This will assure the purity of your hearts as well as theirs." There is a link, it seems, between the boundaries created in the home—where guests shouldn't linger, shouldn't wander in expecting food without being invited—and the boundaries created on the body. These are the spaces in which you are welcome, this verse seems to say, and these are the spaces in which you are not. Unlike the word "veil" in English, which is linked to the idea of covering up, the word "hijab" comes from *hjb*, which in Arabic means to screen, or to separate. In the Quran, the word "hijab" is also used to refer to the sunset, that brief borderline between day and night. I can imagine that, if I were living in a social and religious hub—where people were constantly coming and going, demanding my attention, trying to engage me in conversation—any sort of barrier would be a relief.

My grandmother, the heart of religion in my otherwise relatively agnostic family, hardly ever wore any kind of veil. Hijabs were a special occasion, going-out affair; they were made of light, wispy muslin that would flutter, slightly, as she wrapped it over her head. Once or twice as a young child I imitated her when she took me along to her jam'iya, her old ladies' charitable society, feeling glamorous, like Audrey Hepburn on her holiday in Rome. It's strange to think now of the source of that tradition: those wives of the Prophet with their need for privacy, for boundary, for space. Even stranger to think how deeply emblematic the veil has become for Islam—the sign of everything from regression to rebellion.

It was only after years of living in the UK that I began to really notice the hijab. You don't pay much attention to things that you're used to, and when I

59

was growing up, at least a third of those on Jerusalem's streets usually had some sort of head covering, whether they were Muslim or Jewish or Christian. It was always there. Not something that evoked any particular emotion, neither alarming nor empowering, just—present. But any kind of externally worn religiosity is, of course, noticed and noted in Europe, and so I began to see it too. A veil: synonymous with Islam, highlighting difference. Ironic, that a cloth designed to create privacy brings with it so much exposure.

⁂

Would Nusayba have donned a hijab of some sort, either before or after she converted? It's highly unlikely. In pre-Islamic Arabia, in the early days (3000 BCE) of Mesopotamia, as in Europe both then and later, veils were often status symbols distinguishing the elite or the free from the poor or the enslaved.[56] As feminist scholar Fatema Mernissi highlights, the Babylonian king Hammurabi imposed the veil for aristocratic women and actually forbade prostitutes from using it.[57] Under the Assyrian empire, again, veiling was made mandatory for married women and concubines; likewise, under the Christian Sasanid empire, aristocratic women were made to cover their hair.[58] And even before that, in ancient Greek and Roman cultures, veiling marked out women of the upper classes, and this trend continued on throughout Europe well into the twentieth century. Alexander Roslin's famous portrait, *The Lady with the Veil*, painted in 1768, shows his wife looking seductively through a dark veil worn *à la Bolognese*—in the style of Bologna, where the best veils were produced, where Roman courtesans and young women would cover their heads with floor-length silk in white, black, yellow, often also covering their faces as well as they sauntered along stone-slabbed streets. You are veiled because you're valuable, untouchable, pure. In part, this is to do with visibility, of course—or rather, invisibility, hiding from view the desirable or the erotic or the beautiful—but veiling also creates a physical barrier, one that protects both from the elements and from other people. Veils are curtains drawn across the body, delineating the private from the public.

Multiple authors have pointed out that, in the Quran, the term hijab is applied only to the wives of the Prophet (and, in fact, reference to wearing it was a metaphor for becoming Muhammad's wife, as in *she who wore the veil*).[59] It's never applied to any other woman. Instead, it seems the hijab only started being worn by Muslims after Muhammad's death—probably, in part, as a way to emulate his wives. Like many aspects of religious tradition, the veil's importance has grown through time, through interpretation and imitation. So it's extremely unlikely that Nusayba, part of the Banu Najjar tribe in the mostly poor, agricultural town of Yathrib, would have been important enough for a hijab worn in the style of Muhammad's wives. Instead, she probably would have worn a tunic and a wrap called a jilbab, worn loosely and exposing the chest. It would have perhaps been made from a heavy, scratchy material, and some have suggested that this type of cloak sometimes would be worn over the head, covering an eye.[60] Perhaps, then, in the hot, sandy desert, with showers being few and far between, covering her head occasionally isn't entirely unlikely. I picture her half-naked, a raggedy cloak wrapped carelessly around her well-built body.

⁓⊰⁓

I followed my friend's visit with a visit of my own, to my parents' home in Jerusalem. It still feels like my home, too, though it is not the same house I grew up in, and too many of my schoolfriends left the country years ago. So leaving it is always a bit painful; there is always a sense of wrenching as we drive to the airport, as I stare at the mangy, worn-looking hills that dip and rise beside the Route 1 motorway that goes between Jerusalem and Tel Aviv. It's made more painful by the security processes at the airport, which are particularly bad if you happen to be a Person of a Suspicious Nature (read: Palestinian), and especially if you are a Puzzling Person of a Suspicious Nature (read: East Jerusalemite). I am put into a special line, given the highest security number, and searched extremely thoroughly. The idea of privacy here is gone entirely: two women in dark suits with lanyards round their necks, wearing white rubber gloves and strong perfume, pull out and examine my (slightly stained) thong, my pads, my beleaguered bras, my books and my water bottle. They take everything out and pass the items between them, displaying each one for the other guards, as well as all the fellow travelers who are sitting on the special seats in the special High Security area. The entire inner contents of my luggage and handbag. The security workers pause when they get to my half-eaten granola bar, a comment is made, in Hebrew, and the bar is passed along and then back to the original security operative. My private life on full, laughable display.

A few seats down from me, a woman in a maroon tunic and veil is being asked by two of the guards whether she is wearing any jewelry underneath her clothes. She is struggling to understand them; they are communicating with her in English, a language in which she is clearly not comfortable. They point at the tiny cubicle beside the X-ray machine and make gestures to help explain that she will be going in there with them: this is the strip-search area. They will go in with her, two women, and one of them will stand while the other asks the veiled woman to pull down her trousers and take off her tunic and undershirt. The guard will then gently feel—through the slightly rough, see-through plastic of her gloves—inside the top seam of the woman's underwear, underneath the wire of the woman's bra, moving her fingers along the sensitive flesh in an act which, in other circumstances, would feel exceedingly intimate. Their bodies will all be absurdly, almost erotically, close. I know this room and this routine because I have been in it many, many times. I have never worn a veil, though, so I don't know how this would impact the process—I picture the woman undoing it all, struggling to move her arms in the circular motion necessary to unravel the material, avoiding the other bodies and the thin gray walls of the cubicle. I imagine the added layer of exposure this would entail, the sense of intrusion at a physical boundary so callously crossed.

Once on the plane, I see a different woman a few rows in front of me, also wearing a headscarf. She looks hot, her face flushed, but then again, I probably don't look that different. Privacy doesn't much exist in twenty-first-century planes either; the man in the seat beside mine has pulled out a mortadella sandwich, and now it's me who has contorted my body in ways I didn't realize were possible in order to move out of his way, his elbow occasionally darting dangerously close to my sternum. At one point during the flight, I indicate to him that I need to move past in order to get to the bathroom; instead of getting up, though, like I expect him to, he simply sits back and grins. I smile tersely and do my best to squeeze through, my back towards him. I feel something on my bum as I maneuver out, my legs stepping over his, but I decide to ignore it. Maybe it's him, maybe it's the armrest, or even the mortadella. I don't want to know. I spend most of the flight standing in the aisle.

I am constantly aware of these intrusions, perhaps especially because boundaries are in vogue these days: defining them, respecting them, navigating them. I am repeatedly told by well-meaning friends that I should set clear boundaries at work, or with family. Even Oprah has a step-by-step guide on boundary-setting, on how to cure "the disease to please."[61] We are meant to protect ourselves by being clear about what lines cannot be crossed: *no work emails on weekends, no coming into my bedroom without knocking.* Boundaries, as one psychiatrist told the *Wall Street Journal*, mark "when your own autonomy and self-esteem are being invaded."[62] Not everyone's boundaries are the same, of course—Ernest Hartmann, a psychiatrist and dream researcher working in the 1980s and 1990s, who is often credited with popularizing the concept of personal boundaries, differentiated between those with "thin" boundaries, who experience the border between themselves and others as porous, and those with "thick" boundaries, who are rigid and well defended.[63] I am almost definitely of the former type—too sensitive to the incursion of others—but maybe it's more general than that. It's a particularly Western thing, perhaps, and a particularly Muslim thing as well, to care so much about boundaries, to want clear lines between the public and private. Norman Lewis argues that this need is absent in the Far East; in Vietnam, for instance, the home spills out onto the street, the family living room part of a larger communal space.[64]

On a purely personal level, I think that a hijab—or even its more extreme version, the niqab—would bring me comfort, in the same way that the feeling of closing my eyes does, even now, as an adult, giving me the sense of invisibility. *If you should ask something of me, do so from behind a hijab.* A definitive, nonverbal way to create a boundary, and to feel some protection from the encroachment of the world. To feel, as Mohja Kahf, the Syrian-American poet put it, "a tent of tranquility."[65] Of course, the desire to create a boundary between myself and others isn't a good enough reason to start wearing a hijab—related as it might be to the reason it first appeared in Islam—and I don't have the faith required. More to the point, though, I'm just not brave enough. I would wear it so that I could hide, yet nothing makes you more visible, these days, than wearing a veil. What I would want from it is the space that it provided Muhammad's wives; but maybe what I really want is to be able to say: don't come in unless you're invited. And definitely don't linger.

Being from Ramle, a city far from Jerusalem, my grandmother was always hospitable, almost to the point of farce. Her doors were never locked, even her garden gate—which leads out onto a main road—was almost always open. People from the street would often knock on her glass-fronted front door, or even just let themselves in, some to say hello, some to ask for money, which she would always give. It was common for me to come over for a visit and find two or three people I didn't know sitting beside her on the sofas. When we were clearing out her belongings from the awda rafi'a—the narrow room—in the back of the house after her death, we found a giant pile of thin mattresses neatly stacked in one of the corners. For the refugees, my dad said, after a moment. Her hospitality was as firmly rooted as her faith; she believed in letting people in, no boundaries necessary.

Nusayba probably also often had people around her in her own home: her sons, her clan, her tribe. She would, most likely, have had a deeply porous life, people coming in and out with increasing frequency and quantity as the Prophet became more famous and drew to them more followers. (She would also likely have been part of the crowd milling around Muhammad's compound: a lingerer.) Her small agricultural village, her home, was transformed into a central hub for the converted; it would have been a change, for her, to see it flooded with so many strangers. Whether she ever had, or wanted, any privacy is impossible to know. What I imagine is this, at least: being in the desert, in this relatively remote village, it was easy to get away, at least. To wake in the night and slip out, unseen, mount a camel and wander, for a bit, under the stars.

My friend's visit felt interminable, despite it only lasting just under three weeks. I began waking up with the dawn, just so as to have some time to myself—to work, to think, to just be. I found space and privacy in this way—through time—impossible as it was to find it through space. I felt, and still feel, ashamed of this reclusiveness. I desperately want to be porous, boundary-free, unveiled. But in reality I have always been a deeply private person, and shared space, exposure, frightens me. I like walls and barriers—ironic, maybe, for a Palestinian—and the ability to shut others out. I like locks on my doors, and I tend to keep the curtains closed. My social media accounts are quiet places, dominated by the voices of others. Maybe there's some epigenetic trauma in my desire for fixed territory—here is mine, here is yours—maybe national loss has seeped into my marrow, somehow. Or maybe it is just the Jerusalemite in me.

THE SEDER

K invites me to join in her family's Seder, which this year, because of the pandemic, will be virtual. A Skype Seder, she tells me. Don't worry, my sister's boyfriend will be there, so you won't be the only non-family member.

Thank you, I say, grateful for the chance to be part of a family gathering, even if it's over the internet, and touched that I have been asked. That sounds great.

Oh, and you'll need some coriander sprigs, she says.

OK.

The next day, I find an email from her with two links to online versions of the Haggadah. *For tonight!* the email reads. Having never been to a Seder before, I am unsure what role the Haggadah will play, but I open the links, read through the first few lines. *Tonight, we gather to celebrate Passover. Passover is a holiday commemorating the Israelites' liberation from slavery and their exodus from Egypt, as told in the beginning of the Book of Exodus in the Hebrew bible.*

In the afternoon, I get a text message:

You'll need these!

Sacred items list:

Red wine (4 cups' worth)

Bread of some sort (unleavened or cracker if possible!—but any bread will do)

Small pot of salt water (to dip the coriander!)

I root around in our lockdown kitchen and find some slightly vinegary cooking wine, an old piece of sliced white bread and a lettuce leaf. I take them upstairs to my bedroom.

Then, later:

Oh! And horseradish and an apple if you can!

I go back and find a pear, slightly soft, and some mustard. I snap a picture and send it to K. Will these do?

They'll be fine, she says.

I open my Skype a few minutes early to make sure the camera is angled appropriately—no accidental boob shot—and wait apprehensively. I feel like a bit of an interloper, a fraud. Not just a Muslim but a secular Muslim. I feel I will sprout a beard and horns halfway through the ceremony.

"Hello!" I say, waving at the screen, which pops up to show me K and her parents seated around a table laden with food. They are each holding a book; K's father and her sister's boyfriend are wearing kippahs. The sight transports me instantly to Jerusalem.

There is a bit of technical kerfuffle as K's sister tries to connect to Skype. Laptops are adjusted and microphone levels are fixed, and then we begin: K's father begins talking from the head of the table. So for those of you who are not familiar with the Seder, he says—looking towards the screen but slightly missing the camera—the way it works is I'll read a little and then we'll eat or drink and then someone else will read from their Haggadah and so on and so forth. Right, then.

He starts us off, speaking in Hebrew, while I follow the translation K has sent me: *Blessed are You, God, our God, King of the universe, who has chosen us from among all people, and raised us above all tongues, and made us holy through His commandments. And You, God, our God, have given us in love and festivals for happiness, feasts, and festive seasons for rejoicing this the day of this Feast of Matzot and this Festival of holy convocation, the Season of our Freedom in love, a holy convocation, commemorating the departure from Egypt.*[66]

⟡

There was and there was not, in the depths of the past, a woman who lived amongst religions both ancient and new. Nusayba bint Ka'ab al Khazrajia, my supposed ancestor the warrior woman, may have sat at a Seder a bit like this one, I realize, as we go round the virtual table, beginning to read from the text and enact the rituals. Watching the family sip their wine in unison—a part of the ceremony—through my small computer screen,

I feel struck by religion's ability to create a thread through time, despite the twenty-first-century setup. At this moment, around the world, Jewish families are sitting and telling the same stories about their people that are told every year, that have been told every year for generations, that Nusayba herself may even have been told. She may have heard about the exodus from Egypt, may have taken a bite of unleavened bread. It's certainly possible; there were a number of Jewish Arab tribes in Yathrib who would have been her neighbors; her tribe, the Khazraj, were known for being close to one in particular. In fact, her knowledge of religion would probably have initially come from these Jewish tribesmen; they would likely have been the ones to introduce her to God, to fasting, to religious ritual, before Muhammad did, so that his ideas would have felt familiar thanks to theirs.

Their influence on Muhammad himself, it seems, was also profound. When Muhammad first proclaimed himself as a prophet of God, the skeptical Meccans are said to have sent two messengers (who famously hated Muhammad) to ask the Rabbis of Yathrib—as experts in monotheism—for their take on the matter.[67] Then, when Muhammad arrived in Yathrib, Muslims were told to face Jerusalem when they prayed, like their Jewish neighbors. This was in part, some have suggested, because Muhammad wanted to establish the closeness of the two religions, but also because he wanted to earn his neighbors' respect and acceptance.[68] Rules to do with diet and purity were, it has been proposed, largely adopted from the Jewish ones, and Muslims were encouraged to forge connections through marriage with the Jewish clans.[69] Much of the religion's early development, in other words, happened with a cognizance of, and in the context of, Judaism.

The similarities between the Abrahamic religions are no coincidence. As the Quran explains, Islam sees itself as the culmination and the final expression of all three: the Jewish and Christian prophets also being Muslim prophets, the Torah and the Gospels referred to in the Quran as sacred scriptures. All the People of the Book, or the mu'minin—those who have faith in the one God—have a place in heaven, the Quran assures us. Islam sees itself as "at once the primordial religion, a return to the original religion of oneness, and the final religion,"[70] as Seyyed Hossein Nasr puts it. Islam and Judaism appear particularly fraternal: they share an emphasis on monotheism, on gender segregation, on legal doctrine, on ritual and dress. The Talmud, like the

Hadith, is presented as a chain of transmission. Both have a rather disturbing obsession with menstruation.

There have also been overlaps between the two religions, traditions adopted by one and then the other. Judaism changed its laws on divorce, for instance, because of Islam.[71] In the latter, women had more power, could be granted a divorce without the consent of the husband, and were entitled to compensation. It was an appealing prospect, and for a time Jewish women were converting to Islam just to have a bit more control.[72] Though obfuscated by contemporary discourse which pits Muslims and Jews against each other, it is easy to see the intricate tapestry of the religions when standing in the Old City of Jerusalem—the Greek Orthodox priests in their full gowns and high headdresses, the Hasidic Jewish men in suits and tall black hats, the Muslim imams with their long beards and gravelly voices, the tourists sobbing hysterically as they walk into the Church of the Holy Sepulchre, all so deeply theistic they might appear theatrical if it weren't for the political weight, and cost, of their beliefs.

Outward dress and specific praying-place aside, many of the lines and patterns are the same, highlighted all the more extremely by their contrast with the secular, agnostic, outside world. You might see one or two preachers in Times Square, but it would be unusual to find yourself surrounded by groups in religious garb, congregating en masse to perform a daily prayer ritual. In the Old City, by contrast, the secular bystander is the woman out of place and time, awkwardly detached from a God that seems to be the driving force for everyone around her. Once, at a Shabbat dinner with a friend and his rabbi in Jerusalem, the rabbi made a similar point, telling me he had more in common with the sheikh down the road than his fellow Jew in New York. He tore off a piece of bread and dipped it into his soup, and placed his other arm weightily on the table as he turned to look at me more closely. It is not just that we both live in this land, he said, taking a bite of the soggy bread. It is that we both live in the world of God, you see? Whereas your average reformist Jew in New York, he does not! He smiled at me warmly as if to ask if I understood, and I nodded. It's obvious: the links between Judaism and Islam are much, much closer than the links between theism and atheism.

We forget this, though. Colonialism and orientalism and occupation have emphasized the differences between the religions, even while paradoxically and erroneously reducing the Palestinian struggle for self-determination to a dispute between tribes. Perhaps, in a sense, this has always been the Western project: eyed with equal suspicion by the Christian West, Jews and Muslims have historically been viewed as too "primitive" to be European-civilized, more in common with each other than anyone else.[73] Too often in the discourse, Palestinian rights get swirled in with Muslim ambition, Israeli action with Jewish aspiration. We are told that we are the same—non-white, non-Western, non-Christian—but that our similarities make us irreconcilable, like twins who resent each other for their sameness. Never mind colonization, expulsion, terrorism, territorial expansion—tricks all learned, in part, from Europe. To the West, the Palestinian—Israeli conflict can largely be summed up by simple reference to Isaac and Ishmael. Whatcha gonna do, eh? The Westerner shrugs.

-⟨⟩-

As the Seder progresses, I find myself relaxing into the ceremony of it, basking in the warmth and gaiety, enjoying the jovial good cheer that so often accompanies religious festivities. It feels a bit like Christmas, a bit like Ramadan. K's family has a variety of Haggadahs, so there are comparisons of translations—"mine says "cut him *off*," not "cut him *down*," which seems to me quite different, don't you think?"—and lighthearted nods to ritual. ("Does the matzah need to be uncovered now? Oh damn, we left it uncovered from the last one, didn't we? Oh well," K's dad says, fumbling with the napkin covering the flatbread on the table.)

But I find myself stopped short when, in the midst of all this joy—after the spring onions are thwacked during the chorus of "Dayenu," but before the third glass of wine is drunk—Jerusalem suddenly makes an appearance. K's father speaks the words in Hebrew as I read along in English, a cold lurch in my stomach:

Have mercy, Lord our God, upon Israel Your people, upon Jerusalem Your city, upon Zion the abode of Your glory, upon the kingship of the house of David Your anointed, and upon the great and holy House which is called by Your Name.

-⟨⟩-

The year was 1949 when an armistice agreement formally divided Jerusalem into an Israeli-controlled West and a Jordanian-controlled East. This happened as a result of the 1948 war that established the state of Israel, in what had previously been known as Palestine. (Other things that happened in 1948 include: the nationalization of British railways, Burmese independence, a cease-fire between the Netherlands and Indonesia, the assassination of Gandhi, Sri Lankan independence and the first women being sworn into the US Navy.) When my father was only nineteen—about the age he met my mother—the 1967 war broke out, leading to Israel's military occupation of the Gaza Strip and the West Bank, including East Jerusalem, his hometown. New municipal boundaries were created, which excluded various Palestinian villages—one of these was where I spent my first few years on Earth.

In June of 1967, the territory was militarily annexed, and the Israeli parliament extended Israeli jurisdiction to East Jerusalem, a move that was considered illegal under international law[74] and condemned by the UN General Assembly.[75] That month, the government held a census in the newly annexed area: Palestinians who happened to be away, for whatever reason (the dangers of war, for example), lost the right to return to their homes and live in Jerusalem. Thirteen years later, in June of 1980, the Israeli government declared Jerusalem its "eternal and undivided capital" and reaffirmed its de facto annexation of the territory. Again, another UN resolution condemned the action, demanding that Israel rescind its actions.

That didn't happen—and still hasn't.

Rebuild Jerusalem the holy city speedily in our days. Blessed are You, Lord, who in His mercy rebuilds Jerusalem. Amen, the Haggadah reads. I sip my vinegary cooking wine and smile as K compliments her mother on the food, as K's sister makes a comment about her own inadequate cooking, and everyone laughs, though all I can think about, now, is Jerusalem.

If you wanted to make it hard for a certain type of person to live in a certain place, you could go about this in a variety of ways. For instance, you could start by making their actual residency tricky—make it notoriously hard for that type of person to gain citizenship, even if they were born there, by denying it to about half of those who apply, or by halting the acceptances almost entirely. Make this the case even if this place—their birthplace—is their only home, they have no legal status in any other country, and did not choose to live there. Give them, instead of citizenship, a different status—say, "permanent resident," such as immigrants have. Make this status precarious and easily lost. For example, if they lived outside the country for a few years, they would lose it; if they wanted to go on holiday, they'd need to apply for a re-entry visa in order to come back home. Make it so that they'd have to *prove,* constantly, that this place was their so-called "center of life." Make it especially hard for families: make it so that a child could be given "permanent resident" status only if the father already held it, but not if just the mother did, meaning that a woman who married a foreigner would not be able to raise her child in this place. Make it so that these residents can't vote or campaign in national elections and can't run for mayor, either.

You might also want to focus on making day-to-day living a bit hard. Maybe you start by concentrating on housing: make sure that there just isn't enough physical space for this type of person by declaring large areas of this place "unfit for building," forbidding construction there. Make sure that there are no government construction initiatives there, so that the onus on building apartment blocks and housing is on the people themselves. But make it impossibly hard for that type of person to get building permits and prove land ownership, encouraging people in need of places to live to build illegally, and then use this illegality as an excuse to keep knocking down these houses and evicting their residents. Do all this while making it simple for other types of people to build there and live there. Make it so that the other types of people can move into the recently evicted residences with ease.

Does all this sound Kafkaesque? These are real policies that apply to Palestinians in Jerusalem—everything from the building permits to the residency issues. Take citizenship: of the 4,152 East Jerusalemites who applied for citizenship between 2014 and 2016, only eighty-four were approved.[76] "Permanent resident" is a real status conferred on Palestinian residents of East Jerusalem, and if you live outside Jerusalem for several years, even in the West Bank (a ten-minute drive away from Jerusalem, where you may have lots of family, which is internationally recognized as part of the same occupied territory but designated by Israel, for all intents and purposes, as a foreign country), you risk having it taken away. If you're a "permanent resident," you're treated like an immigrant.[77]

I was born there, I grew up there—even my grandparents were born there—and yet I have a special East Jerusalem ID card (called a hawiyah) to signify my special "permanent residency" status. And I'm lucky it was my mother who was a foreigner, because if it had been my father, it would have been nigh on impossible to grow up there. My residency is a precious, precious thing that I live in constant fear of losing. Every few years I go to the Ministry of the Interior, and wait for many hours in fluorescent, institutional rooms to show documents that attest to the fact that I am a student, and that that is the sole reason I live abroad. I do what I can to demonstrate that Jerusalem is still my "center of life"—but the term is ambiguous for a reason. I am always afraid I will not have done enough.

Or take the housing situation: much of East Jerusalem is designated as "unfit for building", making construction impossible for many Palestinians, in spite of a rapidly expanding population.[78] And while in West Jerusalem, construction is initiated by the Israel Lands Authority or the Construction and Housing Ministry, and most buildings are erected and sold by contractors and supervised by the state, there are almost no such initiatives in East Jerusalem.[79] And building permits are close to impossible to get.[80] The process is both very costly and extremely complicated, with a high likelihood of an application being rejected (my parents spent over forty years trying to gain one). So, many much-needed housing units are built "illegally" and then knocked down. Of course, none of this is the case for Israeli residents of West Jerusalem, who are, increasingly, encouraged to move into the Palestinian neighborhoods in the East.[81] In fact, according to a 2021 EU report, roughly 14,894 settlers now live in East Jerusalem.[82]

Or take the unequal distribution of services. Before I went to study in the UK less than a decade ago,[83] East Jerusalem held almost 40 percent of the city's population,[84] and yet only 10 percent of the municipal budget was invested in the area[85]—despite Palestinians paying the same tax rates as Israelis, whose per capita income is roughly eight times higher.[86] Thus, according to a 2012 B'Tselem[87] report:[88] a thousand public parks in the West, forty-five in the East. There were a thousand residents per playground in the West, and thirty times that in the East. Thirty-four swimming pools in the West, three in the East. Twenty-six libraries in the West, two in the East. Over five hundred sports facilities in the West, only thirty-three in the East. Social workers, welfare offices and post offices all follow this same pattern. In fact, only seven per cent of postal workers served these East Jerusalem neighborhoods (my neighborhood, for instance, was not). Much of East Jerusalem was then—and continues to be now—not green, not clean, not well connected, not well cultured. Much of it is poor, shabby and overpopulated.

In Jerusalem—city of Christmas songs—Israelis and Palestinians live alongside each other, cheek by jowl, in an odd, dystopian setup, in which, as B'Tselem puts it, "Israel has been treating the Palestinian residents as unwanted immigrants and has been working systematically to drive them out."[89] In Jerusalem—city of William Blake's poetry—Palestinians cannot rely on the authorities, knowing that these authorities (the law, the police, the army) will likely meet them with excessive, often deadly, force.[90] In Jerusalem—city of Jez Butterworth's classic play—Palestinians face forced expulsions and discrimination. Unlike somewhere like Tel Aviv, in Jerusalem you are confronted with the lesser-lives of the Palestinians who live a second-class life right next door. In Tel Aviv, if you are young enough to have no memories of the city prior to 1967, you can look around you and really feel you are in Israel. The beaches, the restaurants, the nightclubs. Hebrew signs on Israeli shops being run by lovely Jewish hippies. What Palestinians? What conflict?

In Jerusalem, this is harder. In Jerusalem, all you have to do is walk for ten minutes from one area to another, and you are confronted with a stark contrast. Not in terms of look—Western friends who've visited Jerusalem delight in telling me that *you all look the same!*—but in terms of languages, services, freedoms, rights. And while there is a clear split, we are still constantly mixing. There are often Israelis buying bread in the Palestinian bakeries, and Palestinians working behind counters in Israeli shops. In fact, much cheap labor within Israeli services is done by Palestinians—the latter make up roughly 69 percent of the workers in construction and 55 percent of those in transportation, storage and postal services in West Jerusalem.[91]

Despite this, Palestinian residents of the area—myself included—obstinately continue to be a significant percentage of the population, even while the Israeli government makes every effort to expel us. And we're the fortunate ones! Free to move, entitled to health insurance and education:[92] we Palestinian residents of Jerusalem have freedoms that our counterparts in the West Bank do not, rights that our families in Gaza could only imagine in their daydreams. Every day, in fact, I think about how lucky I am not to have been born on the wrong side of a then-invisible line. But this situation is nonetheless grueling, draining and dehumanizing. And most importantly: it is meant to be.

Jerusalem, then, is a contradiction—an integrated, divided city.

Or, in the words of Amnesty International: apartheid.[93]

K catches my eye through the screen and smiles at me with a little wave, her mother temporarily distracted, bending down to pet the dog, her father and sister also paused, for a moment, discussing the appropriateness of the digital setup. I smile back from my empty bedroom. You OK? she mouths. I nod and give a thumbs-up, though I am not, in truth, entirely comfortable any more. I read on from the Haggadah: *If He had brought us before Mount Sinai, and had not given us the Torah Dayenu, it would have sufficed us! If He had given us the Torah, and had not brought us into the land of Israel Dayenu, it would have sufficed us! If He had brought us into the land of Israel, and had not built for us the Beit Habechirah (Chosen House; the Beit Hamikdash) Dayenu, it would have sufficed us!*

Though it is unlikely, it has been suggested that some of the Jewish tribes who lived in Yathrib in fact came from Greater Syria, after being driven out by the Romans in 70 CE. Nusayba's neighbors, then, might have had ancestors who were Jerusalemites. These Jewish tribes—the Banu Nadir, the Banu Qurayza, and the Banu Qainuqa[94]—were date merchants, sometimes also dealing in wine.[95] They were part of the fabric of the oasis—this fabric being, by all accounts, rough and uneven. It was a politically uneasy place: the two large non-Jewish Arab tribes—the Khazraj (of which Nusayba's clan, the Banu Najjar, formed a part) and the Aws—were in a constant battle for control of Yathrib, and the Jewish tribes were split in their loyalties between the two. Jew against Jew, Arab against Arab. Nusayba then, like me, would have been used to living in a place steeped in conflict.

In fact, Muhammad, on arriving in Yathrib in 622 as an escapee from

Mecca, had to do some diplomatic work to ease the tensions. The famous Constitution of Medina is one of the only sources we have from that period; in it, Muhammad sets out rules for cohabitation that would allow the various clans and tribes of Yathrib to live with each other peaceably, sounding for all the world like a weary mother—the earliest example of Eastern "conflict resolution,"[96] according to one academic. Each tribe, the Constitution reads, will be responsible for its own ward, and will pay whatever blood money is needed to even the scores and free whatever prisoners they may be holding in order to keep the peace. All would have the same rights, and "the Jews of Banu 'Awf shall be considered as one political community (Umma) along with the believers—for the Jews their religion, and for the Muslims theirs, be one client or patron."[97]

It worked well, for a while. But then Muhammad turned into a powerful political figure, as well as a religious prophet, and the ruling tribes of Mecca—who were threatened by his revolutionary politics and his popularity—became more and more aggressive in response, waging war on Yathrib. Alliances were broken. People were betrayed. Depending on the source and the interpretation, those three Arabian Jewish tribes—the Banu Nadir, the Banu Qurayza and the Banu Qainuqa—were among those who decided to work with Meccans, and they were punished.[98] Two tribes were exiled; one was executed.[99] Such were the brutal stakes.

How did Nusayba feel about this, friends that she grew up with being sent away or killed? Did she think it was justified? Was death and conflict so unavoidable, so normalized, that she barely felt it at all? Or did she feel devastated by the loss, tenderly carrying the weight of the memory on her shoulders until she died?

In the introduction to *The Ethics of Memory*, the Israeli philosopher Avishai Margalit relates a conversation that he has with his parents, in which they take different positions on the issue of memory. While his father suggests that communities should look towards the future, his mother maintains that "the only honourable role for the Jews that remain is to form communities of memory—to serve as 'soul candles' like the candles that are ritually kindled in memory of the dead."[100]

I think of these soul candles on the day of the Seder, as I watch my friend K and her family discuss the story of the Exodus of the Israelites. The internet connection is unstable so there is a lag every once in a while, an odd pause in the conversation, expressions frozen mid-word, mouths jerked comically to one side. In these moments I look again at the Haggadah—my eyes unintentionally catching on the word "Jerusalem"—and wonder if it, too, isn't a type of rekindling. According to Jewish practice, the tale of the Israelites is to be repeated every year at the Seder, the Haggadah read annually so as to pass on this story of slavery and freedom, pain and reward, to one's children. It is an active, communal remembering, I think, as I listen to a passage, noticing that the pronouns used—"me," "us"—make it sound like it was this very family who suffered at the hands of the Egyptians: "All nations surround me, but I cut them down in the Name of the Lord. They surrounded me, they encompassed me, but I cut them down in the Name of the Lord," K says, almost as though reliving the moment. She confirms this later, telling me that, despite not being religious, the words of the Haggadah have emotional resonance for her. Somehow, on hearing them, she is moved by the memory of an event she never actually experienced.

Only that morning, I'd had my own moment of rekindling. I'd come across an article in the *New York Review* written by a Jewish-American journalist based in Jerusalem that detailed a horrific crash that occurred in the West Bank roughly a decade ago.[101] The story was more than a tale of grief and accident, though. Beginning with the Nakba—the Palestinian exodus of 1948, in which hundreds of thousands of Palestinians were permanently displaced, and thousands were massacred, as a result of the creation of the new state of Israel[102]—it offered a kaleidoscopic view of the last six decades of Israeli occupation and its effects on the daily lives of Palestinians. As brilliant as the piece was, I'd found it hard to get through. I kept having to stop, pace, take deep breaths, dive back in. Take a drink of water, slow my heart down. Pause again, read some more. Though the Nakba took place decades ago, it is still, in many ways, lived daily. To be Palestinian is to carry the Nakba in one's genes, the shock alive and buzzing, molding our subconscious. Reading about it brought the candle's flame closer to the skin.

Derrida[103] was the first to introduce the idea of hauntology—wherein specters of the past (in his case, Marxism) seem to maintain a looming presence in the now—but the concept has since grown to refer to a whole range of phenomena, including the way the ghosts of war and genocide interact with memory. In hauntology, the "haunting is about a nullified possible future that a bygone existence (be it the self or an other) was experienced to promise," explains Sadeq Rahimi.[104] "What haunts is not that which is gone, it is that which was expected to come but whose condition of arrival has been foreclosed, and the ghost is an advocate of the promised future that was unrightfully cancelled when the past was destroyed." As K pauses her reading to pour her parents more wine, I think back to the article I'd read that morning, and feel, suddenly, acutely aware that our respective ghosts—the promised future of a Palestinian return, the promised future for the Jews of Egypt—are also present on this Skype call, are sitting right beside us, in fact, as we talk about translations.

"Cutting him out," K says, tearing off a bit of unleavened bread as she points, with her other hand, to a passage in her Haggadah. "That's a kind of forgetting?"

"Yes", her dad says. "Yes, that seems right."

In the Haggadah, I read: *This is the bread of affliction that our fathers ate in the land of Egypt. Whoever is hungry, let him come and eat; whoever is in need, let him come and conduct the Seder of Passover. This year [we are] here; next year in the land of Israel. This year [we are] slaves; next year [we will be] free people.*

This, after all, is the culmination of the exodus story—the reward for all that suffering. *Eretz Israel*, the land of Israel.

My heart begins to thud. Those horns, I sense, have sprouted: I have never felt so aware of, or alone in, my nationality. Looking at K and her family, I wonder if my presence, as a Palestinian, will be acknowledged.

Being Palestinian, I think a lot about land and place. Jerusalem is a city that makes you aware of itself vertically, as well as horizontally. Because of the country's wall and its ghettos and its physical divisions, performed in miniature in Jerusalem, your sense of space is heightened; you feel its limits and constrictions keenly, the proximity of one enemy to another, the teetering towers of too-many Palestinians pushed together. But at the same time, you cannot escape the city's sense of depth: giant slabs of ancient stone on sidewalks, convoluted old alleyways, constantly emerging archaeological dig sites, not to mention its central and formidable fortress. All of this shouts that this current Jerusalem has been built on many others, that it contains layer upon layer of past selves, that this particular stratum is just the one closest to the surface; a historical millefeuille.

This stratification is an indication of the hunger that has been felt, throughout history, for this segment of earth. An atrocity of blood has been spilt for the sake of just a taste of its tiny, hilly landscape, a small bite of its shore. I often wonder at this, as I drive along Route 1, or walk out into the valley of Wadi Qelt. It's beautiful, sure, particularly this bit of desert, with its endless, wide undulations of sandstone, the smooth ridges like the back of a giant beast that may at any point get up and shake off a long sleep. Nature in this country is at once bountiful and barren: swathes of golden earth peppered with lush, dark olive trees; tangled, scraggly forests of cypress highlighted by antediluvian gray stone. But what is this beauty worth, really? And plenty of it isn't even beautiful at all, just parched and dusty and overpopulated.

Poor Jerusalem, I'll think, as I walk along crowded Salah'eddin Street, past double-parked cars honking outside Abu Hassan's hummos shop, it's not even a particularly good trading route. Just valuable by virtue of being desired, a case of the Emperor's New Territory. It shouldn't have become this enviable, wanted thing, this unwilling celebrity who tries to keep walking as frantic hands grab from all sides, tearing at its shirt and skirt and hair, nails scratching at its skin.

I don't mean—or want—to want it; I don't believe in territorial deserts. And yet I can't deny I feel a connection to this place. That when I return home after time away, it settles something that is otherwise loose and rattling inside, the particular color of the sky when it rains—the weak yellow light that seeps through the afternoon clouds—like being spoken to in a language I finally recognize. My grandparents, their parents and grandparents, all of whom are buried here, have long since become part of the soil in this place, their essence in the scent of pomegranate trees that rides the breeze, or in the wild sorrel that we gather for lunch, fingers caked in dirt. I am not a particularly nature-loving person, and am firmly anti-spiritual, but I can't help a frisson when I breathe in the air outdoors in my hometown. It is at once wildly precious and soothingly mundane in its familiarity. Perhaps because I have been forced to prove it, so often and so consistently, Jerusalem is, quite literally, the center of my life: the axis on which my consciousness and memory and story rotates.

Maybe I also feel a connection to this land because, like its people, it's been through a lot, it has taken a beating—just look at how relentlessly it has been used to justify atrocities, abused for its measly resources, bombed and blasted and dug up and burned. And yet it persists, resolute, solid and firm beneath our feet, offering us and all of our demanding ghosts whatever it can.

Did the warrior woman herself ever make it to Jerusalem? It's not clear. She may have been part of those initial Islamic conquests, may have made it to my hometown, but if so, there is no record of it. Instead, it seems one of her sons (or a brother, depending on who's telling the story) was among the early conquerors who settled in the Holy Land.[105] She herself may have never been, may only have heard about it from merchants and travelers. Or she may have heard about it from Muhammad himself, who would have told her about his midnight journey on the winged horse Buraq, of his ascension on what would later be called the Dome of Rock. The same place where, in 2017, metal detectors were installed in front of the Al-Aqsa Mosque, limiting access to Palestinians and sparking a show of mass, nonviolent Palestinian civil disobedience,[106] and where later, in 2021, a complete ban on entry to Muslims would spark the May war with Gaza which saw two hundred and fifty-six Palestinians and thirteen Israelis killed.[107] Perhaps Muhammad told Nusayba how it was in this place, in the Old City of Jerusalem, that he met all the prophets of the past—Adam and Jesus and Moses and Abraham—and understood his place among them. The last link in a chain of belief.

Rituals, as Durkheim explains,[108] serve "to sustain the vitality of [common] beliefs, to keep them from being effaced from memory and, in sum, to revivify the most essential elements of the collective consciousness. Through them, the group periodically renews the sentiments which it has of itself and of its unity."[109] They are a reminder that we are more than the individual stories we tell ourselves about ourselves; that we are also the collective narratives we create and pass down, a way to kindle candles for the dead.

On May 15, 1948, the creation of the state of Israel was proclaimed in Tel Aviv,[110] so every year on that date, Palestinians around the world commemorate the Nakba. In 2022, the United Nations General Assembly voted, for the first time, to officially recognize the date as well. "Today, this General Assembly will finally acknowledge the historical injustice that befell the Palestinian people," the Palestinian UN envoy told reporters.[111] "Our people deserve recognition of their plight." The move was considered particularly important partly because the story of the Nakba has been (and still is) intentionally downplayed, questioned or erased entirely—despite Israel's own historians and reporters finding ample evidence of the "blood-drenched events that accompanied the conquest of the Arab villages,"[112] as *Haaretz*'s Adam Raz puts it. Even something as innocent as a Netflix film *about* the Nakba was met with ire only this year, condemned by Israeli officials as creating a "false pretense" and inciting "against Israeli soldiers."[113] In the Israeli alter-narrative, the "Palestine of 1948 was 'a land without a people for a people without a land,'" and today, "the hundreds of Palestinian villages and towns destroyed in 1948 are still forced out of Israeli public awareness, away from the signposts of memory."[114]

Because of this, Palestinians often feel, as Margalit's mother did, that the only honorable role for those who remain is to form communities of memory, oftentimes centering on the Nakba—remembering the names of the villages that were Hebraised, the faces of the children who were killed, the stories of the families who escaped and are now unable to return. As Nur Masalha explains, "in the case of the indigenous inhabitants of Palestine, the Nakba has been a key site of collective memory and history,"[115] a moment that has become, for Palestinians, an "eternal present."[116] For Masalha, as for many Palestinians, remembrance of the Nakba is central both to maintaining the collective consciousness denied to us, and reclaiming a truth that has been intentionally expunged. A way to keep the ghost alive, advocating for our lost future.

Watching K and her parents at the Seder table, I think of my last Ramadan dinner. There is less ritual in Ramadan than in the Seder, and no story, exactly, but there are some similarities. Around the world, Muslims break their fasts, say the same prayers, just as, tonight, Jews around the world are taking sips of their red wine and asking the four questions. The communality and warmth and odd anachronism of the ceremony are all comfortingly familiar, and so there is a part of me that feels extremely grateful to have been invited to this digital Passover, particularly during this anxiously isolating time of the pandemic. But there is, underneath all this, a chill brought by our respective specters, and I can't help but think about the cost of being a soul candle: generations reliving and revivifying stories of past atrocities; traumas renewed and passed down and on. Eventually we may burn ourselves out completely.

I am interested in this lineage of suffering, in the collective ordeal that becomes collective memory, the story tenderly handed down from one generation to the next like a fragile, well-wrapped heirloom; or sometimes buried in a back room, perhaps forgotten but still present, rediscovered one day by a grandchild who stumbles on it by accident, unknowingly finding in it something fragile and breakable. I am ambivalent about these heirlooms, suspicious of their connections to the past.

Though Margalit ultimately comes down on his mother's side, arguing that there is a duty of remembrance, I find myself still not wholly convinced. It's true that, as Masalha puts it, "remembering, as a work of mourning and commemorating, with its regime of truth, opens up new possibilities," and that the act itself can mean "putting the wreckage of a painful past together in ways which helps end suffering and helps the process of healing."[117] We are desperate for some healing to begin. And yet: as I watch K relive a trauma that may or may not have happened,[118] I find I just don't know that what we gain from storing these heirlooms—our identity, our history, our community, even the possibility for a different future—is in fact worth the continuation of pain.

On the other hand, I am not entirely sure we could get rid of them, even if we wanted to.

At the end of the Seder, there is an almost imperceptible shift in tone. The family doesn't read the last prayer in English or talk about translations. Instead, K's father rushes through it in Hebrew, the words tumbling quickly out of his mouth as though hoping, if fast enough, I might not catch them.

But I read it afterwards, while the family sings a children's song in Aramaic. *"Rebuild Jerusalem, the holy city, speedily in our days, and bring us up into it, and make us rejoice in it, and we will bless You in holiness and purity,"* it tells us. No one has mentioned my nationality yet, but clearly they are aware.

Jerusalem: a future promised every year to every generation during the Seder. I think with a pang of my parents, sitting in their garden, their eyes closed, heads tilted towards the sun. My past and my history and my home, promised to someone else.

I thank the family for the pleasant evening and close my computer, my fingers, I notice, slightly tremulous.

The text instructions say to raise a glass and say in unison: *"Next Year in Jerusalem!"*

UMMAH/MA

There was and there was not, in the depths of the past, a warrior who was, importantly and from the very start, a mother. At the Battle of Uhud— the first battle in which she hitches up her skirts and runs into the fray, bow aloft, to protect her Prophet—Nusayba bint Ka'ab al Khazrajia is not alone. Her husband, Ghaziya, and her two sons are there. She sees them hesitate, sees them look towards the others who have been distracted by the loot and have broken rank, and yells for them to stay put. There are only six men with Muhammad now, and so Nusayba beckons to her sons and husband to come with her, to stand with him and defend him. They do as she bids, the ten of them the only shield Muhammad has. They surround him, shoulder pressed against shoulder, as men on horses and on foot swarm towards and around them. Dust fills the air; Nusayba has to squint to see clearly; she hears a yelp and turns around just as a sword makes contact with her elder son Abdullah's left arm, slicing into the flesh and immediately emerging again, dripping red. The man wielding it is enormous, twice the size of her sweet boy, almost tree-like in girth; she feels a squeeze at her heart and swings her sword in his direction, but he has already taken a giant step away from the group and disappeared into the crowd. "Abdullah!" she calls out to her child. Another fighter comes on horseback, swinging a blade, and Nusayba has to duck. Others are coming at them from all sides. She hears Muhammad telling Abdullah quietly, "Bind your wound," and looks over her shoulder to see blood still gushing from her son's small, frail arm. His face is pale but resolute, dark eyes blinking rapidly. Holding her sword up above her head and crouching low, she makes her way towards Abdullah as quickly as she can.

Using one hand, she pulls out the bandages she packed that morning, before they had set off for Uhud, and presses them against the wound, circling the rough material several times above the elbow, feeling the pulse of her child's blood echoed in her own pounding chest. "You keep fighting," she tells him, pressing her sweaty forehead to his, and giving his hand a squeeze.

Later, during the same battle, Nusayba stumbles backwards and falls, having pulled an enemy fighter off his horse and onto the ground beside her. She rolls over as the animal brings its hooves down just by her head; she hears a clank of armor as the enemy fighter rights himself and makes for her. She tries to push herself up onto all fours, but her vision is swimming. Muhammad, seeing this from his position further up the battlefield, calls out urgently to Abdullah and Habib, "Your mother, your mother!" She lifts her head to find them, but instead the sun is blocked by a giant, looming shadow. She rubs her eyes, tries to focus: a large man, the size of a tree, is heading right for her, walking a lumbering, heavy walk. She hears Muhammad call out to her as she forces herself up, limbs trembling, rage and adrenaline clearing her head. "That is the one who struck your son!" she hears from behind her. But she already knows. She lifts her sword and swings it, like an axe, at the giant's legs; he falls down onto his knees.[119]

Five years after Uhud, in 630 CE, Nusayba will be surrounded by enemies once more at the Battle of Hunayn. This time they are fighting the Bedouin tribe of the Hawazins, who ambushed them in the night as the Muslims were still setting up camp. Once again, as in Uhud, a group of Muslim soldiers gets nervous and begins to flee. But Nusayba, sitting atop her horse, armor on, sword in hand, bow slung over her shoulder, is not going anywhere. By this point, she has made a name for herself and is an established fighter among the Muslim forces; her presence at these battles is expected. And when she later shoots an arrow at the Hawazin leader's camel, knocking both to the ground, and then stands over him, breathing heavily, to take one of his swords, she is a fearsome sight to behold. You wouldn't have known she was pregnant.

-◊-

My own mother has a terrible time when she gets pregnant with me. First, after getting onto a smoke-filled plane taking her from Harvard back to Tel Aviv via the UK, stopping for a brief visit to say goodbye to her mother's old house in Oxford, she collapses with a miscarriage—my twin. She spends weeks in a hospital in London, recovering, alone. On the flight back, her contact lenses congeal, gluing her eyes shut, and so she has to struggle her way through her journey back home to Jerusalem, half-blind, only to find that, on opening the door to her house, my father—off on a last-minute book tour—has left my three brothers in the care of an inept cousin. The domestic landscape before her is feral with pre-teen and teen boys. No one's in charge; the house is up-side-down. Looking around the chaotic scene in front of her, she suddenly feels something seizing; panicking, she finds she cannot move one side of her face at all. When she is finally able to seek some medical attention, she is told that something about her pregnancy has caused a temporary paralysis of the face. This lasts for months but at least, she thinks, she hasn't miscarried again.

Despite this, I have always wanted to be pregnant. As a nine-year-old I would daydream that my round, soft stomach was housing more than just an extra plateful of lasagna; I would wander around my stony schoolyard alone during break-time picturing the joy of growing a little friend inside me. It never occurred to me to think too closely about the mechanics of it. It was an immaculate conception situation, just a little bean magically planted behind my belly button. Part of the longing came from a desire for my baby fat to have good cause; most of it, though, came from an intense loneliness, a yearning for intimacy. It seemed to me back then that the most connected you could be to another human was to carry them inside you, a secret little person that no one could reach but you.

Most of my friends either want children and are dreading the pregnancy, or they don't want children at all, partly *because* of the pregnancy. God, it just rips your body apart, they tell me. Have you seen what it does to a vagina? And the stretch marks? But I don't care. I have lived most of my life in some sort of physical discomfort. It would be freeing to know that the discomfort had, finally, properly good cause. It's bizarre, another friend says. An alien inside you, isn't that intrusive and gross? I disagree. No alien here; this little being is manufactured using my own body. Right, so more of a little parasite, then, my friend says with a roll of her eyes. A little parasite *friend*, I correct her. I cannot explain to them the physical yearning I feel to do this with my body, to create a kind of closeness I imagine is impossible to replicate. Their tiny heart would be beating inside me, and I'd have built that heart. Can you imagine?

My friend isn't wrong about pregnancy being in some sense parasitic. Some researchers theorize that, rather than the relationship being symbiotic, there exists a constant "maternal-fetal struggle over resources,"[120] that the fetus essentially wants to take more from the mother than she is able to give. Once the embryo implants, it gets unlimited access to the maternal nutrients, and, as the pregnancy continues, the fetus demands more, "sending signals designed to increase the mother's blood sugar and blood pressure and thus its own resource supply."[121] It even releases hormones designed to suppress the mother's immune system, so as to stop the mother from attacking the fetus. The hollow, pear-shaped womb, with its thick muscular wall, is the site of this tug-of-war; its lining forming layers that grow into the lungs, stomach, heart, blood vessels, bones, teeth and nails of a new baby, using those nutrients that it has siphoned from the mother.

But I don't mind all that. It's probably part of the draw, actually—this selflessness, this self-sacrifice, this offering of my body for the purpose of forming another. It appeals to my helpful, people-pleasing side. I like the idea of being able to do something instinctive, natural, that is good, that is so essentially and unthinkingly creative (at least in theory—I block out my mother's and many women's experiences in this imaginary scenario); that the womb quite literally nourishes a person into being. I hate, though, that this desire for pregnancy makes me deeply normative, that it inadvertently reinforces ideas about "maternal instincts" and "natural female urges." I want my wants to be more in line with my beliefs, to reject heteronormativity in all its forms, to reach for something greater and more transgressive than broodiness. How dull, how unimaginative, to want to experience pregnancy. I might as well be one of the less interesting Bennett sisters. But there's no point pretending. My body has felt foreign and wrong, dysfunctional and malfunctioning, for much of my life. It has leaked and collapsed and swelled. It has taken me to emergency rooms and befuddled specialists and surgical operating theatres, has cut short outings and parties and trips. Often my body doesn't feel like my body at all (too big, too tall, too busty) but instead as though I am wearing someone else's physical form, the real me a trapped, flat-chested homunculus inside. And, somehow, I know—call it instinct, call it (perhaps more accurately) magical thinking—that the cure would be to turn my body into a place for two.

-⋛-

You were born into a tribe, and there you stayed. That was the situation for Nusayba before Muhammad arrived. You defended this tribe, shared collectively in its resources, and followed its rules. Whether by marriage or by blood (or a combination of the two), you were tied to others based on this tribal structure. Pre-Islamic society in Arabia had strict rules based on this, and by all accounts the system was not particularly egalitarian. There were clear hierarchies, with heads of clans and hakam (judges) at the top, and women, orphans and slaves at the very bottom; women also couldn't inherit or own property. Justice was understood in terms of retribution—blood money—and was a communal problem. Protection of an individual was ensured by all members of the tribe; conversely, a violent act by one member meant all would be implicated.

But when Muhammad arrived in Yathrib, things changed. He established a new, revolutionary type of community: the ummah. The ummah, the new community of Muhammad's followers, was based not on blood but on belief. Take the shehada—say "There is no God but God, and Muhammad is his messenger"—and you were part of the club. In other words, the ummah was a kind of supra-community, based not on birth, race, age or family, but on faith. It established a connection to others over and above the demographic lines that separated them, with a gentle circle drawn round anybody who believed Muhammad's message, bringing them together. Nusayba had her family and her tribe, and now she also belonged to something bigger, something, in theory, limitless.

A central aspect of the ummah, though, was that it was more than just a gathering of like-minded believers; it was a completely new, radically different *type* of social community, one that changed the structure of the lives of its members. In the ummah, everyone's life was as valuable as anyone else's, regardless of whether you were an orphan or the leader of your own tribe, and women were finally allowed to inherit and keep dowries. And, for the first time, there was a sense of communal responsibility to those most in need, beyond the tribe: Muhammad instituted a type of payment, called a zakat, which every member of the ummah had to pay according to what they could afford, and this money would then go to helping the neediest in the community, a type of proto-socialism. In other words, the ummah—to which you would belong purely by believing—took care of people.

⚜

When I first left Jerusalem to study, first in the US and then in the UK, I made a point of joining multiple societies. I joined the Feminist society, the Psychology society, the Homelessness society, the Literature society, the LGBT society. I signed up happily to almost any group presented, optimistic that I would find my people. I did the same when I went on to my master's and then my doctorate: I expressly asked to be housed in college in a shared house; I started a book club; I joined the choir; I joined a reading group. I made an effort, in other words, to find community—a social unit within which I could feel at home, connected to others in a meaningful way. Not because I didn't have friends, but because community, to me, offered something different: a belonging without effort.

But communities were not, it turned out, so easy to find or establish, despite my determination. The 2010s were the beginning of the decline of physical communities in favor of digital imitations of them, so most of my interactions with these various societies ended up being online; I made one or two real-life friends from each club and ended up with endless Facebook group notifications that I ignored. Part of the problem was that my desire for community made me an oddity: in Britain, young people—my generation and the ones after it—are facing what's been called a "collapse in community," with "each new cohort of young people less interwoven with, and supported by, wider society than the one before it."[122] Millennials like me are less likely to be members of a group or to take part in group activities than any previous generation, which makes people who join societies by definition a bit unusual. Perhaps partly because of this, we're all much more solitary than ever before. One in five people between the ages of eighteen and thirty-four have only one close friend (or none at all), compared to one in fifteen in 2011. Only forty percent of those under thirty-five have four friends or more. Ten years ago, that number was sixty-four percent. We're lonelier, less trusting, more isolated and less civically involved than any previous generation on record; and with each generation that comes after, the picture only gets worse.

Perhaps I feel particularly aware of this because I come from such a heavily community-based culture. As an Arab, you are never a single individual with an atomized identity; you are always part of the wider story of your heritage—your "house," your people. When Arabs ask me who I am or where I'm from, often the first thing I say, even before I tell them my name, is: ana min dar nseibeh.[123] You see yourself always panoramically, your small stitch in the tapestry of the genetic landscape. And there are benefits to this: a communal solidarity, a sense of togetherness, a humility. At its best, I think, it can mean shared responsibilities, halved burdens and a solidifying sense of meaning and connection. Families being raised by groups, cousins just across the hall. But there are drawbacks. Not just what you might expect—too little freedom, too much emphasis on shame and propriety—but also more subtle issues to do with understanding oneself beyond these constraints, or rather, outlining one's own form around and within these strong family lines. I am so acutely aware that I am my father's daughter, that I am a member of the Nuseibeh family, that I am a reflection on and of them, that it is hard, sometimes, to see myself clearly.

There is also the issue of navigating a sense of obligation. Particularly if the community in question is marginalized or oppressed, there exists, for many, a feeling of collective responsibility—the famous Palestinian song from the 1980s, "Ana ismi sha'b filisteen" ("My Name Is the Palestinian People"), is testament to this. You represent the group when in majority-occupied spaces, even if you emphatically try not to—often I am the only Palestinian an English person has ever met. When abroad, you feel both an acrid, stinging survivor's guilt and a hollow yearning to reconnect. Particularly as a privileged Palestinian—economically, but also, one with a British passport who can travel easily—there is an extra impetus to do right by your community, to not squander the opportunities afforded to you, even to elevate them in some way if at all possible. Self-care feels like self-indulgence. You need to not let them down. You need to support them. In a way it is almost a sense of filial duty: when unrest erupts on the streets, for example, and I am far from home, I feel distraught, guilty—as though my mother has broken a hip, and I'm not there to help. When I imagine leaving East Jerusalem, moving away for good, I feel temporarily lighter, freer, but also saddened, ashamed and remorseful, as though contemplating leaving her broken-hipped self to be cared for by someone else. It feels, in other words, like neglect. I am born of my community, and I want to be a dutiful daughter.

But despite the sense of obligation, despite having grown up in this collectivist culture, my relationship with the community is complicated. I long to be a part of it, but I am a bad Arab, a pathetic excuse for a Muslim, and so I retreat. I am hyper-aware of any Arabs I come across—a word of my language spoken in a Levantine accent carried in the wind along the Cowley Road will turn my head whiplash-quick—and I want, always, to reach out, but I get shy, so instead I just stare, beaming at them enthusiastically, while they quicken their pace nervously in response. Just recently, in an optician's clinic, I watched a white English woman in a yellow jumper get confused between two girls wearing hijabs, asking one a question about her prescription when it was the girl's colleague with whom, moments before, she'd been interacting. Yellow Jumper apologized quickly, laughingly, when corrected, but it was painful to see, and I wanted to let the second girl—who was now helping me—know that I saw her, that I was *of* her. Thank you, I said, from my seat facing the back of her computer monitor. I didn't catch your name, sorry?

Khadijeh, she told me, smiling, placing the frames onto my face, soft hands grazing the tips of my ears. She pronounced it the way someone English would: *Ka-dee-jaa.* Thank you so much for your help, Kh— I said, stopping short. I wanted to make a point of saying her name, but found myself stuck, suddenly, on whether to pronounce it the way she did or the way I would, with an Arabic accent. I felt the heavy glasses glide slightly down my nose as sweat began to prick at my armpits. She tucked a stray hair into her hijab and held out the card reader, and I tapped my card against the machine, aware that soon the moment would be gone, I'd be out the door, it would be too late. She handed me the receipt and with a heavily beating heart I finally blurted: Thanks. Kh-k-AAdijah! Too loud and too late. I sounded insane, or racist.

She smiled at me tightly and turned to her computer, raising her eyebrows at her colleague. Christ, no, no! I wanted to reassure her frantically. You have my great-aunt's name! I know all about the woman you're named after, Muhammad's first wife! I'm one of you!

But I just took my receipt and left.

In a great interview between the engineer Mo Gawdat and writer Alya Mooro, both of them Egyptian, on the former's podcast,[124] the host tells Alya: "Your Arabic is . . . not the best." He continues: "So would you consider yourself more British, or more Middle Eastern, or . . . have you ever found an identity?" I unintentionally suck in a breath when I hear this; the question is a familiar one. Inti 'arabiya willa inglizia? my great-aunt would ask me sternly.

Alya laughs, though, and replies: "Yah, it's a really difficult one, one which, especially when I was younger, yah, I found really difficult. I used to always say I'm both and neither, because by being two things, it kind of makes you not fully either of those things."

I can relate. Much of the time when I am home, I am aware of how un-Arab and un-Palestinian I am. Over the years, I have lost touch with much of my friend group in Jerusalem; almost all have moved away. Now, when in Jerusalem, I write in my parents' garden, go for walks around the Old City, eat an occasional dinner at the same East Jerusalem restaurant at which we have been regulars for many years, but that is the extent of it. I am not involved in the city's social life at all. I don't visit my cousins. The last decade of studying and living in the UK has meant that my Arabic—at one point my mother tongue—has become weak, so much so that I sometimes don't follow exactly what a newscaster has said and have to add subtitles to make any sense of it at all, or put certain words into Google Translate while reading an article. I haven't read much Darwish or Kanafani, and when I have it's mostly been in English. I've stopped dreaming in Arabic, mostly.

But then it turns out I'm not that great a Brit, either. In England, I have none of the same cultural references as my English friends, I have no close family to stay with, and my accent sounds more American than anything else. I feel exceedingly foreign in my shared house, which is filled with English students, and I am seen that way, too: jokes have to be explained, Britishisms translated. Juha means nothing to them, my hand gestures are unintelligible. When I moved to the UK at eighteen, I had to learn which TV channels to watch, which radio programs to listen to. At work I was always the go-to for overseas questions or concerns (never mind that my lived experience gave me very little expertise in the ways of, say, Pakistan). My name and my food and my keffiyeh and the language I would speak on the phone when I called home all marked me as foreign, as Arab. I am too British in Jerusalem, too Palestinian in England. Always, as Edward Said puts it, out of place.[125] Never quite part of the group, always just a little bit lonely.

And it is precisely this—the group—that largely determines the identity of the individual. "Even though I wasn't white, I wasn't considered fully

Korean, either. I was trapped in what felt like an inescapable limbo," writes Korean-American Arden Yum.[126] "A Chinese-American friend of mine used to lightheartedly call me a banana: white on the inside, yellow on the outside. I felt like an impostor." This will likely be a familiar experience for many people of mixed heritage. So much of our essential sense of self, our identity, is actually not to do with us at all—our social identities are, yes, determined by the social units in which we place ourselves, but also the groups in which we are placed by others, by how we are perceived and treated. If we are always treated as not-quite-insiders, then this will determine how we think of ourselves, how we live. As Kwame Anthony Appiah puts it, a given social label "creates what you could call norms of identification: rules about how you should behave, given your identity."[127]

No wonder people of mixed race or heritage often feel themselves in between worlds, between selves, both and neither—as though there were an authentic, "pure" social identity to which, as people with mixed or multiple identities, we do not have access. When I say I am a bad Arab, it is not because I consider myself to be both a bad person and an Arab, but because I fail in some way to express Arabness at its fullest, as Alya says, or purest—a strange and high standard I wouldn't expect from anyone else, because what even is full or pure Arabness?[128] Essentialism of this kind is deeply problematic, yet this sense of lack—this limbo—is, like Yum's, partly due to community, to how I am perceived. When I take a dance class with my close friend in Jerusalem and prove to be more skilled than she is in Middle Eastern dancing, and she splutters at me angrily, "But you're not even really Palestinian!" what she is saying is that my having been born and raised in the Palestinian territories, by a Palestinian father and Palestinian grandmother, my having an Arab ancestor to whom I owe my name, is still not enough to wipe out the Englishness of my mother, my years studying abroad, and my distance from a core Palestinian experience. And so, despite my inescapable connection with my community and the tyrannical weight of its representation, I am pushed out of that social category. Floating in a painful limbo, I belong to no one.

Sometimes I wonder if the problem comes down to my wandering womb. Hippocrates certainly thought so, pinning all female issues on this imagined element inside us, what Aretaeus of Cappadocia called an "animal within an animal." In ancient Egypt and Greece, the uterus was seen not as an organ, but as a ravenous roaming creature that could get too easily bored, that would—in its hunt for sperm and entertainment—cause pain and breathlessness and, of course, hysteria. It needed to be kept busy, kept still, or else the consequence was depression, confusion, tears. This is, needless to say, ridiculous. But a part of me feels that maybe my womb and I have wandered a bit too much; maybe what we needed was to settle in one place. Maybe my appetite to explore the world was my undoing, maybe I and my womb should have just stayed put in Jerusalem.

Pregnancy was seen as one of the ways to keep a womb from wandering, birth a way to keep a woman strong. But in my reading about motherhood, I have been struck by how ravenous women become *after* having children, how weakened their sense of self. "My appetite for the world was insatiable, omnivorous, an expression of longing for some lost, pre-maternal self," writes Rachel Cusk, in her memoir about motherhood.[129] Jenny Offill, whose narrator in *Dept. of Speculation*, wanted to be an "art monster,"[130] finds herself, instead, wholly engulfed by her identity as a mother. Rachel Yoder's anonymous mother in *Nightbitch* literally has to turn into a dog-wolf in order to find herself again, so destroyed had her identity become in her maternal role. By assuming the form of the wolf-creature, though, the anonymous mother regains access to a wildness that had been denied her, finding "a hunger that filled up every space inside her until she was nearly crazed."[131] In these accounts, motherhood is presented as a Faustian proposition: you get your child, but you lose yourself. Becoming a mother is, as Pragya Agarwal puts it, "the annihilation of what once was in order to raise a child," a metamorphosis into "a being that does not seem to belong to us any more."[132]

And it is particularly motherhood—not parenthood—that carries with it this risk of self-annihilation, the institution steeped in the patriarchy for so long that, no matter what one does to sweeten it, the bitterness still lingers. "I would nurse [my son] until my nipples bled and deprioritize my marriage and friendships to suit his needs,"[133] writes Kim Brooks in her essay "A Portrait of an Artist as a Young Mom," referring to her desire to be an ideal mother. Essentialized and normalized—as in, created an obligatory norm of—for centuries, motherhood is a weighty thing that can jeopardize individuality, humanity, and even our lives (just think of anti-abortion laws that prioritize the life of the fetus). Simone de Beauvoir even famously equated the decision to have children with selling oneself into slavery.[134]

Promise you won't let me disappear, my friend tells me anxiously, as we discuss her beginning the process of trying to conceive. I've been reduced to a juice box, another says, three weeks after having given birth, and two months after taking leave from her prestigious institution as a sought-after academic. All I do, all I am, is feeding this fucking baby.

It is a socially constructed role that demands self-abnegation for the sake of one's offspring, nutrients redirected to the embryonic cells in the uterus. Maybe it's not surprising that, in Arabic, the terms for mercy are related etymologically to the word for womb: rahm.[135]

If only there were a way for a cis woman to become a parent, rather than a mother. Instead, when I imagine a future in which I have had a little bean, and seen it grow, I often think of the quote from Adrienne Rich: "My children cause me the most exquisite suffering of which I have any experience. It is the suffering of ambivalence, the murderous alternation between bitter resentment and raw-edged nerves and blissful gratification. Sometimes I seem to myself, in my feelings towards these tiny guiltless little beings, a monster of selfishness and intolerance."[136] And I wonder, sometimes, if my cure for loneliness would end up making me lonelier still.

Not long after the Battle of Hunayn, Musailama, of the Banu Hanifah tribe, declares himself a prophet. At this point in time, Muhammad's message has reached most of Arabia and most inhabitants have already converted to Islam, yet Musailama somehow manages to gain enough followers that Muhammad is forced to take him seriously. He decides to send Musailama a cease-and-desist letter and chooses a man called Habib to deliver the message.

Habib reaches Musailama without incident and hands him the short note inscribed on a palm-leaf stick, and readies himself to leave, but Musailama, upon reading it, has Habib immediately chained up and held captive, unable to move. The next morning, Habib is brought before Musailama and a counsel of Musailama's advisors and followers. He is thrown roughly onto the ground.

"Do you believe Muhammad is the Messenger of God?" Musailama asks

Habib, without getting up from his seat. His tone is bored.

"I do," Habib says.

"And do you testify that I, too, am the Messenger of God?"

Habib says nothing.

"Do you testify that *I* am the Messenger of God?" Musailama asks again, his voice louder this time.

"I cannot hear," Habib says quietly, his gaze lowered.

Musailama's face darkens, and he signals a man standing to his left, who goes to Habib, grabs his leg, and swiftly brings an axe down across his ankle. White-hot, delirious pain shoots through Habib, who doesn't need to look down to see that his foot has been chopped off. In his head, he recites a prayer: *Bismillah al rahman il raheem.*

Musailama signals his henchman to stay where he is. "Do you testify that I am the Messenger of God?" he asks Habib again.

Again, Habib says simply, "I cannot hear."

Again, the henchman picks up his axe, this time aiming it at Habib's other ankle. He swings.

Limb by limb, Habib is dismembered, all the while continuing to assert that he cannot hear Musailama's question. He does this until all the blood pools out of his body, until he cannot see for the pain, until first his consciousness and then the last nerve signals of life fade away. What does he see just before his final breath? Does he think of Muhammad, this man for whom he has just died? Maybe. But maybe what he thinks of is something more instinctive and natural, more naked and vulnerable. Maybe what he sees in those last few seconds is an image of his mother, Nusayba.

The news of her son's gruesome death reaches her surprisingly quickly. The people who tell her will emphasize his bravery, his stalwartness. But she is too broken, too devastated, to feel comforted by this idea. Instead she becomes angry, determined. Two years later, at the Battle of Yamama, which takes place far away from Yathrib and lasts for over two weeks, Nusayba will push her way through the ranks of soldiers frantically, bow over her shoulder, spear in hand, looking for Musailama. In the middle of the first week, she will be surprised by an enemy fighter who comes at her from behind, and will feel in her arm a sudden, searing pain so strong that it loosens her bowels. She will look down and see that there is blood and empty space where there should have been a hand. So this is what Habib felt, she will think numbly, tearing off a piece of her skirt and wrapping the gaping wound. And she will clench her jaw and trudge on through the battle.

Part of Nusayba's story, then, is one of motherhood—she fights for her Prophet but she also fights for her children, to avenge her children. She fights to avenge Habib. Later, she also fights to avenge her other son, Abdullah, who dies not long after. Importantly, she fights *alongside* her children, and, as is clear from the story of the Battle of Hunayn, doesn't stop having children once she becomes a regular in the Muslim battles. To put it another way, even after she gets pregnant—even after she gives birth, first to Tameem, and then again to Khawla, becoming not only a mother but a mother of small infants—she remains a warrior.

In Kim Brooks' essay, the author focuses on the tension between art and motherhood, arguing that the conflict arises essentially because "the point of art is to unsettle, to question, to disturb what is comfortable and safe. And that shouldn't be anyone's goal as a parent." The ideal mother is the amniotic fluid within the womb, absorbing all shocks so that her child feels none. This is the mythical, archetypal construction of the mother: she is "the naturally passive, peaceful and altruistic nurturer,"[137] as Cortney Pasternak puts it. Many mothers do not fit perfectly into this mould, and yet the expectation persists that good mothers must sublimate their own needs for the sake of the child; they must protect the child at all costs, must keep the child as safe and comfortable as humanly possible. So attached are we to the idea that mothers should protect their young that it took until the 1970s for scientists to stop labeling animal infanticide as pathological,[138] despite its being a natural part of many creatures' survival instincts. Often, the caring urge is presented as a phenomenon akin to reflex. "People say that a mothering instinct kicks in on giving birth, making you protect your child above everything else," writes Pragya Agarwal when describing her own pregnancy.[139] "The fear and mistrust I had felt for so long, and the desire to protect my unborn child, all jerked into place at the same time as my body shuddered with pain." It is natural, it seems, to want to keep one's child in a cocoon of love and protection; it is something that kicks in the moment one goes into labor.

And yet this is not what Nusayba does. In fact, she does the opposite. She brings her children onto the battlefield. Does that make her a bad mother? The archetypal mother shelters; if she fights at all, it is to fend off attackers for the sake of her children. She doesn't touch her forehead to her son's and tell him to keep his sword raised. Is Nusayba going against that protective instinct that Agarwal describes? Does she lack that instinct altogether? Perhaps she is less like Agarwal and more like Gioconda Belli, the famous Nicaraguan writer, who, in the 1970s, transported weapons for the Sandinista movement. When Belli was approached by the FSLN resistance,[140] she protested at first, telling them she had a daughter.[141] "Your daughter is the reason you should do it," the recruiter told her. "You should do it for her, so that she won't have to do the job you are not willing to do." She joined, her protective instinct precisely why she decided to unsettle, to disturb what was safe. Likewise, Patria Mirabal—one of the infamous Dominican sisters known as the "Butterflies," all of them mothers involved in dangerous resistance activities against the 1950s dictator, all of them eventually assassinated by that same dictator—was motivated to get involved partly *because* she was a mother. "We cannot allow our children to grow up in this corrupt and tyrannical regime, we have to fight against it, and I am willing to give up everything, including my life, if necessary," Patria is quoted as saying.[142]

The archetypal mother is, in some ways, a privileged one. Able to focus on shelter and nourishment, secure in the knowledge that—unless she chooses to disturb it—the home *will* be comfortable, *will* be safe. For many mothers, this is not the case, whether economically, racially, personally or politically, such as in the case of Patria and Belli. Often, there is the encroachment of the political into what should be safe spaces; too often, also, there are no safe spaces to begin with. As Cortney Pasternak observes in the Palestinian context: "Manifestations such as home demolitions and bombings violate the lines between the public or 'male' area that is the battlefield and what might otherwise be considered the protected area of the domestic or 'female' sphere, thus infusing political resistance into the domestic sphere—politicizing what is 'personal' or 'domestic.'" What's a mother to do when the fight is already on the home front? When she's already, by default and without a choice, involved in that fight?

For these mothers, there is doubled duty: to the child, and to the community into which that child was born. For women from marginalized backgrounds, "the subjective experience of mothering/motherhood is inextricably linked to the sociocultural concerns of racial ethnic communities—one does not exist without the other," as Patricia Hill Collins explains. The maternal work "goes beyond ensuring the survival of one's own biological children or those of one's family", recognizing that "individual survival, empowerment, and identity require group survival empowerment, and identity".[143] This runs counter to the narratives of Heti, Offill, Yoder and Cusk, where the needs of the mother become sublimated by the needs of the child; here, in this narrative, the needs of the mother get amplified by the needs of her child, her awareness of the relative position of the group heightened by the fact that she has created a new member.

It's easy to vilify mothers who appear to fail at that fundamental imperative to protect the child, though. Israeli political strategists do this often. As Adania Shibli has shown, these strategists often turn Palestinian women, whose children have been shot dead by the occupying forces, into symbols of bad motherhood. These "bad mothers" not only fail to protect their sons, the strategists' narrative goes, but intentionally send them out to be "martyred."[144] The narrative is effective in shifting the focus—from the forces that kill to the mothers who fail to protect—precisely because we value maternal shelter so highly. But this vilification betrays a false assumption lurking underneath: that, as Patricia Hill Collins puts it, "all women enjoy the racial privilege that allows them to see themselves primarily as individuals in search of personal autonomy, instead of members of racial ethnic groups struggling for power." To unsettle and disturb, when the status quo keeps your community—and by extension your child—oppressed, seems exactly like it *should* be the goal of a parent.

Perhaps this is partly why I am cautious in my judgement of Nusayba. Though it is true that there is something uncomfortable—even, perhaps, repellent—about Nusayba's warring alongside her children, I am sensitive to the loadedness of the beliefs that underlie that discomfort. Not only in terms of privilege, but also in terms of what these beliefs mean more generally for women who are living in unsettled and disturbing worlds. As Munmi Pathak points out, the "pacifist archetype of the mother in conflict and wartime situations limits the role of the mother only to the traditionally sanctioned role of a victim, a protester, and a mourner."[145] Many women in Nusayba's time probably *were* victims or mourners. Sons and husbands in the sixth century inevitably took part in raids or confrontations, inevitably put on armor and defended their clans, and, inevitably, got injured or maimed or killed. By joining her sons and husband, rather than staying on the sidelines, Nusayba is, in fact, enormously transgressive—violating moral and social boundaries even more as a mother than as a woman. She breaks free of those traditionally sanctioned roles of victim, protester and mourner, and becomes sidekick, ally. There beside them, a mother, with her spear on the battlefield.

-}-

The painting *Arab Motherhood* by the twentieth-century French-Egyptian artist Georges Hanna Sabbagh depicts three women in white dresses surrounded by small children. Two of the women stand, each carrying a child on her shoulders, while one sits cross-legged on the ground, breastfeeding a baby. All three women gaze downward, their expressions mournful, while the infants press on their heads with their small, pudgy limbs, pull at their dresses commandingly, or mess around with each other in the background. These last two children, clearly having some sort of brotherly squabble, are shown standing behind the breastfeeding mother, towering over her despite their small size in relation to the other standing mothers. The women are underneath their children in every way, and yet, the image—with its idyllic bright blue streak of water in the far distance, the foregrounding of this family, if that's what it is, the colorful village right behind them—creates also a sense of busyness, of community.

For Palestinians, the connection between motherhood and community is strong. Because Israel has often framed its problem with the Palestinians as a "demographic" one—the idea being that if the Palestinian population would just shrink enough (or better yet, disappear entirely), there really wouldn't be any issue at all[146]—the idea of motherhood has always been linked to Palestinian society. "The womb of the Arab woman is my strongest weapon," Yasser Arafat pronounced on more than one occasion.[147] A particularly popular Palestinian saying from the first intifada was: "The Israelis may beat us at the borders, but not the bedroom."[148] In other words: seeing as we are militarily and economically pathetic, we can instead, perhaps, procreate our way to national self-determination. If we simply persist in existing, we will not so easily be erased. If we bear children to pass on our stories, our history will live on. As Yousef Munayyer explains: "Today, through its occupation, Israel continues to make life unbearable for Palestinians, but millions resist the pressure by not leaving.[…] For those who have never lived in a system of violence like the Israeli occupation, it is hard to understand how simply not going anywhere constitutes resistance, but when the objective of your oppressor is to get you to leave your land, staying put is part of the daily struggle."[149]

In the context of the Palestinian situation, then—where the struggle is one to do with presence, as much as anything else—being a mother, a creator of people, is an act of powerful and nonviolent resistance.

Which makes it complicated for Palestinians who could, in theory, be mothers.

"I feel like a draft dodger from the army in which so many of my friends are serving—just lolling about in the country they are making, cowering at home, a coward,"[150] writes Sheila Heti, the army in question being motherhood. This feels more literal in my case, but I, too, feel like a coward. Though a part of me is desperate for the little bean, another is paralyzed by the prospect of mothering in the context of the political, frozen in the face of too many still-unanswered questions. Do I raise this child in Jerusalem, make sure that they are born there so that they receive the blue Palestinian ID reserved for Jerusalem residents, and in so doing expose this child to the structural oppression, violence, and dehumanization with which I was raised? As Palestinians, that's the only way we'd be able to live in my home country. And if I did so, would I let this child join protests? How Arab would my child look? How likely is it that he would be one of the thousands of Palestinian children killed by Israeli forces in the last two decades alone?[151] Or that she would be incarcerated, interrogated, beaten? Sexually assaulted, shot in the leg, or executed by the Israeli military, as happens routinely to Palestinian women? My economic privilege can do a lot to protect her, but it can't do everything. Would I put her in the Friends school in Ramallah, probably the best private school available to Palestinians, and drive her back and forth through a hostile checkpoint every day, subject her to harassment and fear and instability? Would I cover her ears when the settlers march, shouting, "Death to Arabs", smoothing her hair, and whisper to her to stay proud no matter what? Would I stay on the sidelines, or should I unsettle and disturb? Could I protect her, or should I bring her into this fight?

Or perhaps I move to London. Give up and let down the land and culture that I love, wrench us out of our community as much as I possibly can, push aside her Palestinian past so that she could perhaps grow up more secure, more happy, properly free. Rip us both in half for the beguiling promise of being seen as whole human beings, and risk us both floating forever in a limbo.

The early idea of the ummah is a bit like what was thought would happen centuries later with the advent of the internet. We were meant to find community online; that was the early promise of the World Wide Web. To connect with each other across space, based on our likes, our hobbies, our reading interests. To find friends of friends and add them to our social networks unobtrusively, effortlessly growing our circle, like a uterus stretching wider and wider when growing a baby. Whether through chatrooms or social media, the idea was that we were coming together, finding "our people." True, to some extent: the importance of the internet has been well documented when it comes to marginalized communities in the West especially. If you're a gay kid from East Kilbride, it can be lifesaving to find others like you online. And in the Arab world, young Arabs are using these platforms to break down social restrictions and find like-minded others[152] even while making the effort to maintain their Arab identity. The Arab Spring was possible, in part, because of social media. And in Saudi Arabia, online platforms have empowered and connected Saudi women with their rights campaigns to end male guardianship.[153] For Palestinians, finding communality online with the Black Lives Matter movement has been central to changing the discourse on the occupation: thanks to the internet, Palestinians in Gaza a decade ago were able to connect with protesters in Ferguson—giving advice via Twitter, such as "Remember to not touch your face when tear-gassed or put water on it. Instead use milk or Coke!"—thus not only providing solidarity but creating a virtual community of the oppressed that has had wide-ranging, pragmatic implications.

More recently, being able to document and share events as they happen on the ground—whether in East Jerusalem, Gaza or the West Bank—with a virtual community in the West has enabled a fundamental shift in perspective.[154] When the May 2020 mini-uprising happened in Sheikh Jarrah, for example, Muhammad El-Kurd—its most public face—used Instagram to provide daily updates on the situation. I would watch him and watch the comments and the likes stream in, endless floating smileys and hearts on the incongruous background of tanks and soldiers. The internet, and social media, has provided the opportunity to bring outsiders into the lived political reality of certain groups and to connect people across spectrums,[155] creating the kind of supra-community envisioned by the ummah.

At the same time, we know very well these same social media platforms have disproportionately subjected Palestinians, and other similarly marginalized groups, to content moderation.[156] They have silenced, harassed[157] and alienated people. And we are well aware of what has happened more generally as a result of the internet: the creation of echo chambers, empty performance venues and extremist islands where anonymity translates to consequence-free putridity. Incels spouting hate on Reddit, the rise of the alt-right thanks to unmoderated platforms, teen girls spending miserable hours comparing themselves to other teen girls online. For all the kindred spirits found via Twitter, there will be ten times as many *un*kindred spirits, even *anti* kindred ghouls—angry people threatening to dox or rape or kill (and sometimes doing more than threatening). If any sort of community is created, it is a community of public shamers,[158] but the "togetherness" of a mob is fleeting and ungratifying. The age of alienation has the internet to thank for its inception. We are all online, alone.

But I wonder if the idea was flawed from the start. Though it is taken for granted that one could, and perhaps should, be part of multiple communities, particularly online—an online recipe-sharing group, a neighborhood Facebook page, a writing circle—the end result of these various interactions is a slicing of one's personality into ever more distinct slivers: specific interests relating us to specific people in a specific way. Even if a sense of solidarity or camaraderie is established, this approach to society is always going to feel a bit lonely, a bit isolating, because only a small part of ourselves is seen— particularly over the internet, where so little of our unmediated selves exist, where one has to exert active effort to be unfiltered. In physical spaces, we at least bring our whole personalities with us whether we want to or not; even if we are quiet, we can be seen, and our bodies will do the talking. But the whole idea of building community through these virtual slivers feels like it will still leave many of us in that familiar limbo, a bit between-worlds. Both and neither. To feel truly part of a community is to feel accepted, fully—to feel the protective walls of the womb embracing us as we grow.

Perhaps this is why the idea of the original ummah, Nusayba's ummah, appeals to me. Technically, every Muslim is still, even today, a part of the ummah, but this doesn't really translate to reality, in fact it likely never did. Not long after Muhammad died, there began to be splits within Islam, divisions based on different interpretations; eventually these became larger sectarian divides. There has also always been—as there is everywhere humanity resides—racism and hierarchy. It was never the utopia that was envisioned. Even on a more micro, individual level, there is too much variability within the religion and culture to feel a true sense of wider *communitas*. As Aziz Al-Azmeh puts it, "the very idea of Islam as meta-culture obscures the reality that there are as many "Islams" as the conditions which sustain them—as many "Islamic cultures" as different geographical, social conditions, size of wealth and educational levels can produce."[159] It's not the reality of a modern-day ummah that I am drawn to; it's Nusayba's model ummah that I want: the ideal of a connection that transcends nationality, race, gender and age, a circle drawn around us to which we can belong with as little as a belief.

Some scholars have suggested that the word ummah is derived from the word "mother", *umm/umma,* because they sound the same. There is, in fact, little consensus on where the term comes from, but I like this idea of its link to the maternal. It makes sense to me, that even if it doesn't originate from the word "mother"/"umm," that it would at least have the same linguistic structure; that it would contain this central sound *"umma"* that appears in almost every language to refer to a family member, whether mother or father or grandmother. "'Ma,' 'mater,' 'amma,' 'meme,' 'mama,'" writes Pragya Agarwal. "Across the different language divides, it is the first word a child is supposed to utter, the word that is naturally formed on our lips as we first begin to speak, the connection we have to the land, the tongue, the language and customs of our forebears."[160] This natural noise we make as babies to mean something close to us, something we want, something important: it seems right, to me, that we would make the same noise to mean community, to mean belonging.

⁕

I am forced to consider pregnancy and motherhood again more seriously this last year, when a doctor informs me that I have an exceedingly rare genetic disorder. He has a slightly boisterous manner that softens as he explains the results of my blood test: the risks associated with the condition, the annual scans of various body parts I will now have to get used to. He has kind eyes, I notice, as he lists the things I'll no longer be able to do (blow balloons, scuba dive, high-mountain hiking, sky-diving, marathons). He smiles at me ruefully as he tells me that, in a way, I'm quite special: I am part of an exclusive community—only six hundred families in the world suffer this particular condition. But then his tone turns more serious. You haven't got any children yet, have you, Miss Nuseibeh? he asks me gently. No, no, I say, always slightly shocked that I have reached the age at which anyone would even think to ask. Good, he says. Well, when the time comes, there will be some things to consider.

He goes on to explain that (of course, because this is how genetics work), there is a fifty-fifty chance that any children will inherit the disease. But there are options. The NHS, he says, will fund an IVF procedure that would involve testing the eggs for the genetic condition before insemination, terminating any that have the marker, all if they all have the marker. Though they will only do this for one child, and not if I already have a child. The process does take years, though, he continues, pulling out some leaflets, so if you're interested, now is the time to let us know. Of course, the other option, he says, possibly registering my panic-stricken face, is adoption—though that comes with its own complications.

Or perhaps, Miss Nuseibeh, he says after a pause, you don't want children at all?

I think of a line from a Maya Abu Al-Hayyat poem—*We became lonely and had children who doubled our loneliness,/so you gave us more children*—and place my hands just below my belly button, remembering my youthful longing for the little bean in me, the heart that I would build myself.

I thank the doctor and leave, my fingers clutching the leaflets.

THE ROAD TO DAMASCUS

For more than two thousand years, the Hagia Sophia—domed, turreted, squat like a satisfied gourmand—has remained in its place beside the Bosphorus, straddling Asia and Europe with a solemn, passive serenity. Inside the building, floating chandeliers create a gentle, golden glow that is lifted by the many concentric arches that form the space: small arched windows above large arched windows within an arched recess of the main hall that is, itself, a series of arches. The effect is at once dizzying and viscerally, almost painfully, satisfying. You ache to trace your fingers along each perfect parabola, one half-circle after another. I remember thinking of parabolas—seeing also, in this domed space, the mathematical symbol for the intersect, that upside-down U—when I visited the Hagia Sophia in 2013. At that point, the building was still a museum, and so I had approached it as such: blurry photos that failed to capture the splendor of the central dome were taken and subsequently used as screensavers; leaflets were diligently acquired and then quickly skimmed and discarded; toilets and a café were hunted for, but not found. I brought very little reverence along. Although a campaign to turn the museum back into a church had already been launched several years earlier by the American-Greek politician Christos Spirou, it hadn't occurred to me at the time that the space could, or would, ever change. It had been a museum since long before I was born, and so I had walked around the building with the confident inattentiveness of a person who believes they can always go back.

Less than a decade later, in July 2020, Turkish president Recep Tayyip Erdoğan signed a presidential decree converting the Hagia Sophia into a mosque: inside, Christian mosaics and icons were veiled,[161] and visitors were invited to enter not as ogling tourists but as worshippers, a muezzin's voice calling them to prayer from the previously silent minarets. Although the decision was met with international outcry—the Greek culture minister said it was "an open provocation to the entire civilized world"[162]—this wasn't the first time that the striking complex had had an identity shift.

Built in 537 CE, not long before the Prophet Muhammad was born, the Hagia Sophia began its life as a church and ceremonial site for the Byzantine emperor Justinian I. It remained a church until, in 1453, Ottoman forces captured Constantinople from the Byzantines. At that point, Mehmed II, the sultan at the time, walked purposefully into the building, prayed, and turned it into a mosque. Over the next few years, the Ottoman architect Mimar Sinan[163] worked to transform the space architecturally, adding essentially Islamic features like minarets to the structure. Just under five hundred years later, the secularist president of Turkey, Mustafa Kemal Atatürk, transformed the building once again: the carpets which ran along the floor (an essential feature for those who pray largely on their knees) were removed, and the Hagia Sophia became, this time, a non-religiously affiliated museum, a "monument for all civilization,"[164] as Atatürk put it. For roughly six decades, millions of travelers visited every year, myself among them, paying an entry free and lazily sipping ayran as we ambled halls of mighty transfiguration, before the museum was turned, once again, into a mosque.

⊰⊱

Near the start of the COVID pandemic, the Pope makes a comment about conversion. Now is the time for metanoia,[165] he says: a change of heart, a spiritual acceptance of Christianity. Crouched on the floor, meticulously de-bagging and wiping down each grocery-store item with gloves and a noxious-smelling antiseptic, the street outside silent for the sixth week in a row, I can't help but feel tempted.

I have always felt uncomfortable with—even unnerved by—conversion, suspicious of the fervor involved. Wary, also, of the ferocity required for such a fundamental identity shift: a restructuring not only of one's whole religious schema, but of one's life plans, behaviors, priorities and understandings (a previously atheistic acquaintance suddenly quoting scripture, squeezing my hand as they tell me about Jesus). The convert, it seems to me, rejects their prior self—and often the society in which that prior self existed—in favor of a new self, a new society. It is an axe swung to the walls within, a stripping of the carpet, a building of minarets. In truth, even more gentle personality changes unnerve me: for years I had a recurring nightmare in which I caught my mother, a vehement nonsmoker, casually holding a cigarette to her lips. Relax, she says in the dream, blowing smoke in my face, it's really no big deal. I would wake, heart pounding, feeling that I didn't know her at all.

Still, I am forced to admit—as I gingerly remove my rubber gloves and realize that the delivery had not included more anti-bac (the one essential!), because the shop was all out, as they were constantly these days, and laughing, momentarily, at the absurdity of my new, tiny, super-sanitized, apocalypse-adjacent life—that, right now, I could go for some sort of higher power. Something to believe in, something to save me. I think then of my ancestor, the woman warrior, and wonder.

-⁕-

There was and there was not, in the depths of the past, a woman who became a believer. Nusaybah bint Ka'ab al Khazrajia doesn't officially convert until she travels to a mountain pass a few miles from Mecca to meet the man himself. In 622 CE, she heads southwards from Yathrib, her home town, with hundreds of other travelers, most of them polytheists who are on one of their regular visits to the Kaaba, the small, square mud hut in central Mecca that at the time houses figures of the many deities they worshipped. It is safe to assume that Nusayba has, at this point, already heard stories of the man they call the Apostle (already, another group of Yathribites has met with him and converted) and that she is most likely intrigued. Here is someone talking about a different social system, freedom for the poor and a single god only. Though there are many soothsayers and mystics around, preaching the words of various divinities, his message—for whatever reason—stands out to her.

On the third night of camping, she sneaks away from the other travelers and out of her caravan. In the biting desert breeze, and with only the moon's small split of light in the black sky to guide her, she finds the others—seventy-one men and only one other woman, Asma Umm Mani'. The group makes its way, silently, stealthily, up the rocky incline to the top of the mountain route known as Al-Aqabah.[166] They stand there, huddled and exposed, waiting for the man who will introduce them to a new reality.

He will ask them to follow him into it, and somehow, impossibly, they will.

To date, nearly a hundred thousand Brits have converted to Islam in the UK—the majority of them women—and that number keeps increasing, doubling in the decade between 2000 and 2010.[167] I read this statistic with incredulity. Why would people *choose* to become Muslim, especially in this context? Here, where so often headlines focus on Brits who convert to join ISIS, and famous converts—such as Sinéad O'Connor or Lauren Booth[168]— are met with open hostility, both in private and public. (Booth, for instance, in a tragicomical account of telling family that she's become a Muslim, describes her mother's reaction of tearful joy on hearing that her daughter had converted—only to discover that her mother had heard the word "Buddhist" instead of "Muslim."[169] When she realized her mistake, Booth's mother was much less pleased with the announcement.)

In Britain, while conversions to Buddhism or Christianity might be seen as odd, they are generally viewed as inoffensive—someone finding their spirituality, rather than becoming fundamentalist. The conversion of Saint Augustine, and the religious turmoil conveyed in his *Confessions*, is seen not as a disturbing move towards extremism, but as a slow appreciation of God, the text taken as a universal example of human inner conflict.

Islam, however—coded as violent and misogynistic and darkly Other— is different. Call Prevent[170] if your colleague grows a beard or stops drinking. As Jason Webster of the *Guardian* puts it: if a dinner party companion declares he's become a Muslim, "cultural memories of centuries of rivalry between Islam and the West kick in, and all of a sudden your friend is placed beyond the pale."[171] And this is not a new, post-9/11 phenomenon. When the first British convert to Islam, William Henry Quilliam, opened the first British mosque in 1887 and managed to entice around six hundred others to follow the faith as well, he and his new converts were met with rage and physical abuse. People threw bricks and horseshit at them in the streets of Liverpool.[172] The general public in the West is not on board with the switch from "God" to "Allah"; yet somehow, despite this, increasing numbers of people do continue to make it.

Perhaps I find this particularly hard to comprehend because, in Jerusalem, I am just automatically and unconsciously Muslim because my family is known to be a Muslim family, and because a large portion of Palestinian families are Muslim, and because that is simply the culture in which I grew up.[173] My religious identity is, as Sophie Gilliat-Ray puts it, "ascribed, assumed, unquestioned and deeply embedded and justified by cultural traditions."[174] I am not devout; in fact, I have, until writing this book, pretty much avoided all things earnestly religious, alarmed at the intensity of the believers who surrounded me growing up. So I struggle to understand those who find, suddenly, they believe. What would draw you in, if you hadn't been raised in a Muslim country, a Muslim household?

I find myself (unfairly, problematically) suspicious of the white men who become orthodox Muslims, who have grown long beards and speak the Classical Arabic they have learned through the Quran. What about Islam has attracted you? I wonder, looking at these English converts, proselytizing behind their stands on the Broad Street in Oxford, handing out leaflets about Muhammad. (One of them sees me looking and hands me a Quran, frowning at me as I respond to him in the negative: la' shukran. His expression makes me suspect he doesn't, in fact, understand Arabic.) A part of me (a racist, problematic part) wonders if it's the misogynistic version of Islam they're attracted to, whether they find in this particular community an easy way to control women and feel somehow righteous in doing so. How many of them have read about Nusayba? What are they hoping to find, in Islam?

I search for answers in the diaries of Isabelle Eberhardt, aka Si Mahmoud Essadi—the Swiss-Russian writer who, eschewing all norms of Victorian womanhood, "drank more than a Légionnaire, smoked more *kef* than a hashish addict, and made love for the love of making love."[175] In the late nineteenth century, Isabelle and her mother traveled from their rambling home in Switzerland to occupied Algeria, and converted to Islam. The move was unusual, perhaps, but then again, they were an unusual family. Isabelle— isolated and homeschooled by her anarchist maybe-father father figure (it was never clear if they were biologically related)—had grown up in a decaying mansion that no one in the family was domestic or wealthy enough to maintain, happily frolicking beyond the bounds of convention. It was the 1870s, a time of corsets and bustles, parasols and chaperones, but Isabelle kept her hair cropped, and often she'd labor, her fingers callused and her brow moist, in the garden, digging weeds and chopping wood; or else she'd dress herself in male clothes and go out riding with her brother.[176] By the time she was a teenager, she'd wander the streets of Geneva alone in a pair of trousers, and people would just assume—with her short hair and slim, muscular frame—that she was a boy. She'd make out with men in alleyways; she'd devour the novels of Pierre Loti. She was well educated, also, learning metaphysics and chemistry in addition to literature. She became fluent in Greek, Latin and—significantly—Classical Arabic, able to read the Quran with ease by the age of sixteen. Maybe it was this that first drew her to Islam, the beauty of the Quran; either way, she was attracted enough to be publishing stories about Islamic mystics by age eighteen, and by age twenty, Isabelle and her mother had both taken the shehada in Algeria and officially become Muslims.

One might have expected this to change Isabelle, but far from it. Soon after her conversion, she was thrown into crisis: in November of 1897, her mother died of heart failure. Only a year later, her brother took his own life. Isabelle, already grief-stricken and desperate, was then dealt another blow in 1899, when her father figure passed away of throat cancer. Lost, alone, broke at the age of twenty-two and finding nothing for her back in Europe (a Europe she felt hated her Eastern/Russian roots), she settled in Algeria. "This land of the Maghrib, which was always the sacred Kaaba," she wrote. There, she began to live semi-nomadically, journeying on horseback across the desert, often alone, writing, drinking, smoking *kef*, developing "the most stubborn and unconquerable energy" and enjoying the "physical aspects of love."[177]

She found freedom in Algeria and in Islam: freedom to be not only Isabelle, the French woman of Russian descent, but also Si Mahmoud Essadi, a Sufi Arab Muslim man. In her diaries, in which she would detail her visits to brothels and souks in the guise of Si Mahmoud, she would often sign the name of her alter ego. It was easy for her to live this way: the local Arabs accepted Si Mahmoud, with his fez and loose clothing, without question. As her friend Robert Randau put it, "the innate courtesy of the Arabs is such that none of them ever made any allusion, even by so much as a wink"[178] that they knew her biological sex. So unshakeable was this acceptance that, before long, Isabelle/Si Mahmoud even managed to get herself initiated into the Kadriya, the first and oldest of the Sufi orders, her dedication to the religion so powerful it didn't matter that she wasn't born Muslim, Arab or male.

It was, in a way, a love story. Isabelle/Si Mahmoud had fallen for Islam, was, from the outset, taken with its mysticism, with its ideas of predestination—everything is mektoub, foretold—almost drunk on her love of the religion. "Oh, that extraordinary feeling of intoxication I had tonight, in the peaceful shadows of the great al-Jadid Mosque during the icha prayer!" she wrote in her diaries. Like any besotted teen, she was filled with longing. "Oh, to lie upon the rugs of some silent mosque," she penned, the desire almost palpable. "The soul's gaze turned heavenward, to listen to Islam's song forever!" She was a goner.

But saying "I do" was only the beginning. While she traveled, inhabiting the two identities, she spent time thinking deeply about the religion, finding God in the shapes of the sand dunes, in the "beautiful, grave gestures of the Muslims' rite" that "exalt even the humblest of them." And she learned more about Islam as she spent time with it, became intimate with it, the love deepening, the process of conversion slow and layered. "As for my religious feelings, my faith is now truly genuine, and I no longer need to make the slightest effort," she wrote, a few years after she took the shehada. She was nearly destitute at this point, and constantly ill. She'd make money by writing and then spend it all within a week. But this was how she lived, traveling through North Africa, embedding herself in the lives of the locals. She was, in spite of everything, happy. She had her belief with her, riding beside her across those desert dunes.

Eventually, her connection with Islam strengthened even more, and she felt the initial declaration of Islam was not enough: marriage was about more than the wedding day, after all. "Man's salvation," wrote Isabelle/Si Mahmood, "lies in faith. Not in the dreary kind made up of empty formulas, but a living faith that confers strength." She added: "To say *There is no God but God and Muhammad is his Prophet* is not enough, not even to be convinced of it. It takes more than that to be a Muslim."

◈

Before Nusayba and the other inhabitants of Yathrib travel to Al-Aqabah to meet the Apostle, Muhammad tries to convert the inhabitants of his hometown, Mecca. He does this almost reluctantly, at first; he's not one for stirring things up. And his message is certainly one to stir things up. His message—of social equality, of liberation, of ultimate accountability—not only threatens to destabilize the usual way of things (social revolutions are always discomforting, frightening affairs) but also, specifically, to drain the power away from Mecca's ruling clan. This clan, the Quraysh—of which, it should be noted, Muhammad was a part—dominated Mecca by controlling the Kaaba, which served as a focal point for pilgrims journeying through the Arabian desert. Holding the keys to the Kaaba, in other words, meant that the Quraysh controlled the town's tourism industry, and also its finances, since locals would also pay the Quraysh to enter the sacred hut. Muhammad's preaching—which, above all else, specified that there was only a single god, and that this god did not particularly enjoy iconography—threatened to undermine the entire business model of the Quraysh.

At first, they let this go. Muhammad is dismissed as another hakim or soothsayer; plenty of these around in the seventh century, religion is every-where. But then they become a bit nervous. People appear to be listening to him, rejecting their old beliefs. Slaves—who he preached should be freed—and women and the poor are the first to gather, but soon others (men! Rich men!) start to pause and listen to what he has to say. So the Quraysh decide the thing to do is to ask him, reasonably, to *see here, old chap, we can't have you spouting this nonsense and mucking up our business.* They expect him to back down, especially when they visit his guardian, a member of their own clan, and tell him *it's really not on* (they do this with a little extra menace, but nothing that is, they are quick to assure each other, unwarranted).

But Muhammad is stubborn. He continues to stand in the square and recite the words that he hears from God, words that are poetic, learned and wise, so much so that they stun his fellow Meccans, some of whom have known him for years and have always thought of him as bright, yes, but certainly not eloquent, not *sage.* The Quraysh watch this happening with increasing trepi-dation and not a small amount of anger. Their tactics turn harsh. They mock him, they throw food and dung at him, Quilliam-style; they initiate a boycott against him—no one may buy or sell anything to or from him or his so-called "followers", those early converts. He is battered with the rocks that they hurl at him. His old guardian has died and so he has no clan protection, and soon there are death warrants out for him. His followers begin to flee, leaving Mecca for the closest nearby town—Yathrib—and begin to spread the word. Despite the Quraysh's best efforts, one by one, converts emerge.

It took time and effort to turn the Byzantine cathedral properly into a mosque. Not only for those minarets to be built, but also to construct an arched, recessed altar, to show the direction of Mecca, and beside this the minbar, a steep pulpit. A chandelier was placed precariously high in the center of the main building, and the figurative mosaics inside—depicting the Virgin Mary and Jesus Christ—were plastered over and replaced with Arabic calligraphy. Small, square plaques bearing the names of Muhammad and his successors were added, and then updated a few hundred years later, replaced by giant green-and-gold discs, pinned at the base of the central arch. When, in 1935, the Hagia Sophia then became a museum, workers once again filled the space, scrubbing the recently uncovered marble flooring, trying to heft those same giant spheres out of the building. "For nearly five centuries their discordant green had shouted across at the dimming colors of the splendid marbles with which the walls are covered," wrote a *Guardian* correspondent at the time. "When they were got down, it was found that they could not be passed through the doors. So—and also because this museum of Byzantine art is to house Ottoman objects of interest to this building too—they are stacked one against another against an aisle wall, and you can touch the gold names."[179]

The stories of the Hagia Sophia's spatial conversions reflect the much larger-scale religious conversions happening slowly and clunkily across the empires. The seeds of Christianity were planted centuries before the Roman Empire became truly Christianized, with over three hundred years passing between Jesus's birth and Constantine's embrace of the religion; another decade or so later, Emperor Julian "The Apostate" was still ruling over a largely pagan Roman empire. By the time Islam was born, though, another few hundred years on, paganism had been outlawed, Jesus was widely accepted, and Christianity was largely dominant across Byzantium—despite decades of confusion over the nature of the Trinity exhausting, and causing disagreement between, the leadership (how could God be at once the father, son and holy spirit? Was Jesus the son of God or a *part* of God?). In the neighboring Sasanian empire, Zoroastrianism was still officially the state religion, though Christian, Buddhist and Jewish minorities were also increasing, and the Sasanian Christians were themselves having their own issues with the Trinity.

It's clear why Islam, emerging at a time when both Byzantine and Sasanian empires were embroiled in these messes, spread quickly. By 632 CE, the year of Muhammad's death, most of the Arabian Peninsula was dominated by Islam. Just over a century later, the Muslims had spread from Mecca to as far east as Afghanistan, and as far west as Spain. This was in large part due to the Muslim armies' military prowess, but the other empires, having wasted resources weakly batting at each other for decades, were also unable to handle the unexpected challenge. Though conversion in these newly conquered territories was likely an attractive option for many—it was simple to do, and Muslims in the caliphates paid lower taxes than their non-Muslim compatriots—no one was forced to convert[180] and, in the end, it took until the eleventh century before Muslims made up the majority of subjects in the Islamic empires. A few hundred years after that, and many of the previously Muslim-majority territories had been Christianized again. In other words, though the symbolic change might've taken only a few decades, the substantive shift towards the new religion was, as Christianity had been before it, far, far more gradual.

It is easy, when examined from this bird's-eye perspective, to see conversion as slow and effortful metamorphosis, to picture—as in a time-lapse video—the way in which religious seedlings are planted in swathes of empty brown land; how they shoot in a sudden, trembling, delicate burst from the earth; rise, unfurling, green arms stretching, towards the heavens; push faithful tendrils deeper into the earth as, up above, leaves spring out, first one, then ten, then a hundred; the trunk and the branches and the foliage all starting, ever so gradually, to take shape; the seed finally, painstakingly, transformed into the tree; the tree then felled; a new seed planted. The kernels of each new religion budding quietly and steadily over the centuries, springing up to turn the landscape green and verdant, for a short while, and then replaced. As the eleventh-century poet-philosopher Abu al-'Alaa al-Ma'arri wrote:

Now this religion happens to prevail
Until by that one it is overthrown,
Because men dare not live with men alone
But always with another fairy tale.

-⸖-

A few months into the pandemic and I find myself unintentionally on the outside. It is the summer after that first lockdown, and those who had previously also been meticulously wiping down with anti-bac are now "eating out to help out,"[181] crowded around tables in bars and restaurants, laughing with wide-open, uncovered mouths, spittle spraying into the already spittle-filled air. I stay masked and outdoors, my hands rough and dry from the alcoholic gel I conscientiously slather on after contact with anything outside my flat. I have seen what the virus can do; I'm not going to let it get hold of my body. A friend invites me to a big birthday do, indoors, and I feel insane as I instantly decline, noticing in the tiny Zoom reflection that my expression is panicked, that I am shaking my head quickly and repeatedly, almost backing away from the screen. The truth is, I'm shocked. This friend had been terrified to even leave the house for her allotted walk only a month or two earlier. Now she's about to have a blowout with three dozen people in her tiny Camden apartment?

As always when faced with a person's sudden change, the inconsistency has unmoored me, and I am left wondering how it happens, this about-face, this total transformation. Relax, my friend says, it's no big deal.

-⸖-

Though it was William James who pioneered analytical thinking on religious metanoia, or conversion, specifically in Christianity, it is the work of Lewis R. Rambo and Charles E. Farhadian that moved the thinking into the more holistic, psychosocial model that is generally accepted today. This model sees conversion as a process involving seven phases: context, crisis, quest, encounter, interaction, committing and consequences. While the context is the general environment in which the change takes place, the crisis is the actual catalyst for the change. A global pandemic, for instance, is a crisis on a mass scale, but smaller things might do this too. Losing one's job. Grief. Isolation. Loneliness, in fact, can be a catalyst for a great deal, particularly where religion is concerned—organized religion offers not only ritual, a shape to the days, but also companionship and community. The socially rejected can find acceptance in conversion; it can be a way out of depression and hopelessness.

Often the crisis is followed by the quest: a search for answers, for a road-map, any way to meet the challenge one is facing. A frantic Google search at two in the morning. Usually a way is found through an advocate, someone who highlights a particular path; this is the encounter. During the next phase, interaction, the advocate and the potential convert get into the nitty gritty, what the changes will actually *mean* for the person. A head covering? A new diet? The commitment phase marks the moment the potential convert de-cides to dedicate their life to this new belief system, while the consequences phase refers to the cumulative effects of all past actions and beliefs that either help or hinder this phase.

Like the stages of grief, though, these phases are dynamic and not nec-essarily linear; one can move backwards and forwards, repeat a phase, jump a phase. The point here is that conversion is not just an immediate and indi-vidual psychological phenomenon, but deeply social, deeply contextualized, deeply gradual. This is why religious groups find that they have the most success finding new recruits during the autumn terms at universities, when students are feeling dislocated and overwhelmed; the process is one of seeking and solidifying answers at a time of uncertainty. It is rare to have a road-to-Da-mascus moment, a sudden epiphanic lightning strike that transforms one's worldview. Instead, it is dynamic, complex. Like the metamorphosis from church to mosque to museum, there are negotiations involved, stumbling blocks and solutions: efforts to deconstruct and reconstruct structures appro-priately; shields that are found to be too large to remove are, instead, turned into a feature.

The pre-Islamic period in Arabia, known as the jahiliyyah period, or "the age of ignorance", was, depending on the source you read, either a femi-nist utopia—with women able to be business owners, poetesses, warriors, polygamists—or a gendered nightmare, with female infanticide a common practice. A mixture of both is probably true. Food was scarce; raids were common. There was poetry and sex; there was suffering and confusion. The constant throb of rotting teeth dampened by the overwhelming enormity of a star-saturated night sky. A helpless dependence on the elements tempered by the belief that it could be no other way. Death was everywhere; without modern medicine, a third of the youth wouldn't live beyond the age of ten. Women had children only to watch them die. So common was loss that mourning was a profession.[182] If you made it through childhood, you were unlikely to reach forty—whether because of violence, illness or just bad luck. But there was also love, companionship, family. There was also dancing, the beat of a drum shifting the grains of sand beside a fire, the scent of sweat in the air.

Nusayba, we know, had already grieved two husbands by the time Muhammad came along. Her sons were—according to the traditions—alive and thriving, but other children were possibly lost both to Nusayba and the annals of history. Though her tribe, the Khazraj, were likely polytheists who worshipped the three goddesses of the region, monotheism was a close neighbor. In Yathrib alone, both Jewish and Christian tribes were prominent; a particularly famous Christian, nicknamed "the monk,"[183] was, we are told, close with her clan. It is likely, then, that many of Muhammad's messages—an extension, as they are, of the other two monotheistic religions—wouldn't have been entirely unfamiliar to her, making it the right sort of context for the development of a new belief system.

The crisis, it's clear, was Muhammad's message: in calling out the Quraysh's hold on power, he created a "rupture in the taken-for-granted world,"[184] as Rambo and Farhadian put it. Suddenly, how things had always been done seemed, maybe, like a bad reason to keep doing them. Perhaps Nusayba had already been on a quest for a different sort of life, anyway, sick of the death, sick of the hopelessness, sick of the unpredictability of her world. Perhaps she was looking for a cause, or for power. Perhaps she knew that being close to God—for instance, being a priestess in Christian Byzantium[185]—had always worked out well for women, had provided them with more freedom, more control. So perhaps Nusayba thought that being close to this new God, and close to his prophet, would work out well for her, too.

Or maybe it was the encounter and the interaction that really convinced her. The charisma and the poetry of the Apostle's words. The vision of the ummah—the community of Muslims—that he described. The guidance he offered, straight from the heavens. The way his voice carried over the sound of the wind, whistling over the ridge, in Al-Aqabah, as the men stepped forward, one after the other, clasping his hands and repeating the words *La illaha illah la, wa Muhammad rasul Allah*. There is no God but God, and you, Muhammad, are the messenger of God. Maybe her heart began to beat against her chest and a lump formed in her throat as she watched this procession, maybe her body hummed with nerves. Maybe she pulled her jilbab tight around her shoulders, the nape of her neck suddenly pricked and cold. Maybe the air felt thick with tension, maybe a shiver snaked up her spine. Maybe she could sense it, even then, what was happening.

Right in front of her, now, Nusayba was witnessing the start of something inconceivably enormous: the birth of a new and lasting world religion. Maybe she wanted to be more than a witness, maybe she wanted to be a part of it—to commit and protect him. Maybe she was ready to be transformed.

Despite my misgivings, research on the similarities between experiences of coming out and of religious conversion point to the ways in which this latter process can be positive and emancipatory, defined by a "feeling of joy and release from the burden of self-hatred." It can lead to "a renewed sense of strength and vigor and self-worth which was never experienced" before, as Christopher Lamb writes in his exploration of the phenomenon.[186] Sure, change unnerves me, but it can also be good, even necessary. Under the right circumstances, conversion offers the possibility of complete renewal. How many spas and apps and gym memberships and self-improvement programs offer to do just that? To believe that the type of metamorphosis required by religious conversion is actually possible, maybe even happens quite often, could actually be—for the anxious among us, the depressed among us, the Occupied among us—quite reassuring.

If one looks closely enough, in fact, there exist all sorts of non-cultish, non-*followy* conversions—conversions that are more about embracing a true self or a gratifying truth than they are about groupthink or uncritical devotion. Plato's cave dwellers who finally see the shadows for what they are can be called converts of a sort; even becoming a feminist is a type of intellectual conversion. When I think back to my younger, more naive self—the one who still saw catcalls as flattery, who tried to be the cool girl in all the problematic ways that entailed—I am astounded at her worldview. Her belief system, I see now, was moronic; but it took time, slow exposure to particular ideas, a realization of the truth of these ideas—yes, of *course,* duh, patriarchy explains so much—before the change could happen. I read feminists, and I met feminists, and at some point, I, too, became a feminist. *I* was a convert. In this light, conversion itself is transformed: no longer the bogeyman of zealotry, but proof of our capacity to alter, develop, grow. To become, in a certain way, more authentic versions of who we were before.

An assassination attempt in 1901 left Isabelle/Si Mahmoud with a deep slice above the elbow, the attacker's sword having snagged on the laundry line above her head as she sat writing, and so missing its target—just—and reaching her arm instead. The wound was bone-deep; she was unable to move her fingers for close to a year, an injury eerily similar to the one that Nusayba suffered centuries before on the battlefield. Despite enduring immense pain and a terrifying period of hallucination-filled recovery in hospital, Isabelle/Si Mahmoud publicly forgave and defended her attacker, whose arrest she knew could be used in pro-colonial propaganda.[187] She wanted no part in any bid to justify the colonization of North Africa or the demonization of Muslims. Islam was, for Isabelle/Si Mahmoud, the only place she felt safe, felt peace. "I have no fatherland besides Islam," she wrote, signing off as Si Mahmoud. Moving back to Algeria after the death of her father-figure was a return home; indeed, in many ways, Islam *itself* was the home to which she returned.

Though the Hagia Sophia's latest transformation into a mosque was referred to in news items most often as a "conversion," this isn't, strictly speaking, accurate. The use to which the building was put was not new. The most recent iteration of the space was, in fact, a *reiteration.* Prayer mats had lined the marble floors before; Arabic calligraphy had hung beneath the domed archways. For centuries, the devout had kneeled and stood in the ritualized gestures of the rak'a underneath the splendid central dome, had traipsed out past the purple columns on a Friday afternoon. "The resurrection of the Hagia Sophia takes the chains off its doors and the shackles off the hearts and the feet of those who stand alongside it,"[188] Erdoğan said, on announcing his decision. Though the initial transformation from cathedral during the time of the Ottomans had been a painful metamorphosis, this was not the case the second time the Hagia Sophia became a mosque. The second time, it was a going back.

This is, in fact, how Muslims see the process of taking the shehada: not as a transformation, but as a *reversion*. We are all born Muslims, this story goes, so if we "convert" to Islam, in reality, we are just *re*verting to it. The natural state of the human being is a state of submission to God;[189] some of us simply forget. Taking the shehada isn't so much taking us somewhere new, as it is bringing us back to where we were to start with. Conversion, then, can be a story about transformation and novelty, but it can also be a story about return. It can be a process of metamorphosis, like the seedling to the tree, but it can also be a different sort of journey—to a truer state of being, a former self. Even, perhaps, to a fatherland, a home.

When I think of conversion these days, I can't help but think of my own home. This little triangle, like a tooth, like a shard of glass, this small, breakable thing in the Middle East that I call my country. Here, in this place, on a national level, we see the stories of conversion converging: here is slow, painful metamorphosis into something entirely new, as well as—for some, at least—blissful reversion to a more authentic former self. Here is also (for a certain group) a love story, an intoxicating devotion. The process of conversion is ongoing, so it is not clear, yet, where it will ultimately lead, hard to imagine what it will create. Easy, also, to forget that there was a time before the conversion began. Oddly enough, Isabelle/Si Mahmoud is a reminder. Only a few months before she died—drowned, aged twenty-seven, in a freak flood that engulfed almost a quarter of the town in which she'd spent the night—she had been wondering about coming to this country. "I shall look into the possibility of settling in Palestine," she wrote. Strange to think that the place she so wanted to go, "an Arab country, no doubt like the one I love," has since been so transformed.

These days, I think of conversion and picture the arches inside the Hagia Sophia, my mind's eye tracing a line along that parabola, down, up, up, and then down again. That mathematical symbol for the intersect in the meeting point of Europe and Asia, Christianity and Islam, conversion and reversion.

⟡

Two years into the pandemic, and much of the world has reverted. Most of us have, it seems, forgotten the selves we temporarily inhabited, though the evidence of these former selves remains: on my bedside table and in coat pockets and in the tote bags that hang on my bedroom door, I find nearly empty bottles of hand sanitizer, slowly congealing. The one drawer in my small galley kitchen has too much space occupied by a box of plastic gloves, no longer used; underneath the sink is the giant carton of anti-bacterial solution. Tests and surgical masks and nasal spray sit behind the mirror door of the bathroom cabinet. But outside, the street is now always busy. Children screaming as their harried parents walk them back from school; honking traffic jams at rush hour. For many, the journey they were on is now over. They have come back to themselves—changed and unchanged.

Returning to my own former self is not so easy, though, and in the end, I find I am the one who metamorphosed. Thanks to the virus having found its way into—and wreaking havoc in—my already-vulnerable system, I discover I cannot be in the world the way I used to be, even when normality has settled again. In my body there is a swollen and defective heart, newly malfunctioning lungs, a weakness that makes the day-to-day freshly challenging. New rules, about what I can and cannot physically do, are in place, and because of this, there has been a restructuring: of life plans, behaviors, priorities, understandings. An axe has been swung to my inner walls, though I wasn't the one to swing it.

My friend whose birthday I had missed a year and a half earlier comes to visit for the first time, and even this entails a different setup. I cannot cook or host or drink, I will mostly stay lying in my bed. I struggle even getting down the stairs to open the front door when she rings the bell, and feel my heart pounding with anticipation when I reach the bottom. I'm not sure I'm ready for this reunion, my new self still too unfamiliar, too unnerving. Revealing my transformation to my friend feels almost too much. I clutch the door handle, close my eyes, and take a deep breath. Relax, I tell myself, opening the door, smiling, my body trembling as I lean on my new walking stick. It's really no big deal.

GOOD GIRLS, NASTY WOMEN

There was and there was not, in the depths of the past, a woman who was very, very fucking angry.

It is a Saturday in March in the year 625 CE. She is leading a crowd of women behind her husband, Abu Sufyan—a member of the elite Meccan clan, the Quraysh—who himself is leading three thousand men from Mecca, southern Arabia, to a valley north of Mount Uhud. The mountain, formed of volcanic rock, is 3,530 feet high and more than four and a half miles long, the color of dried blood. They are headed there to fight against Muhammad and his supporters, who, a year before, had beaten them—surprisingly and embarrassingly—in a battle at Badr, one of many such fights between the new Muslim converts of Yathrib (later called Medina) and the polytheists of Mecca, fights that were really more about power than about religion.

That loss had been felt keenly. After the defeat, as the troops had made their way slowly back from Badr to Mecca, one of the men had turned to Abu Sufyan and said, angrily, "Muhammad has wronged you and killed your best men, so help us with this money to fight him, so that we may hope to get our revenge for those we have lost." Abu Sufyan had looked at the bedraggled group of defeated men around them—all missing their dead brothers, fathers, sons and uncles—and agreed. So today the Meccans have come well prepared and, thanks to Abu Sufyan, well funded, leaving nothing to chance: they have camels, tents, weapons and, behind them, the throng of women who will watch from the sidelines, urging them on with ululations and cheers. In charge of these women is Abu Sufyan's wife, Hind, whose father, son and uncle had been killed at that same battle at Badr. She marches quickly, purposefully, at the front of the group, one hand carrying her tambourine, the other clenched in a tight fist. She has plans of her own.

The Meccans set up camp and station two infantries facing the mountain, pinning Muhammad's far less numerous troops—only a couple of hundred men—against the incline, with nowhere to go. The Prophet sets up his camp in a little protected inlet, sends his insignificant infantry to face the Meccans, and orders his archers onto the hillock that juts out just beyond the inlet, directly opposite the Meccan camp. He is relying on these archers to protect him and his men, but they will let him down. Some will panic and fall back; others will take advantage of what appears to be a Meccan retreat to go looting; either way, they will leave their post, and therefore the Prophet, unguarded. Before long Muhammad will be surrounded by the Meccans, and it will be Nusayba bint Ka'ab al Khazrajia who swoops in there, last-minute, daring, to make sure that her Prophet survives. She will become famous for this, the first of her many battles alongside Muhammad, sustaining injuries that will last her lifetime.

As Nusayba charges forward furiously, plunging her sword into the flesh between the armored plates of a large, muscled Meccan fighter, praying to her new God that she and the Prophet and her sons survive what feels like a rockslide of limbs and hooves and knives and swords, Hind watches impatiently from the sidelines. "Quench my thirst for vengeance, and quench your own!"[190] Hind shouts at the Meccan troops. She suddenly screams as a Yathriban, Abu-Dujani, draws near her, sword raised—but he puts it down at the last minute, when he sees she is a woman. She backs away, her eyes still scanning the soldiers in their clanking armor. She is looking for an enslaved Abyssinian named Wahshi. Only hours before, she had been heard making a deal with him: his freedom, in exchange for the death of Hamza, the most powerful of the Muslim fighters. "Come on," she had wheedled. "Satisfy our vengeance." It doesn't take long to spot him; there, in the distance, dragging his bloodied javelin behind him, she sees Wahshi leaving the battlefield. Meaning that Hamza is, yes, he must be, finally, he has to be . . .

Yes, *yes*, she has been avenged.

But it is not enough, she soon realizes: she still feels that clenching of rage deep in the pit of her stomach. As Muhammad, Nusayba and the rest of the Muslim fighters finally retreat, defeated, Hind marches into the battleground, now littered with the strange stillness of the dead, followed by the other Meccan women. She is searching for Hamza's body, her own vibrating with adrenaline, undeterred by the sour stench of open wounds rising in the heat. Finally, she spies his corpse, a large limp figure, this once powerful man who had killed her father, lying still as a rock. She climbs onto him, straddling him, pulls off his armor and pushes her knife just below his left pectoral, forcing it down and slicing through to his belly, deeply enough to push aside the skin and yank out what looks like a smooth, rounded, red piece of steak: his liver. Wild-eyed, incandescent, she bites into the bloodied organ and shrieks from the top of her lungs.

I have become increasingly obsessed by this tale of Hind bint 'Utbah—this other, more controversial female figure of Islam, forever referred to in the texts as the Liver-Eating Woman—whose maniacal, vengeful cannibalism fascinates me, particularly beside Nusayba, who is presented as, above all else, courageous and self-sacrificing. It is intriguing to me that the same battle should produce these two infamous women. Hind acts almost as foil to Nusayba: she is murderous, vengeful, but not in fact brave, since she out-sources the dirty work of killing to Wahshi. She is full of aggression, but it is self-serving; she is not a protector but a scavenger. She is fearsome and wild, like Nusayba, but the contours are different; both she and Nusayba are angry, but Hind alone is truly nasty.

When Donald Trump made his "nasty woman" comment in reference to Hillary Clinton during the 2016 presidential campaign, the term sat heavy with insinuation—of physical repugnance, of sexual deviancy, of obscenity. "Nasty" is a particularly gendered word, with undertones of the filthy and the sexual when placed next to a woman. Nasty girls are dirty girls, mean girls, but they are also, perhaps, sexually loose girls, girls whose bodily functions are too obvious, out-of-control girls. Morally unclean as well as physically so. Girls whose appetites and emotions are outsized, whose sexuality becomes vulgar, tumorous: bulbous bosoms and fleshy faces. Hind is the Liver-Eater, with her hunger for human flesh, but she was also called "She with the big clitoris."[191]

(Perhaps this is because, as Susan Sontag has suggested, everyone has felt "an erotic lure in things that are vile and repulsive."[192]) Nastiness is thus associated with repulsion as well as unkindness; "that girl's nasty" might mean "she's cruel," but equally it could mean "she's disgusting" or "she's wild in bed," and often it means, by extension, a little bit of all three. "If you ain't scared, take it out/I'll do it like a real live nasty girl should," the Prince lyrics go.[193]

⚜

Years after the battle at Mount Uhud, Hind decides to convert from polytheism to Islam. This, too, brings out a rage in her, and the descriptions of this outburst remind me of Seneca's[194] idea of "anger as madness."[195] She goes home, picks up an axe and begins swinging it haphazardly at the clay idols she has standing around the house. "We were deluded about you!"[196] she says furiously, smashing them to smithereens. "Deluded!" She picks up a fragile stone figurine and hurls it to the ground; it breaks into small, sharp fragments.

This scene feels strangely, viscerally familiar. Aged maybe four or five, I had a temper tantrum. Something to do with Pokémon cards, I think, though I can't be sure. What is vivid is that I was so enraged with my mother that I picked up a snow globe—significant because it was a present I had given to her for her birthday—and hurled it, with all my tiny-girl strength, to the ground. I don't think I expected it to break; I certainly didn't expect it to shatter spectacularly over the bathroom floor, for the world inside it to leak out miserably between thousands of shards of glass, the glitter gathering in the crevices of the broken tiles. Unfixable. Instantly, the rage was gone. Instead, I was devastated: at the pain on my mother's face, caused by me; at the destruction I had created; at the irrevocability of it all. I felt I had lost my mind, lost my self.

⚜

In that same battle at Uhud, Nusayba is said to have yelled angrily at the troops who abandoned Muhammad and left him vulnerable to the attacks of the enemy on the battlefield. Later, at a different battle, when she sees soldiers run away from the fight yet again, she screams at them in frustration ("WHAT IS THIS HABIT OF YOURS? WHY DO YOU KEEP FLEEING?") and charges forward by herself, taking down the leader of the enemy battalion. *Those fuckers!* I can imagine her thinking, right before she channels that fury

126

into her fighting. That's what she *would* do, of course: on the battlefield, rage is sanctioned. Her ferocity and aggression are part of the deal. And yet I struggle to fully picture this.

There is a story we are told, as women, about anger. This story suggests that anger is not a female trait; that the expression of anger—aggression—is particularly unfeminine. Women are, the narrative tells us, the "guardians of relationships,"[197] as Janet Zuckerman puts it, our ability to love and care cast as natural. Essentialized, and prioritized. Some women (like me) internalize this story: we play the part of the good girl, "embody[ing] the fiction that women are calm," that hostility and rage are foreign to us. We dutifully pack away unwanted feelings, along with the fancy china (or feel inadequate if we don't), and forget that we have them at all. "Girls never learn the right way to express aggression," Zuckerman adds. "They only learn not to do it." While aggression in a male context is seen as justified and straightforward, for these women "it is a shameful personal failing that prompts dissociation even when felt to be legitimate." We are meant to be the healers, the helpers, not rage-filled warriors, pain makers, inflicters of wounds; female anger is, as Alison Jaggar has dubbed it, an "outlaw emotion."[198] This isn't to say that women don't show aggression and that men do, but that *well-behaved* women can't show aggression while *well-behaved* men can.

Good boys can punch the bully, but good girls wipe away the blood.

Many women, including myself, put an awful lot of time, energy and money into keeping the physical body in line. Waxing, shaving, plucking, coloring, cutting, not farting, not bleeding. An endless Sisyphean imperative that is at odds with my ideologies (queer, feminist, anti-capitalist). I epilate. I sugar. I get my eyebrows threaded regularly, despite my dermatographism—an allergy to touch—meaning that the area will swell and redden for days after the ordeal, and despite my Arab genes (with their consequent hairiness) leading to consternation among beauticians. ("This is something I've never seen," one will mutter in dismay, as a new thread breaks in my superhumanly strong brows. "It looked like you had *nothing*," another will say in whispered awe, twenty minutes into the five-minute-long appointment, still uprooting entire coastal paths of thick, invisibly blonde strands across my forehead.) These parts of my body over which I have power only highlight the ones that are beyond me entirely. Too regularly I have found myself in intestinal agony, frantically reaching for a bucket or a pack of Imodium. Unexpected bloodfalls are an inevitability, always painful and messy, staining pants and trousers and sheets and once, horrifyingly, a library desk chair. (I stayed until everyone had left and then panic-dabbed the mark with sparkling water, ineffectively.) And I have felt shame at my inability to control and contain these bodily functions, and somehow this shame has grown into a larger shame about not being clean or contained or calm enough more generally. The wildness of my womb somehow exposes me as wild, when all I want is to be good and poised and happy-to-help and no-bother-at-all.

This, I think, is the thing with the nastiness of the physical female body. What is nasty is so often what is untamed or uncontrolled—bloodiness or hairiness or gassiness—and so it serves the dual purpose of keeping us busy controlling and taming, as well as learning a more general lesson about how we, as women, should be controlled and tame.

⚜

I have never been good with anger, so when I read of Hind's unadulterated rage, or Nusayba's furious determination, it gives me pause. Do I admire it, I wonder, or does it frighten me? It seems so uncomplicated for these women of the past. By contrast, I am Zuckerman's "good girl": I over-apologize and rush to support; I anxiously make inane conversation when I feel tensions rising in a room. The typical, overenthusiastic people pleaser. (A recent email search found that my most commonly used phrase is "Happy to help!". And I am, genuinely, very happy to help, most of the time.) That childhood incident notwithstanding, I do not know how to handle anger, shying away from it in others and myself when I sense its approach, doing the tip-toe dance around topics I know are likely to be explosive. More often than not, I am on the receiving end. (I'm so sorry, I say, horrified, as my friend's face closes and tightens for some unknown reason. *What did I do? How did I upset her?*) Always apologizing, mending, guarding those relationships, vigilant against anything that might cause upset, even when upset is unpredictable.

In a park in London one day with a friend, a middle-aged white couple, whose large, energetic dog had, without warning, bounded up and stolen our food container, suddenly become inexplicably aggressive towards us. "Fuck you!" the man shouts at us, after flinging our chewed-up container at our feet. He says this in response to a polite, laughing "excuse me, I think your dog—" from my friend.

"Fuck you!" the man shouts again, spitting, his finger inches from my friend's face. Don't let it escalate, I pray. As he walks away, my friend shouts back to him: "You need some manners, sir!" But I stay frozen, confused, terrified. Sorry, I mouth silently, not sure if I am apologizing to my aggressors or to the friend I have failed to protect. I call for Nusayba in my head, but she is nowhere to be found.

⊹

In Jerusalem, anger surrounds me, is omnipresent, it simmers and boils: the air is thick with its stenchy fug. Like skunk water, it stings the eyes with the acidity of burning rubbish. How could it be otherwise? We are under unending occupation. The whole nation is angry, at the corner shop, outside the café, in the schoolyard. People's nerves are grated, exposed, and the rage leaks out. If you want to escape the anger, go to a beach bar in Tel Aviv, have the hippie half-Californian waiter wearing surfer shorts and flip-flops bring you a beer, and pretend you are innocent, a guileless visitor. Pretend this decades-old atrocity has nothing whatsoever to do with you.

⊹

When it comes to feeling and expressing anger, Muslim Arab women are even more constrained than their white peers, triple-bound by the Western construction of what it means to embody that identity. If "Muslim" and "Arab" are by now shorthand for "scary" and "brutal," every Arab Muslim in the West is already in the unenviable position of constantly trying to prove themselves the opposite. An effort is made to be soft-spoken, gentle, unthreatening. Wear glasses if you can, bring out that lisp, tell them about how you're an academic (the most delicate of professions). But this of course leaves a female Muslim Arab to drop straight through the trapdoor into that other stereotype: that of the Arab Muslim *Woman*, who is of course quiet and fearful and in desperate need of saving. (And from whom? Why, from her Scary Brutal Arab Muslim Man, of course! Thus unintentionally confirming the original stereotype.) If female anger is an outlaw emotion, Arab Muslim female anger—at least in a Western context—is a capital offense.

The situation is perhaps even more dire for us as Palestinians; the word "Palestinian" itself having been interchangeable with "terrorist" for much of my life. We are racialized as mad, aggressive, rageful and violent, so any hint of anger, no matter how justified, is simply confirmation of this racialization: the inherent barbarism of my people further proof of the necessity of our occupation and annihilation. So even when I am provoked, in my country or outside it—when told that Palestinians are "bloodthirsty", that we "don't exist" or should "go to the rest of the Arab world," whether by my fellow Brits or my neighboring Israelis—I keep my features polite, my voice quiet. I make an effort at a joke. When a fellow student in my art class in New York makes a point of switching seats, moving from right beside me to across the room, right after I say I'm Palestinian (this was 2009, the height of anti-Arab sentiment), I just bite down on the fleshy inside of my cheek and give a small, apologetic smile. If I get angry, if I scream out "apartheid!" I prove them right. As the academic Whitney Phillips has pointed out: "The anger of those seeking justice—especially those who are Black, brown, female, or members of other minority groups—is minimized, pathologized, and knee-jerk condemned."[199] It is also, she adds, decontextualized and offered no path to redemption—so rather than recognize the provocation, and apologize or communicate, those outside the group will only see pathology. There is no way, in other words, to be angry, as a Palestinian, and retain my individual humanity. So instead I empathize, I play peacemaker. See, I'm no villain, I say with my open body language, my attempts to smile. And so it goes: I try to not get my people in trouble, while simultaneously I let them down.

Meanwhile, Nusayba perches beside me invisibly, sword in hand.

The year 2017, dubbed "the year of women's anger"—with the Women's Marches on Washington and beyond, and then, later, the #MeToo movement—was considered revolutionary. Women! Showing anger! Together! A public reckoning was, supposedly, taking place; women everywhere were embracing rage—*expressing* rage—and thereby reaching new, dizzying heights of power. They were rewriting that story about female anger, and this time they were *mad*. They were uncontrolled and uncontrollable; they were outlaws. "NASTY WOMAN" proclaimed the T-shirts, hats, notebooks and iPhone covers of smiling young women walking down high streets in America and elsewhere. Signs with the same expression were held high at the March on Washington; Ashley Judd, speaking to a crowd of half a million feminists at that same march, announced to all: "I am a nasty woman."[200] The term almost immediately became a badge of honor, iconic mainly in its irony: Clinton, with her reserve, her aloofness, even in the face of Trump's verbal assaults, was of course anything but nasty. She has spent years refining her public self to be as self-controlled, as placid, as she can be, even when baited. She is far from gross, sexual, or mean.[201] Her Trumpian "nastiness" is simply ambition, and so feminists took up arms and said: if ambition is nasty, I am nasty. But where did the real nastiness go? The appropriation of the term should have felt liberating, but to me, it felt limiting: an ironic, controlled nastiness is a nastiness with all meaning and sting wrung out.

(White cis) men are often angry and aggressive without catchphrases and hashtags, and this anger perhaps serves them, is a propulsive mechanism that underlies many, if not most, interactions. As Zuckerman has argued, men are not only able to feel anger, they are actually able to *use* aggression to their advantage. Others, too, have pointed out that anger, even aggression, can be emancipatory: Mona Eltahawy writes rousingly about the need for female rage, and the way in which patriarchy holds this emotion back, imprisoning us.[202] Rebecca Traister, looking at the history of female anger in the context of the American "year of women's anger," also understands it this way, and argues that female anger is not only a catalyst for social change, but an opportunity for community: women can find themselves liberated, and connected, through anger.[203] Audre Lorde famously wrote of anger being a "powerful source of energy serving progress and change,"[204] and often this is taken to mean that we should express our anger without restraint, and use this to energize ourselves and others. There is a part of me that is drawn to this idea, that feels high on righteous indignation, that feels freed by the "fuck you"s we're suddenly not only entitled, but *encouraged*, to shout. Somewhere within, I know that the female directive to be nice is a boot pressed to the trachea; I know that to be truly liberated would be to feel free to be wild and angry, NOT happy to help.

And there may be an important moral dimension to anger, too: as Peter Strawson[205] and others have argued, anger is an expression of moral assessment; it is what sensitizes us to injustice. You get angry, the theory goes, because you have been wronged, and it is from this feeling—this judgement—that all other morality then flows. In other words, anger may be essential to recognizing good from bad, to *creating* a moral society. I get angry when I am slapped and this then tells me that I have been wronged, that the slap was a wrongdoing, that I don't want to live in a world in which I get slapped for no reason. And if this is the case—if anger is what creates the moral judgements needed for a moral society—then "inhibiting any and all anger," as Agnes Callard puts it, "is acquiescing in evil."[206] Anger, then, is not only liberating and rebellious, but also necessary. Nusayba's fury, as she defends the Prophet, is what makes her moral. Not getting angry, *that's* what makes you the bad guy.

⟡

When I was in my twenties, an American friend of mine, with whom I was staying for a couple of weeks in New York, told me he was considering going on Birthright. "Just for the free plane ticket," he assured me. "I won't, you know, *buy into it*, but seems like a shame to pass up the opportunity, you know?" It took me years to understand that the panic attack I suffered immediately after he told me—hiccupping gasps of air that seemed entirely deoxygenated, my body trembling as though perched on a vibrator—was a way of avoiding the anger I couldn't (or wouldn't) access. If I got angry at my friend for this, I thought—for partaking in a project whose aim, it feels, is to gift my country, as a "birthright," to those who already have one, while my own right to it is denied,[207] its name alone guaranteed to cause a fear and pain so sharp it is like flesh caught on broken glass—wouldn't that make me the monster? Instead, I relied on a different instinct: panic (an instinct I'd always seen as, at worst, pathetic).

Now I look back and think: did this make me complicit?

⟡

When Muhammad, a few years after the Battle of Uhud, goes to Mecca with his followers, ready to convert the city and rid it of the stranglehold of the

132

powerful Quraysh clan, Abu Sufyan decides to finally concede. On hearing of her husband's decision, Hind goes up to him in the middle of the town square and pulls him down by his beard, glaring at him, eye to eye. "Kill this old fool for he has changed his religion!" she yells out, letting go in disgust and turning her back on him.[208] She is easy for me to conjure up; I can even hear the click of her tongue as she walks away.

In the Western imagination, Arab Muslim women are not often nasty, angry, rude. But this old Orientalist picture of us—as subdued, demure, oppressed, secluded—leaves no room for the shouty, pushy women I knew growing up. Bossy, bubbly Arab women who, frankly, intimidate me in my shy, quiet Englishness. The number of times I have felt awkward at a Palestinian social function and been met by competent friendliness or no-nonsense rudeness, a girl looping her arm through mine, taking me over to her friends and chatting to (or insulting) me—sometimes in broken English, mistaking my social anxiety for a linguistic one—is uncountable. Palestinian women have an outgoing assertiveness I can only envy. I have seen them be extraordinarily generous, and I have seen them get exceptionally furious (at me, at men, at the occupation).

My grandmother, in spite of her life being unarguably constrained by colonialism, patriarchy and occupation, was a formidable woman. It helped, perhaps, that she was from an old, well-respected Jerusalem family. Tender and loving as she was with me, she would scream at the handyman in her croaky smoker's voice until he'd leave the room with tears pouring down his face. (She demanded, and expected, perfection. She was always pristine: manicured nails, stiffly coiffed hair, elegant suits, a spritz of Giorgio perfume.) And she would get enraged watching the news, or hearing my father talk about what the occupation forces had done most recently—broken into his university offices, shot and killed a neighbor, installed a checkpoint. Her face would twist with disgust. May they rot in hell, she would say, stubbing out a cigarette and lighting another.

But even in writing this I worry that I play into the hands of those who would denigrate us. It feels like a privilege, to become angry without becoming—being turned into—the bad guy. The villain.

A man at a bar in Notting Hill once told me I was lucky I was fuckable, or else he'd have punched me. The place was crowded, so he'd leaned in close to say it, a large, sweaty hand heavy on my shoulder. I could sense the nasal sting of strong cologne. In the background, Dizzee Rascal sang about madness.

Sorry? I said, straining my ears. The man had asked me where I was from, and I'd told him I was Palestinian. I must have misheard his answer.

I *said*, you're lucky you're fuckable, or I'd have to punch you. *Ha ha.*

Sorry? I said again, blinking fast.

I've got family in Israel, you know, he continued, grabbing his pint from the bartender and turning around. So it would only be right.

Sorry? I replied, meekly, but he had already walked away.

Hind came from privilege. The traditions tell us that she was, from her birth, as close to nobility as existed at the time: the daughter of the powerful Qurayshi leader, Utbah ibn Rabi'ah, she was born and raised in Mecca, a center for pilgrimage even before it became Islam's sacred site. She was married three times; her first husband died from an illness, while her second was her deceased husband's brother, Al-Fakah. He left her, though, after finding an employee scuttling out of his home when Hind was meant to be there alone. Assuming Hind was having an affair, he immediately divorced her, despite her denials. Though she assured him she'd been asleep, and knew nothing of the man in her home, rumors started circulating. *Adulteress*, they whispered. *Whore.* Her father, frustrated, and himself now the subject of gossip, suggested they get a kahina (a female soothsayer) from Yemen to settle the matter. *She* would be able to determine who was telling the truth. When the soothsayer finally arrived and stood before a seated crowd of women, she immediately walked up to Hind and told her to rise.

"Stand up," she told Hind. "You are not ugly, and you are no adulteress." The kahina also went on to tell Hind that she would give birth to a king, which Hind found unsurprising. (Al-Fakah, on hearing this, went to Hind with arm extended, but she refused to take him back. If I'm conceiving a king, she snorted, it's sure as hell not going to be with you.) Her third and final husband was Abu Sufyan, the man who led the battle at Uhud. She chose him because he, as she put it, "befits to be the husband of a free noble woman."

Her sense of self-worth is clear; she will not settle—impressive, for a woman of the seventh century. It is as though Hind was literally empowered, through nobility, to wrath, and that this stays with her for her lifetime. In fact, my favorite part of Hind's story is the ending. Though Hind is ultimately "saved"—she dies a Muslim—she is never chastened or repentant. She accepts Muhammad's message, but when she does so she is still portrayed, in all accounts, as sarcastic, dry, even snooty and, yes, angry. When Muhammad tells her, "You will not commit adultery," she replies, "Does a free woman ever commit adultery?" When he tells her, "You will not kill your children by infanticide," she sardonically replies, "Have you left us any children that you did not kill at the Battle of Badr?" Unlike so many other stories of female ire and wildness, there is no comeuppance, no humbling return to the constraints of gentle femininity.

Not only that, Hind is genuinely subversive. In the story of her revenge at the Battle of Uhud, a gender-flipping is taking place: while it is women who are usually devoured, here it is she who eats the pliant male form. She stands over a man, triumphant, and makes his body literally a part of her own. And she is transgressive not just as a woman but as a human being in her act of cannibalism, becoming monstrous and wild as she plunges her teeth into her enemy's organ, doubly bad both within and outside the bounds of femininity. Unconcerned with how she comes across—or rather, intentionally wanting to scare and threaten and radiate her violent emotions down from the hilltop— she is not controlled, not pleasing, not tame. She doesn't have to be.

It is easy to be intoxicated by it. Particularly by righteous fury, with all its hepatic bloodiness, felt and shown by those for whom it has been inaccessible—that's where you can get really drunk. "I AM an Angry Black Woman. Unapologetically, rationally and rightfully so. I am blistering mad! I am frustrated and enraged! I am devastated, and my blood is boiling at a temperature so hot that I think my heart might stop beating at any given moment!" writes Rachel Alicia Griffin, in the stirring opening to her essay on Black feminist resistance.[209] Fuck, yes! I air-punch as I read it, and daydream about feeling powerful and out of control enough to write the same, because another way of saying "out of control" is "free." If anger is the way to stop myself from participating in wrongdoing, maybe I need to be angry. Maybe, despite my discomfort, I *should* be angry. Let me stop shaving, bleed everywhere, bite into livers, pick up a sword, spew whatever outrage boils over in the throat. Maybe my reluctance to be angry—the ropes I feel wound tightly around me as a Palestinian, as a woman, as a Muslim—is all the more reason to embrace fury. What else is the appropriate response to oppression, after all?

⊰⊱

Part of the problem is perhaps that women—and especially non-white women, both cis and trans—are without models of effective, unpunished female anger. Female anger is hysterical, maniacal (and often white): a cackling old witch in a forest; Glenn Close with a rabbit boiling in a pot; an obscenely gigantic Ursula being speared by Prince Eric's mast. A dearth of representation of female anger has left us with a gaping hole in our understanding, a lack of examples, not able to recognize or reckon with it, in others as well as ourselves. Perhaps this is partly what draws me to Hind and Nusayba's stories. In them, we are shown aggression and fury of different kinds: Nusayba's narrative is rooted in self-sacrifice and bravery, while Hind's is over-the-top, selfish, an act with no meaning or end beyond the meaning given to it by the preservation of the tale, a truly non-stereotypical type of female nastiness.

They are so archetypal that it strikes me that the two women ideally personify a distinction made by Martha Nussbaum[210] between what she suggests are two types of anger. The first is vengeful, or retributive, anger: Hind clambering amongst the dead at the end of the battles, defiling the corpse of her enemy. This, Nussbaum says, is ultimately pointless, because the victim's suffering won't be lifted through revenge. The second is forward-facing, or transition, anger, which Nussbaum argues is constructive and even, potentially, beneficial—directed towards achieving change, such as when Nusayba uses her anger to defend the Prophet. Nusaybah's anger as heroine, Hind's anger as villain.

⊰⊱

Though the word's etymology is obscure, one possible origin for the word "nasty" is from the Old French *villenastre,*[211] as in, *villain.* Meaning: "infamous, bad."

⊰⊱

The complicated truth, though, is that I just don't like the shape of anger on a face: the sneer of the lip, eyes turned shock-blue, a jaw tensed and jutted. Anger often comes out mean and spiteful, even when it is unthreatening or amusing. ("I *hate* you," my nephew once whispered to me darkly, glaring at me with his huge blue eyes, when I told him six years old was way, way too young to watch *Deadpool.*) So when Nussbaum also speaks of anger as being essentially narcissistic, I see truth in this. Even when it is outward-facing, fury doesn't leave much room for empathy or grace or kindness—so while it may be emancipatory, it also often seems to me poisonous. As with many poisons, it involves a loss of control, contortions of emotion and thought. Anger "alters us, makes us worse," Barbara Herman writes, making us "not who we would have been,"[212] whether we express it or not. By being inside us, it transforms us. We are turned into monster-selves—liver-eaters and Hulks—and this transformation unnerves me, even if it brings with it a certain type of liberation.

Agnes Callard writes that it is impossible to purify anger, that it is intrinsically connected to vengeful grudges, to nastiness, to aggression. (I picture Hind sinking her teeth into the still-warm liver of the man who had killed her uncle. Screaming as she chews.) Even Nussbaum's transition anger isn't free of the dark side, Callard suggests. This doesn't mean that anger isn't still essential, as a moral signifier, but just that it's "impossible to be good in a bad world."[213] Anger may be nasty, but it still tells us right from wrong. It may make us monsters, but in a monstrous world, this is inevitable.

⊰⊱

My friend gets furious with me one day—over something small, my keeping him waiting—and as he screams at me in my kitchen in Jerusalem, it takes all my effort to find the voice to whisper "please stop." I tremble through the shouting and well after, my heart still beating fast and hard against my chest as, hours later, he hugs me to him and apologizes. Anger feels galaxies away to me; my nearest emotion is fear. I wish to be tiny, an invisible speck, drifting across the cosmos. But later, I also feel a frustration turned inward, Nusayba's voice whispering "pathetic" as I wash the dishes, hands still trembling.

I often wonder about what feminist Alison Phipps has called the possible *mis*uses of anger, what others refer to as "equal opportunity domination"[214]— the desire for women to be simply as rageful and aggressive as men, that "sees more female prison guards, more female soldiers, more female defense CEOs and ultimately a female commander in chief as social and political progress."[215] Does my fascination with Nusayba and Hind fall prey to this? Have I been taken in by the glorification of rageful aggression, simply because it is female?

The oral histories that tell us of them did not come out of nowhere, their positioning as heroine and villain were not mere accidents of action, caught by chance. Their stories will, over time, have been crafted. For instance: some scholars have attributed Hind's depiction as barbaric to the political forces at the time of the creation of the written accounts;[216] essentially, Hind—as the mother of Mu'awiyah, a caliph of the Umayyad dynasty—became fodder for the anti-Umayyad propaganda machine. Her story has also been seen as a way of delineating between the wildness of the jahiliyyah times—that Age of Ignorance before Islam—and the Islamic age, her out-of-control, rageful cannibalism a reflection of the time before Muhammad. Nusayba, on the other hand, as a disciple of the Prophet, was always going to be painted in positive colors, no matter her fury.

I'm not sure I want a world with more anger, even if it is women's. And I'm not sure how emancipatory it is, anyway, to feel exactly how you were provoked to feel, or to be exactly as aggressive as you are racialized to be. It is a bully's trick, of course, to put one in this double-bind, but there we are, bound nonetheless. And it's worth pointing out that anger is not a particularly Islamic trait, either. Rather, the quality of hilm is considered a virtue, this being defined as "the act of reining one's soul and holding back one's nature from the violent emotion of anger,"[217] a type of patience and reasonableness that often seems to work in opposition to the red we see when filled with ire. Real believers, the Quran tells us, are those who "when angered are willing to forgive" (42:37). This is not a gendered virtue in Islam but instead one associated with divinity; al-haleem—that is, one who exhibits hilm—is another name for God in Islam.

And what about when anger is misguided, misdirected, misfelt? When anger isn't an accurate signal of wrongdoing, but instead a symptom of selfishness, emotional turmoil or misunderstanding? I have been confronted with many furious soldiers. I know they, too, feel unapologetic, justifiably enraged. Whose morality is showing what, in that instance? When is a monster not the reflection of a monstrous world, but the cause?

I wonder if the distinction to be drawn isn't between *types* of anger, but between reactions *to* our own anger, to the sense of it in the body and soul. Though the first lines of Lorde's famous speech are often captured on Instagram posts, what does not so often get noticed in her talk is her directive "to stand still, to listen to [anger's] rhythms, to learn within it, to move beyond the manner of presentation to the substance."[218] This, it seems to me, is the key to tapping into its power. Because while some women may now be at a place where, when anger rises in the throat, they are able to expel its contents instead of swallowing the bile—an improvement, perhaps, to being forced to play the good girl—it seems to me that this is not learning the texture of anger, feeling its contours. It's true some women may now have "Angry Bitch" on their iPhone covers, and others may say #TimesUp, but this anger feels like it is still essentially performance, worn defiantly, with full cognizance that its repercussions range from the irritating to the fatal, often without much to gain (and this risk can be even greater when we are pre-coded as violent, dangerous and threatening). Playing anger doesn't mean *knowing* anger.

Instead, perhaps we ought to listen. What is our anger telling us about who we are? What is it saying about right and wrong, villainy and righteousness, and is it necessarily correct? Whose story are we in, anyway? I worry that even those of us who were part of "the year of women's anger" may still not be truly feeling anger on its own terms, meaning that the full breadth of the emotion—its rhythms, its substance—is still left untapped, and alongside it all of its human potential: for resolution, for empathy, for self-preservation. To simply equate the *expression* of anger with liberty is, I think, a mistake. It is sitting with our anger, getting to know it, that's the trick. It is only then that we can, as Judith Butler suggests, craft it[219]—accepting our own uncontrolled villainy, while still keeping the hero in sight. What would it look like if we were free enough to get intimate with rage?

I picture Hind and Nusayba here, beside me now in my dark, north-facing London flat. Hind, haughty, sneering, unimpressed by my self-deprecating shabbiness, my untrimmed hair, my people-pleasing demeanor. Nusayba, perched on the arm-rest opposite, less judgmental, perhaps, but an imposing figure nonetheless, with her many welts, her sinewy arms, her one callused hand. All battle scars and muscle. They dislike each other, this much is clear. Perhaps they like me even less. I try to summon anger—I think of seemingly inevitable ecological collapse, of corrupt Palestinian politicians and smug Israeli security officials, of the silence of my friends during every attack on Gaza, of being spoken over by male peers in meetings, of being exploited and underpaid, of injustices both tiny and enormous. I feel the outrage build in my chest, my heart beginning to thud with aggression, but before I have had the chance to sit with it—to savor the taste on the tongue—it has already disappeared, already been replaced by heartbreak.

Hind watches me cry and rolls her eyes, lets out a tutting noise.

"*This* is your descendant?" she asks Nusayba incredulously.

"Well, no proof of that yet," Nusayba answers, glowering.

TIED TONGUES

There was and there was not, in the depths of the past, a warrior who lived among poets. In the Arabia of the seventh century, the world of my ancestor Nusayba bint Ka'ab al Khazrajia, poetry could be heard beside the battlefield, called out by women egging on their own fighters and heckling the other side, as well as in the town square, being proclaimed by a kahin, his words more convincingly divine precisely because they were being manipulated so artfully. It was the central medium of expression for men and women, the powerful and the meek, the young and the old. Hind the Liver-Eater famously shouted out poetry from the hilltop after taking a bite of her enemy's organ; others used poetry to articulate political opinions. "Screwed men of Khazraj, will you be cuckolds/allowing this stranger to take over your nest?" a poetess named Asma proclaimed, in reference to Nusayba's tribe and their acceptance of the Prophet. "You put your hopes in him like men greedy for warm barley soup/Is there no man who will step up and cut off this cuckoo?"[220]

Poetry was so venerated that one of the most important events of a given year was the annual poetry contest held at the largest marketplace in the Arabian Peninsula, in the valley of 'Ukaz, approximately 100 miles from Mecca. The open-air bazaar was seasonal, only opening for a few weeks per year,[221] drawing merchants and buyers and—importantly—poets from across the region. Here, during these weeks, rival tribes would put aside their differences (for the most part) and instead trade ghee, dates, honey, camels and wine, and listen to speakers take the stage to make important announcements—peace treaties, new alliances, new tribal chiefs—as well as give speeches and recite poems (sometimes all of these were the same). Regardless of social status, age, gender or tribe, a good wordsmith could take the stage, and the best of these speeches and poems would, according to tradition, be embroidered and hung on the market's walls. The best of the best would be woven in letters of gold and draped over the walls of the Kaaba; today, these poems—taught all over the Arab world—are known as the Mu'allaqat, or the Hanging Odes of Mecca. An oral victory captured, preserved, and thus transformed.

"I was walking down a slope and thinking to myself: How / do the narrators disagree over what light said about a stone?" I tell Nusayba as I wash my hair, quoting a Darwish[222] poem.[223]

I have been thinking about these early Arabian poets, and my ancestor's aural world, because I have been thinking recently about my relationship to books. "A book," wrote Carl Sagan, "is made from a tree. It is an assemblage of flat, flexible parts (still called "leaves") imprinted with dark pigmented squiggles. One glance at it and you hear the voice of another person, perhaps someone dead for thousands of years."[224] As a child, I went nowhere without a paperback in my hand; a tender object that would amass food stains and rips, whose spine would become lined and colorless, on whose pages I would doodle and write notes. When my favorite elementary school teacher, Mme M, asked eight-year-old me why I couldn't put the book down, please, for goodness' sake, at least for a moment, I told her that it was important to keep hold of a way out. If soldiers take me, I told her with a tone of cheery seriousness, I can just escape into my book. Another person, even if they were long dead, would be with me.

Mme M was obstinate in her efforts to get me to separate from my book, but I—and my mother, fighting on my behalf—persisted. I needed my book with me, it was not up for debate. Where Nusayba waded bravely into the fight, I used books as a way to hide, disappear, protect myself. I didn't even have to understand the books to feel this way; for months I sat on my schoolyard's bench with a copy of *Pride and Prejudice* on my lap, rereading the same lines over and over again, not quite following what was happening between Elizabeth and the awful-seeming Mr Darcy. (Equally, I tried, multiple times, with Saeed, the ill-fated Pessoptimist, but couldn't understand the references to the Establishment, had no clue how an alien got in there, or even what it really meant to be an "informer.") It didn't matter that I wasn't quite sure what was going on in the story, I was still happier in someone else's narrative.

Most of what I read, though, I read in English. Despite having both English and Arabic as my mother tongues, the diglossic nature of Arabic—that is, the existence and use of two forms of Arabic, one (largely) spoken and one (largely) written—make it difficult for me, as it does for many Arabs, to feel comfortable in, and escape through, works of Arabic literature. Classical Arabic (fusha) is about as different from colloquial Arabic ('ammiya) as Chaucerian English is from contemporary English, and yet in most of the Arab world, everything in any way non-intimate—from the news to children's cartoons to both old and contemporary novels—is in fusha. As Niloofar Haeri notes, "almost all that has been published in the Arab world since the founding of Islam is in Classical Arabic."[225] You speak 'ammiya, your mother tongue, at home and with your friends or at the shops, but outside that bubble—in government, say, or in an article—you must be able to express yourself in Classical Arabic, or its slightly modified updated version, Modern Standard Arabic (both are referred to as fusha). The better you are at fusha, the more cultured, educated and intelligent you are assumed to be—though it would seem pretentious and artificial to use it in a social context. 'Ammiya, meanwhile, despite being the language of social interaction, is considered base and backward.

As Hossam Abouzahr explains, what this means is that countries have "made an official language out of a form that nobody considers a native tongue, while making everyone's native tongues seem subpar, uncouth, useless."[226] Even at school, teachers have to work to teach children to learn a variety of subjects in, and express themselves through, fusha, despite that not being the language that is spoken casually in the classroom. It's a system that alienates many; "even grammar teachers, copyeditors, and university-educated people speak routinely of their fear of making mistakes," as Haeri says.[227] Indeed, the Arab world has some of the highest illiteracy rates globally, with recent estimates suggesting that as many as 26 percent of females and 21 percent of males in the MENA region are unable to read or write[228]—and that is likely to be a significant underestimate.

Not only does this mean that most people just don't have the level of proficiency in fusha required to fully take part in most creative or civic parts of life—a major issue for the politics of the region—there is also the issue of the schism between the language that is *lived* and the language used to *represent* that life. No matter how fluent a person may be in fusha, a conversion of the thinking-language into the writing-language is necessary before a thought is penned; and likewise a transformation from reading-language into the thinking-language when a text is read. As Haeri explains, "the language situation leads to a separation between 'culture' and 'life.' This is also often articulated in terms of translation—one's thoughts, feelings and experiences having to be first translated into written language, thereby creating a further distance between the individual and his/her experiences, thoughts, or feelings."[229] For a reader, this is a miserable situation. How can I expand my world through reading, if no writing in my mother tongue exists? How can I lose myself in a written world, if I am always aware of the artificiality of the text, of its separation from lived experience?

"Naeeman," Nusayba tells me, as I hop out of the shower. "Allah yin'am aleki," I reply, grateful to have access to a language in which there is an expression and response to showers and haircuts and shaves. There is no equivalent in English and translating it is clunky, but let's say the closest is: Congratulations on the bliss of cleanly transformation!

"Language isn't just a means of communication, it's a reservoir of memory, tradition and heritage," writes Sinan Antoon.[230] Recent research has suggested that the earliest oral form of Arabic may have first emerged in Northern Arabia and then slowly migrated downward towards the south.[231] An important shift happened between the fourth century BCE and roughly the first century CE, when the Nabataeans—who controlled Arabia and slightly beyond, before being replaced by the Byzantines—began using a proto-Arabic script to write the proto-Arabic they spoke.[232] Before this, they had used Aramaic, written in the same proto-Arabic script, to communicate more formally across the region; this change is what gave us the early version of the Arabic lettering and language that we recognize today.

During this time and for a couple of centuries after, the ancient Arabs appear to have been astonishingly literate, at least in functional terms—hundreds of thousands of graffitied rocks have been discovered in the Arabian desert, suggesting that, according to Michael C. A. Macdonald, "by the Roman period, it is probable that a higher proportion of the population in this region was functionally literate than any other area of the ancient world."[233] But they weren't writing *literature* of any kind—no stories or myths or histories, and very few poems—and instead mostly just scratched the stone with things like names, dates of birth, or lineages: things that were, as Peter Stein puts it, "spontaneous and brief."[234] By the time of Nusayba and Muhammad, very few had the advanced skills necessary to read literary works; the society was based on, and respected, a deeply oral tradition.

And then Islam came along. The Prophet Muhammad's messages from God were memorized and transmitted by his followers (Nusayba among them) orally, at first, but as his revelations and followers multiplied, people soon saw the need for a record. His verses were scratched on sticks made from palm-leaf stalks ('usub), on splinters of limestone and on camel bones, and then eventually inked on parchment and cotton.[235] His words, exactly as he said them, became standardised and more widely transmitted. As the religion grew, so did the particular script and speech of Muhammad: that is, the particular nuances of the Hijazi dialect. In the year 705 CE, roughly seventy years after Muhammad's death, Caliph 'Abd il Malik, the fifth caliph of the Umayyad dynasty, declared Arabic the "official language" of the caliphate,[236] an area that encompassed all of Egypt and Greater Syria. Muhammad's messages, unified and standardized to make the Quran, thus became the basis of the Classical Arabic used today; in fact, as the source of Arabic grammar, Classical Arabic and the Arabic of the Quran are virtually identical.[237]

It is the religious roots of Classical Arabic that are thus partly to blame for Arabic's diglossic nature. As Reza Aslan writes, "in Muhammad's time, the medium through which miracle was primarily experienced was neither magic nor medicine [which applied to Moses and Jesus, respectively] but language."[238] The revelation of the Quran—the extraordinary, breathtaking beauty of it—is considered by most Muslims to be the *only* miracle Muhammad ever performed.[239] It was the poetry of the language that convinced those early followers like Nusayba, perhaps even more than the message itself, that Muhammad was the real deal. How else could this illiterate forty-year-old merchant suddenly start spouting these exquisitely lyrical lines? More than that, Islam's emphasis on tawhid—oneness and unity—means that many believe the Quran itself *is* God, because God *is* the message, God *is* the poetry.[240] How, then, could this language—which, in its sacredness, can't possibly *belong* to the people who use it—become vernacularized? Throw in the pan-Arabist ambition to unite the Arab world based on a shared language and it is clear why the colloquial Arabic dialects are relegated to the land of the spoken, rather than the written, while fusha remains elevated and exalted. And although this situation is specific to the Arab world, it serves as a more general reminder that language—no matter its source—is never neutral.

Dear Western reader: when you hear the word "Islam," what comes to mind? Beards, bombs, burqas? Scimitars and secluded women? Maybe a more neutral mosque or minaret, a crescent moon? Don't be ashamed to admit the truth. The fact is, that is what comes to my mind, too. The word "Islam" in English, with its buzzing "*z*" sound at the beginning, has been dunked so many times in these ideas that it has lost all structural integrity; it falls apart in a wet heap as soon as it is used. It bears no relation to the word spoken in Arabic, with its soothing "*s*" and its long, sighing "*ah*". In Arabic, *Islam* sounds like my father greeting me after a long time away, his happy, enthusiastic "Ah! Ah! *Iss*-salaaamu *alaikum!*" It rolls off the tongue, or rather melts in the mouth: buttery. It has no wet weight to it. I find it hard to say, "I am Muslim," here, in this country, in this language, but not so in Jerusalem, in my other mother tongue. There, the word is linked to my name, rhymes with it almost. Here, I stumble in its formation, not sure whether to use an "*uh*" or an "*oh*" or the more commonly British "*uu*."

That's the thing about language: words used in a different tongue, free from context, become static. As Mikhail Bakhtin says, though words become our own through the force of our own intentions, some words "stubbornly resist, others remain alien, sound foreign in the mouth of the one who appropriated them and who now speaks them; they cannot be assimilated into his context and fall out of it; it is as if they put themselves in quotation marks against the will of the speaker."[241] A word like 'shehada" in English—referring to the oath the Muslim convert makes—means only that in English, and as such the word is heavy and important and imposing. In Arabic, though, the word is used constantly, to mean high school diploma or certificate or document of excellence. Its usage and meaning thereby become flighty, dynamic: the word immediately lighter, airier. Familiar rather than formidable.

Dear Western reader: do you know how many words are jet-setters, migrants? Language was slimmer during Nusayba's time, those early Islamic years, divided into smaller dialects for small groups of people to communicate amongst themselves, but it has grown into a giant, saturated beast, fattened through centuries of mixed peoples and expanded imaginations, words resettling or being taken much like human beings themselves. "Safari" reaching English by way of Swahili, but the Swahili itself having its roots in the Arabic "safar," to travel. You don't notice these migrants, perhaps, because they have integrated themselves so well. You might be aware of the more famous *émigrés*: "algebra" or "alcohol," for instance. They are recognizably Arab, with their telltale *al*s on their heads. But what about sofa, cotton, magazine? Coffee, caravan, sugar? These words have also traveled across borders, adapting from the Arabic (suffer, kattun, makhzan and qahwa, kairawan, sukkar) to settle more readily in English mouths.

We think—have been taught to think—of a great divide between East and West, Islam and Christianity. But our languages betray the truth. Waves have carried people and religions back and forth across the earth in tides of various sizes; have seen Byzantine Christianity settle in the East only to be replaced by Islamic caliphates in the West, Crusaders followed by Ottomans followed by Western imperialism. Cut into either culture and you will see the stratigraphic layers of this history. Just think of California, a state we might consider as distant from Nusayba and Muhammad as could be. The word originates from a Spanish short story written in 1510, in which "California" is an island inhabited by beautiful warrior women, the ruler of whom is Queen Calafia. In the story, Calafia's army fights alongside the Muslims, and so her name was naturally chosen to "evoke the title of the Muslim leader: *the caliph*," *Calafia*.[242] The explorers who settled the west coast state of the Americas were apparently familiar with the story and, maybe liking the idea of this proto-Paradise Island, decided to name it after this fictional place. Thus California is, etymologically, linked both to Islam and to warrior women and not so far from Muhammad and Nusayba after all.

Perhaps I am more attuned to the ways words are used and abused and misused because I am a Palestinian. "Just as I've become used to the new network of roads, so I've become used to the language of occupation and oppression that determines our small world," Raja Shehadeh writes.[243] Here, in this place, no words are chosen by accident. "Occupation" or "conflict"? "Palestinian" or "Arab"? "Eviction" or "forced expulsion"? Each implies not only a political perspective, but entirely different policy proposals. A report from the Centre for Media Monitoring[244] highlights an example of these types of choices—often seen in Euro-American media coverage of the region—via an Agence France-Presse (AFP) headline that states: "Hundreds wounded in Jerusalem clashes." Written in the passive, no one is responsible for the wounding that occurred; likewise, "clashes" implies some sort of amorphous collision of forces. The article in question in fact was referring to the events of May 9 and 10 of 2021, when Israeli police entered the Al-Aqsa Mosque as tens of thousands of Muslim worshippers prayed. The "wounded" in question were Palestinians: they were wounded by Israeli police.

And here, in this place—consider carefully, dear reader, whether you call it Israel or Palestine or Occupied East Jerusalem or maybe just Jerusalem, because whichever name you choose is meaningful and consequential—we not only have the Arabic diglossia to contend with, but the language of those we euphemistically refer to as "our cousins" as well. Hebrew is the language of the Israeli Defense Force soldiers who idle by Bab al 'Amood and squint through our windows at the Qalandia checkpoint. Hebrew is the language of the police, and the prime minister, and the airport security. In the science fiction short story "Digital Nation" by Emad El-Din Aysha, Palestinian national liberation begins with a technology that turns the Hebrew in classrooms into Arabic. After that, "virtual tour guides, eBooks and online atlases all began rewriting themselves, telling tourists they were, in fact, in Palestine, and replacing all Hebrew names with the pre-1948 Arabic ones."[245] Here, in this place, our languages bleed into each other, just like our people; and so, too, here, in this place, language is another site of conflict, another source of domination and dispossession, another source of power and control.

⊰

After my shower, I sit down to work on this essay. Ya'tiki il 'afieh, Nusayba

148

says to me, watching my brow furrow and my fingers clench into their claw-like position on the computer keyboard. Yi zeedek il 'afieh, I respond. No equivalent in English, but let's say it translates to something like: May God give you good things!

-⟡-

I consider myself a reader of books, but also, perhaps—and perhaps related-ly—a reader of people. Not necessarily a good judge of character, by any means, but a person with an insatiable curiosity to *know* a person. Tell me your dreams, give me your stream of consciousness. There is no oversharing here. The same drive, probably, that underlies my love of reading: a desire for intimacy. I read because I was (am) an introvert, and I crave the con-nection with a parasite's fervor. I have always maintained that, were I to be given a superpower, I would choose invisibility or—other side of the same coin—the ability to read minds. As a reader, I am an invisible audience, privy to the darkest thoughts of the characters on the page. Admittedly, this is a performance. I know that not only is my presence known—all writing imagines some audience—but I am also not even getting that telepathic insight I so crave. Even the most stream of consciousness narratives, even diaries and nonfiction personal essays are—I'm sorry to say—carefully constructed, are in fact a conversation in which you, the reader, simply have no say.

How can I read Nusayba, though? So little has been written about her. The snippets on which I base my imagination leave a tantalizing amount unknown. There is no record of her birth, her death, her life before battle. What she thought about, how she lived. The fragments that do exist about Nusayba are from the less reliable hadiths, meaning that their chains of transmission are less certain, their sources less clear, or else they come from family lore. Both are susceptible to the mutability of oral tradition. Neither offers a detailed portrait of a person. Instead, I have to read *around* her, into the lives of her contemporaries, the food, the social landscape, the poetesses of Yathrib and Mecca. To some extent this is the project of this essay collection: to create a narrative of her by writing near her, alongside her, teasingly close to her but not quite her. Ironically, perhaps, considering the difficulty of diglossia, the closest I feel to her is through language: the written form of Arabic, with which I so often struggle, belongs, after all, to her. It is an odd thought, that I share, to a large extent, a language with this ancestor from the seventh century. That—given the opportunity to brush up on it—I would be able to jump through a wormhole, land in Yathrib and converse, comfortably enough, with the warrior woman.

Part of the difficulty in reading her, though, is also, paradoxically, that she herself didn't read, and this—a readingless life—I find impossible to imagine. What is it to grow up without even the possibility to absorb a thousand other perspectives and experiences? It is not narratively empty, of course; those poets were telling tales as dates were picked and camels were milked and caravans were raided. But it was an aural and oral world, a fundamentally more communal, less private world. She would not have had the chance to escape into a story, to sit on a bench with a paperback and pretend the battle wasn't raging, even if she'd wanted to.

And there is another difference, I think, between the experiences of listening to and reading a story. Listening is, generally speaking, a passive exercise, passive in the sense that you drop in and out without affecting the narrative. It continues regardless, independent of your contribution and concentration. As Daniel Willingham notes, "eighty-one percent of audiobook listeners say they like to drive, work out or otherwise multitask while they listen,"[246] which is great for "add[ing] literacy to moments where there would otherwise be none." But it does mean you're not fully captured by the world of that literacy. In bed at night you might put on an audiobook; as you begin to drop off, you catch a word or two being spoken in a lilting voice and these might filter into your dreams, but the audiobook continues to play, whether you are asleep or not.

Reading, though, requires your undivided attention; it needs you to follow and ingest the words, letting them sink into your consciousness, in order to survive. If you dip out, get distracted, take a sip of your tea, the narrative stops. There is something unique in the act of reading, then—in the merging or perhaps complete sublimation of your own thoughts to another's, so that your mind is held, vise-like, and led down a very specific path laid by someone else—that is perhaps as intimate as you can get. To read a text is to immerse your brain in the narrative; recent research even suggests that the same nerve regions are stimulated whether you're reading about an act or experiencing in actuality.[247] For the brain, in other words, the line between what is read and what is lived is thin, perhaps nonexistent. And so you submit, as a reader, to having no control over this fake life, trustingly placing your intellect in the hands of the writer, agreeing to silence your inner voice in exchange for theirs.

Conventional understanding would suggest that you, the reader, are the leech; that through reading you get to know the relater, sucking that sweet narrative juice without giving anything in return. But it seems to me to be much stranger, much more interesting than that. It involves, fundamentally, an intrusion, on the part of the narrative: an entering into a place that is otherwise dedicated to maintaining your self-identity. A colonization of the writer's words in the reader's mind. If I were to read nonstop for my entire existence, I wonder, would I exist at all? What sense of self would I have, if I let my internal narrative—the "I" voice, the to-do lists, the insecurities, the worries—be formed, or indeed sublimated entirely, by the narratives of others?

Reading is thus a surrender of the self to another's story. No wonder Islam is full of the wonder of words and writing; the idea of fate in Islam is called "mektoub," meaning "written." Jews and Christians are "people of the book," just as Muslims are, while a Muslim marriage ceremony is called a 'Katb il kitab," "the writing of the book." On the day of judgement, the Quran tells us that this judgement will be revealed by whether a person receives their book in their right hand (headed to paradise) or left hand (headed to hell). The book being sent, in this case, is an accounting of one's deeds; but it is nonetheless referred to as a *book*. Mosques are covered in calligraphy because Islam bans iconography, yes, but also because what better way to invoke a sense of divinity than through writing? It is good, maybe, to be occasionally reminded that language—writing, reading, poetry—is a miracle. No wonder this is how Islam began: a man in a cave ordered to read. "Iqra!" the angel Gabriel told Muhammad, who, being illiterate, duly panicked. To read God's narrative is to surrender oneself to God, and this, after all, is the meaning of Islam: surrender.

Then again, "Iqra" can also mean "recite."

⊰⊱

I break from my writing to make myself a cup of tea, and find myself reciting Darwish to Nusayba, who listens closely.

All this light is for me. I walk. I become lighter. I fly
then I become another. Transfigured. Words
sprout like grass from Isaiah's messenger
mouth: "If you don't believe you won't be safe."
I walk as if I were another. And my wound a white
biblical rose. And my hands like two doves
on the cross hovering and carrying the earth.
I don't walk, I fly, I become another,
transfigured. No place and no time. So who am I?
I am no I in ascension's presence. But I
think to myself: Alone, the prophet Muhammad
spoke classical Arabic. "And then what?"
Then what? A woman soldier shouted:
Is that you again? Didn't I kill you?
I said: You killed me . . . and I forgot, like you, to die.[248]

SUPERWOMAN

There was and there was not, in the depths of the past, a heroine. The last battle, the battle they won at Badr, took place on a Tuesday, which seemed right, somehow—Tuesday is when things get done, before the gruel of hump day or the lure of the weekend, but after the manic catch-up of a Monday. But this one, at Uhud, takes place on Saturday, a day that, somehow, with its connotations for rest, was already a bad omen. It happens near an oasis, which is lucky because it will be hot and the men and women will sweat as their thighs grip onto the warm wetness of their horses' and camels' slick coats. First, there are duels: three men from each side, the rest watching, tense or bored or buzzing with adrenaline. The women stand a bit away, calling out encouragement, heckling the enemy, calming a rogue camel with a gentle voice, hand firmly smoothing the neck in repeated downward strokes. Near the fighters, a horse defecates, and a young archer feels his own bowels tighten as he takes in the sheer quantity—hundreds, he realizes, maybe more—of enemy fighters gathered before him.

Combat—full-on, all-out combat—soon follows the duels, and before long, Nusayba bint Ka'ab al Khazrajia is tending one mess of blood and bone, and then two; she is holding calfskin bottles to dry lips and whispering her Prophet's words and also watching as the man himself swings his sword into a swelling mass, as he gets surrounded, as his troops fall back, panic in their eyes—where have those damn archers gone? They were supposed to be his defense!—as her own son (her own son!) begins to hesitate, hides behind another soldier. They are used to raids, small tribal spats. Not this. Never this. Over a thousand Meccans, Abu Sufyan among them, furious and well fed and determined to win. She shouldn't do it—she should stay here, among the wounded. But she won't. She is a trained archer, skilled with her sword—unusual for a woman, but useful in this case. She will risk her life to save another, she will persevere even though outnumbered. She will fight, and in her speed and her strength and her physical prowess, she will seem almost superpowered.

⋄

I sit down to make myself watch *Wonder Woman* for the purposes of this essay. I say "make" not because I don't enjoy superhero films, but because watching Gal Gadot, an Israeli with IDF experience and questionable views on Palestinians, strut around with a superpowered ability to police others makes me uncomfortable. What I am thinking about is heroism, female heroism, and how Nusayba fits into the mold of female hero or superhero. Wonder Woman is, I figure, a good place to start, having been created by the psychologist (and inventor of the lie detector) William Marston, as an explicitly feminist icon,[249] but as the film goes on and Gal Gadot's accent increasingly reminds me of the uniformed soldiers that have held me at checkpoints, I also start to think about violence and power.

I find a relaxed happiness in watching superhero films. I love the easy morality of them (Good Guys versus Bad Guys), and especially how, at times and increasingly, this can be played with and subverted (though we know that our superheroes will always, in the end, be Good). Superhero stories are also—unlike their predecessors Achilles and Odysseus, the Greek heroes of myth—stories about identity and belonging, not just violence and justice. Perhaps partly because many of them were conceived by first-generation Jewish immigrants to the US in the 1930s,[250] almost every superhero has a dual identity, has to hide an essential part of him- or herself, uncertain they will be entirely accepted if their whole selves are revealed (thus their alter egos). Two sides that are in tension, a new identity forcing an old one out, figuring out how to bring the two together. How to be Superman *and* Clark Kent, how to be Batman *and* Bruce Wayne. They negotiate these two sides with difficulty, often letting one part of themselves down (Bruce Wayne loses his love for the sake of Batman's goals). These are classic experiences of immigrants from marginalized groups, and yet the superhero genre turns this on its head, makes the hidden not something for which one might end up in a pogrom, but a secret weapon instead. There is something deliciously hopeful about this, which is why, perhaps, I find superhero narratives often so uplifting.

And it's a particularly good time for the superhero narrative. Not only is the industry enjoying unprecedented financial success and popular culture reach—the Marvel franchise alone releasing new material across all media at a near-constant rate, DC not far behind[251]—but never has there been so much diversity and feminism (partly because, of course, the industry has realized there's a consumer base for this). In 2017, the first Wonder Woman film since 1978 was released; *Black Panther*—the first blockbuster ever to feature a Black superhero—was released a year later; *Captain Marvel*, another female-led super-hero film, a year after that. There are Black-led TV shows like *Black Lightning* and *Luke Cage*, which explicitly explore the relationship between race and power (the latter character, for example, is bulletproof and wears a hoodie—a direct reference to the murdered teenager Trayvon Martin). There are queer and non-white characters across the DC universe's Carl Ogawa-produced television shows (such as *Supergirl* and *The Flash*); many of the storylines of these char-acters are handled in nuanced and interesting ways. In a few months' time, a new threshold will be crossed with the release of *Ms. Marvel*, a TV adaptation of the comic of the same name created in 2014 by Sana Amanat, G. Willow Wilson and Adrian Alphona, which features a teenage Pakistani-American super-heroine, who just so happens to be Muslim too.

Historically, though, of course, the superhero genre has not been good to non-white, queer or female characters. The male gaze of the boy-domi-nated industry has meant that superheroines, if present, have been more por-nographic than powerful; depictions of Black, Asian and Arab characters have been laughably offensive. Though comics have included a much more diverse mixture of characters than can be seen in film and television adaptations, most Muslim and Arab superheroes have been problematic from the get-go. Arabian Knight, for instance, in his first 1981 iteration, is an "Arab" of unclear origin whose powers include a magic carpet and a scimitar, almost as though created to explicitly parody Orientalist tropes (to be clear, he was not).

Even when ostensibly created to fight negative stereotypes, which happened increasingly after 9/11, the characters have remained Othered, Orientalized and problematic: the most famous of these is probably the

X-Men mutant,[252] Sooraya Qadir, aka Dust. Not only is Dust saved from Afghan slave traders by a white man in her origin story (already feeding into negative tropes about Afghan women needing saving, Afghan men being barbaric), her superpower is the power to turn into sand—an ability which immediately brings to mind images of Arabian deserts, despite her being Afghan. Most worryingly, she is almost entirely lacking in personality, beyond being Muslim. As Martin Lund has argued, "out of [Dust's] fourteen appearances, she provides exposition in one, while four of her appearances are as set-dressing. The remaining nine are dominated by what can be called "niqab talk," meaning superficial discourse about her Muslimness."[253] This "niqab talk," often with her Western roommate, almost never ends with her having the last word, and almost always makes her reasoning sound a lot like the reasoning of an oppressed abductee. In fact, she is defined almost entirely by her niqab, which is also her superhero costume (and is often drawn so as to reveal all her curves, rendering it meaningless to the point of absurdity). Far from mitigating negative stereotypes, Dust serves to entrench them.

Similarly, though Wonder Woman, created in 1941, has explicitly feminist roots (conceived as a standard of "strong, free, courageous womanhood; to combat the idea that women are inferior to men and to inspire girls to self-confidence and achievement," according to its press release from the time), her equivalent in the Marvel universe has a much more suspect past. Created as late as 1968 by a man called Roy Thomas, Carol Danvers was originally a supporting character to the male Captain Marvel, often acting as the damsel in distress this male captain would have to save. When she finally becomes superpowered, it is from an accident involving his DNA (making her the Eve to his Adam), and she develops an alcohol problem, as well as being the victim of a bizarre and disturbing storyline involving being raped. Though she supposedly represented feminist ideals—she was an "independent" working woman—she served, instead, to entrench misogynistic tropes. It was only in 2012 that she was reimagined by a female writer and given the storyline that led to the "feminist" 2019 blockbuster. And, of course, even Wonder Woman is hyper-sexualized, even in this latest film.

It's disappointing that, despite being "feminist" iterations of the superhero narrative, the most recent films do little in the way of exploring the nuances and complications of truly female or feminist superheroism. The latest Wonder

Woman film, for instance—though enjoyable on a superficial level because it shows a woman able to physically dominate the men around her (apparently something a lot of women wanted after Donald Trump's election)[254]—doesn't actually explore anything related to womanhood. In fact, Wonder Woman barely interacts with another woman after the first ten minutes of the film, and her fight with Aries—her nemesis—is a straightforward good/love versus evil/hate. Compare this to *Black Panther*, which, though it may have its own issues, has its lead T'Challa fighting his nemesis, Killmonger, not only physically but also ideologically, exploring issues of national versus racial loyalty.[255]

By contrast, there are no such ideological dimensions to the Wonder Woman film; hers is an easily consumed pop feminism. Mostly that's how it is across the board: because the industry is still so male-focused, superheroines are rarely fully allowed to explore the consequences of being a superpowered female in a patriarchal world (Jessica Jones, whose powers are manipulated by a man, being a notable exception). They are always exemplars of conventional contemporary attractiveness, never muscular, and they are never allowed to be mothers, either, the implication being that the two things—superheroism and motherhood—are mutually exclusive. (But think of Nusayba, who not only fought alongside her two sons, but fought while pregnant. She is unlikely to have been lithe and slim; her body would have been scarred and rough and strong.) They probably say more than their male counterparts about the importance of love and kindness, but they never wrestle with the imperative to be good girls while superpowered; they are simply the female equivalents of the male superheroes.

Perhaps also because of how male-dominated the superhero genre is, their world is an exceptionally violent one. This is mitigated by the cartoonishness of the comic book format; panels and drawings can only be so realistic. But with television and cinema, and especially the technological advances of the last decade, superhero violence has become amplified, maximized, more gruesome. "Kapow!" and "Clunk!" are very different from the sound of bones crunching under a fist. Marvel and DC fight scenes take up half the feature; people go there for the explosions. And not only is violence omnipresent, it is glorified. In the film, though Wonder Woman espouses love, she's pretty much just great at punching things really hard, and that's what's meant to impress us.

In fact, more often than not, it is the superheroes who are more violent than the villains—a recent study that looked at superhero films released between 2015 and 2016 showed that while villains had an average of 17.5 acts of violence per hour, the heroes had nearly a third more, at 22.7 acts.[256] We accept these acts of violence—applaud them—because they are enacted by the heroes, by the Good Guys; in other words, their aggression is legitimized. We ascribe to them a goodness a priori, and their morality remains unquestioned even as they pummel and punch and cut, because it is in service of their goodness; indeed, their identities *create* the moral boundaries. (If we take the superhero to be a metaphor for the world's superpower, America, we can see how this plays out outside the movies—American aggression is always legitimate, always necessary, because America is always the Good Guy.)

But not all heroes are created equal, so not all violence is equally legitimized. As the scholar Menaka Philips has argued, there exists what she calls a "privilege of violence"; i.e., some superheroes—the ones societies mark as "natural enforcers of justice and order," i.e., white male ones—have access to unrestricted violence, while for others this violence must be modified or limited in some way, in order for the hero to be recognized *as* a hero. Luke Cage's violence, she points out, is "disciplined by the racialized politics of respectability."[257] His violence is restrained, apologetic, sacrificial; he never contemplates killing because, as a Black man, he would not be legible as a hero if he did. (Batman, on the other hand, can spend years agonizing over it and occasionally change his mind, but still be an iconic superhero.)

He also, it should be noted, exists within an almost entirely Black world, as do Black Panther and Black Lightning—their violence is acceptable only when directed at non-white actors. One can imagine the consequences of having a masked and caped Black or Arab man appear in the sky in central Metropolis—even if he's just saved a busload of people from certain death, you can be sure that within minutes he'd be surrounded by SWAT teams with machine guns. Marvel's *The Punisher*, on the other hand—in which Frank Castle, a white male war veteran, becomes a vigilante who hunts down bad guys—bathes in the protagonist's unmitigated violence. He kills (criminals) without qualms. His violence is legitimized because *he* is seen as legitimate; he is good and they are bad. (Philips notes also how this has been co-opted by real-life police forces in America: for example, the Saint Louis Police Officers

Association uses the Punisher logo as a symbol for their law enforcement teams, because, as its president said, "It's how we show the world that we hold the line between good and evil.")

Bodies that are pre-coded as dangerous, such as Black or Arab bodies, are not given access to this same unrestricted violence, however, and when they are, they become the villains, like Killmonger, for instance. (Even without being unrestrainedly violent, non-white characters are more often, and more easily, the villains of the superhero narratives. As comics author Sam Keen said during his 1986 speech for the Association of Editorial Cartoonists: "You can hit an Arab free; they're free enemies, free villains—where you couldn't do it to a Jew and you can't do it to a black [sic] anymore.")[258] Muslim protagonists are given even less access to violence of any sort, partly because of the conflation of Arabs and Muslims, and partly because of a pervasive discourse that maintains that violence is an inherent part of Islam. Beginning with the First Crusade and a papal desire to control the Holy Land (my neck of the woods causing trouble yet again), Islam has consistently been cast as an irredeemable religion that "spread by the sword" and has violence at its core. Muslims were, according to Pope Urban II, "a race utterly alienated from God" who "circumcise the Christians, and the blood of the circumcisions they either spread upon the altars or pour into the vases of the baptismal font."[259] In 1857, the Charles Dickens-edited periodical the *Illustrated London News* described "Mahommedans" as "bloodthirsty, vindictive, selfish and dissolute, and unrelenting."[260] In 1891, the US Supreme Court highlighted the "intense hostility of the people of the Moslem faith."[261]

The rhetoric has not changed much since then; if anything, the discourse has only gained momentum with the atrocities of 9/11 and the rise of ISIS. September 11th, declared John Ashcroft,[262] "drew a bright line of demarcation between the civil and the savage."[263] Thomas Friedman, writing in the *New York Times* after 9/11, called the attacks "the work of super-empowered men and women . . . what makes them super-empowered is their genius using the networked world [. . .] a diabolical melding of their fanaticism and our technology. Jihad online."[264] Muslim terrorists thus became almost supervillainous metonyms of the entire religion. And this particular concept of "jihad," as presented by Friedman and other Western actors, has proliferated. Nowadays almost everyone in the West knows—or thinks they know—what jihad means: a "holy war," that is incumbent upon all Muslims to wage against any and all who stand outside the faith. As Jonathan Lyons argues, this definition has created "an entire theology of violence in which terrorist attacks like those carried out by Al Qaeda constitute "a form of sacrament" in a cosmic battle between good and evil. In this way, a seamless connection is drawn between the attacks on New York and the very roots of Islamic faith."[265]

Of course, as Aziz Al-Azmeh points out, "such mobilisations to violence are limited neither to Islam nor to religion; rather, political movements use whatever aspects of the 'substratum' are available"[266] to them. Despite this, though, jihad has, through the discourse, become a sort of shorthand for the inherent illegitimate violence of the religion—an idea which Nusayba, as a warrior woman, does uncomfortably little to dispel. Yet, like in the case of superheroes, identity is the key to legitimacy: as Jack Goody has illustrated, "the Crusades had been seen by the West as completely legitimate, while *jihads* were a form of reprehensible violence directed against us as the infidel. Both were holy wars."[267] Violence is, as Arun Kundnani argues, in many ways relational. "We like to think our [Western] violence is rational, reactive, and normal, whereas theirs is fanatical, aggressive and exceptional. But we also bomb journalists, children and hospitals."[268]

Besides, though militant Islamists make use of a similar definition of jihad for their own ends, Nusayba would have been unfamiliar with Friedman's understanding of it. The Arabic root of the word "*jhd*" means effort, and words containing this root appear fewer than four dozen times in all the verses Muhammad recited to his disciples; in thirty-one of them the word has nothing whatsoever to do with warfare. Instead, what Nusayba would have heard most often in connection to the word jihad would have been about struggle—specifically, the soul's struggle in the path of God, or the effort to overcome sin. The remaining ten relate to the fair conduct of war, what Reza Aslan has called an early "just war" theory, that differentiated between "combatant and non-combatant"[269] and prohibited all but defensive wars. The battles that Muhammad and Nusayba fought as the verses were revealed were largely against the Quraysh, the Meccan elite who saw Muhammad (and his followers) as a threat, and had tried to assassinate him, consequently leading to his resettlement in Yathrib, Nusayba's town. It was only in the centuries after Muhammad and Nusayba's time that the concept of jihad was developed into one more directly to do with warfare, in the context of wars with Byzantium. Nusayba, though, would have been blissfully unaware of the idea of "holy war," and would have found the idea of forcing others to convert at sword-point to be perplexing, considering that God told Muhammad "there can be no compulsion in religion" (2:256). She fought to protect him and their people; that was her understanding.

Still: the link between Islam and illegitimate violence has become entrenched, and so Muslim superheroes today do not have the "privilege of violence" afforded to others. *Ms. Marvel*, though ground-breaking in creating a fully developed, Muslim superhero character in the Pakistani-American teen Kamala Khan—who exists within a Muslim-American space, thereby representing multiple "Muslimnesses"—is a typical example of this. In the comics, though she fights the bad guys, she does this most often in humorous and non-aggressive terms, "embiggening" her hand in order to lift them up and place them far away, shrinking herself down to scuttle past them. When violence is necessary, it is most often carried out by a different character—a white male character—such as when Wolverine kills a giant alligator that Kamala Khan is merely holding back. "Is it possible to help people without hurting other people ... or, you know, reptiles?" she asks Wolverine. This nonviolent ideology has been read by some to be a step forward for the genre, a moving away from the glorification of violence that so readily permeates the majority of superhero narratives.[270] Much as I would love this to be true, I suspect that something more insidious is at work: that Kamala Khan, as a Muslim, would simply not be legible as a superheroine if she were violent like Wolverine is violent; that she would not be "empowered" through her violence the way Wonder Woman is empowered.[271]

⸬

It's not that I necessarily want Muslim superheroes to be unrestrictedly aggressive, quite the opposite. As explored previously elsewhere,[272] I am not drawn to, or comfortable with, aggression, rage or force of any kind. While I admire Nusayba's bravery and self-sacrifice, I'm not so sure about her having been a warrior, someone famous for, essentially, fighting others. She is, arguably, a type of soldier, and I am not at ease around soldiers of any kind. I'm a pacifist at heart. I believe strongly in the power of communication, in nonviolent resistance. But I realize also that this perhaps comes from a place of privilege, that pacifists often keep their hands clean on the bloodied backs of their more violent brothers and sisters, and that, sometimes, immovable objects need an unstoppable force. That most oppressors have been toppled only thanks to the combination of both types of resistance. That there is a difference between essentialized violence—the violence I am told is an essential part of Palestinians, Arabs, Muslims—and political violence, and that the former is in fact often used as a tool to delegitimize and remove the possibility of the latter. That state violence will always, by virtue of being state-sanctioned, be deemed legitimate, and that without a state, or state backing, it is impossible to ever achieve such legitimacy.

I recognize this, and yet, as Judith Butler has argued, if we see ourselves as part of a collective humanity—rather than as individuals—it becomes clear that the only way to strengthen and protect ourselves as a whole is by *ending* violence, all violence.[273] Legitimate and illegitimate, necessary and gratuitous. Otherwise, one is, in the end, only causing violence to oneself, and to one's world. "When the world presents as a force field of violence," Butler writes, "the task of nonviolence is to find ways of living and acting in that world such that violence is checked or ameliorated, or its direction turned, precisely at moments when it seems to saturate that world and offer no way out."[274] This takes imagination and a little madness, Butler argues, but what else could be more worthwhile? It is impossible for me to disagree, and not to work towards this. I would so much rather that our superheroes and superheroines could all just "embiggen" their hands and move their enemies far away.

Then again: that is not the superhero universe that exists. In the super-hero universe that exists, violence is deployed excessively and with abandon by superheroes because it is necessary and because it is their right. The superhero universe thrives and is predicated on this violence; the "Pow!" and the "Kabam!" and the "Bash!" are an integral part of the genre. That Muslim superheroes do not have access to violence in this universe is, therefore, problematic, particularly if, as Philips has pointed out, superhero narratives and their limitations reflect not only what is acceptable and not acceptable in real life, but even what is acceptable and not acceptable in the public imaginary.

I wonder, then, if Nusayba can be the answer. Can we read her as a superheroine, rather than as a soldier? Can we imagine her, as a Muslim, with the a priori goodness and non-violence that we ascribe to male superheroes, thereby expanding our imaginary? Stan Lee defines a superhero as "a person who does heroic deeds in a way that a normal man or woman couldn't."[275] Could Nusayba, with her unusual archery and sword-fighting skills, with her determination and self-sacrifice—the way that she throws herself into the battle to save Muhammad—be a part of the superhero universe? Lots of scholarship has pointed out the parallels between Superman and Moses (sent off as a baby to survive the destruction of the planet/the Pharaoh, returns with powers), but maybe Batman could be read as Muhammad as well: both are orphaned at a young age, both have their formative experiences in caves, and both want to rid their cities of corruption and possess a certain darkness not present in other prophets/superheroes. And perhaps if Batman could be read as Muhammad, his faithful sidekick Robin could also be found among his disciples: "Wherever I turned, to the left or the right, I saw her fighting for me," the Prophet says about Nusayba, or perhaps Batman says about Robin. She even has a dual identity: most people knew her as Um 'Umara. All she's missing is a cape.

BINT

There was and there was not, in the depths of the past, a warrior who was, very unusually, a woman. This is how I imagine it happened: the Ansar—the Companions, the early Muslim converts, Muhammad's followers—were sitting around in the courtyard of his small compound in Yathrib, as they often did. It was crowded. Men and women, Nusayba bint Ka'ab al Khazrajia among them, crouched on the earth, leaning against the walls, jostling for space. It was hot. It stank of sweat and animals, the tang of dates on the turn. But Nusayba enjoyed these gatherings tremendously. Muhammad was standing at the front, as he always did, leading the discussion about the revelations that had appeared to him most recently. This was how it was, in those early days of Islam: dynamic and exciting and dialogic. Muhammad would preach and the converts would talk over each other, asking for examples, pointing out misunderstandings, clarifying meanings. Aisha, his independently minded and favorite wife, would often ask incisive questions. But this time (according to some sources, at least) it was Nusayba,[276] standing at the side with her stout and muscular body, who spoke up. Through the din of conversation, she raised her left arm—her right arm still suffering the effects of the injury she sustained at the battle of Uhud—and waited until the Prophet saw her and nodded, smiling. *My prophet*, she started, her voice raised. *In your revelations*—she cleared her throat as silence descended on the group, and began again—*In your revelations, I see only things for men. I do not see women mentioned in any way. Why?* What she wanted was clarification: what was the status of women in God's eyes?

It was a question that had been bothering her recently. She knew that, in Mecca, the Qurayshi women were, in some ways, not as free as they were here in Yathrib, because she had heard 'Umar ibn al-Khattab moaning that, before moving to Yathrib, "we the people of Quraysh used to have the upper hand over our wives, but when we came among the Ansar, we found that their women had the upper hand over their men, so our women also started learning the ways of the Ansari women."[277] And she was glad that she and the other female members of her tribe were rubbing off on the Qurayshi women. She also knew that, here in Arabia, despite the miserable tradition of killing baby girls (she loathed this; it made her sick), women had more freedoms than in nearby Christian Byzantium, where she had heard that women were secluded and excluded from public life.[278] Those Byzantian women weren't trained fighters, the way she was. They weren't independent businesswomen who could propose to a man, the way Muhammad's first wife Khadijah had been. If Muhammad's faith was an extension of this Christian one, then what future lay ahead for women? She had thought it would be good—Muhammad had said that in the ummah, women could finally inherit property, for instance—but were the revelations addressed only to men because men were the only true Muslims?

Muhammad nodded, frowning. Perhaps it had been worrying him, too. But he said nothing, and eventually someone else asked a question, and the raucous back-and-forth started again, and then people slowly started to disperse, and Nusayba, hanging back, wondered if her answer was going to be no answer at all. She felt a low, sinking sense of doom begin to fill the pit of her stomach. But then, just as she was about to give up and leave—she had dinner to start on, after all, and her sons would be back from date-picking—it happened. Muhammad spoke again, and it was clear that this was another verse being revealed, and that it was revealed in answer to her (her!) question. He said: "Surely, Muslim men and Muslim women, believing men and believing women, devout men and devout women, truthful men and truthful women, patient men and patient women, humble men and humble women, and the men who give Sadaqah [charity] and the women who give Sadaqah, and the men who fast and the women who fast, and the men who guard their private parts (against evil acts) and the women who guard [theirs], and the men who remember Allah much and the women who remember [Him]—for them, Allah has prepared forgiveness and a great reward." [33:35] There it was, clear and straightforward: men and women were moral and spiritual equals. Nusayba felt light with relief, dizzy with joy.

She couldn't have foreseen what would happen in the centuries to come, the disappointment of it all. How could she? In that moment, and in her lifetime, it all seemed so promising. All the ensuing verses revealed to Muhammad after that revelation also addressed women—something that the scriptural texts from the other monotheistic religions did not. Other passages in the Quran emphasized, again, women's spiritual and moral equality to men; Islam furthered this idea by ridding the biblical creation story of its order of precedence, thereby also eliminating the notion of females as derivatives of males. It seemed to her, as to later scholars and Muslims, that the Quran was clear in its view of women. As Leila Ahmed has argued, "there can be no doubt that Islamic views on women, as on all matters, are embedded in and framed by the new ethical and spiritual field of meaning that the religion had come into existence to articulate," a field that was staunchly and ethically egalitarian.[279] Like many Muslim women today, Nusayba would have insisted that Islam was not sexist, because she and others "hear and read in its sacred text, justly and legitimately, a different message from that heard by the makers and enforcers of orthodox, androcentric Islam," as Ahmed puts it—an Islam that would quickly emerge after Muhammad's death.

Feminist scholars of Islam[280] have emphasized the importance of examining the socio-historical context and development of the religion, arguing that reading the Quran and the hadith and legal doctrines with an understanding of the milieu in which these came into being is crucial to understanding Islam, especially with regards to women. As Ahmed has shown, Islam started to evolve when it began to spread beyond the limits of Yathrib and Mecca, and once Muhammad died, it took on a life of its own. Under Umar (634–644 CE), new ordinances emerged that had not existed in the time of the Prophet, such as the stoning of adulterers.[281] By the time of the Umayyad empire (661–750), only thirty years after Muhammad's death, Islamic law was being interpreted piecemeal (by men) on a large scale, with local (male) administrators incorporating local Byzantine laws in a variety of ways. That led to strange situations wherein women would have different rights depending on which town they lived in.[282] In Yathrib, for instance, women were no longer allowed to enter into marriage on their own, and instead had to be given away by a guardian, while in other regions, such as Kufa, they still could.[283] Almost within her lifetime, Nusayba would have seen her freedoms being curtailed in the name of the very religion for which she had risked her life.

This only became worse as the religion moved further away from its source, absorbing the customs and laws of the regions that were conquered. Since both the Sasanian and the Byzantine empires had been deeply misogynistic (the Sasanid emperor Khusrau I, for instance, reportedly had a harem of twelve thousand women),[284] this, Ahmed argues, meant that the interpretation of Islam became increasingly misogynistic too. It was no longer about the revelations themselves; increasingly, it became about what Muhammad had done, how he had lived (or what people said he had done, how people said he had lived), and these could easily be interpreted patriarchally. He'd had multiple wives, for instance, one of whom was still a child.[285] Although some Muslims (such as the Sufis, Kharijites and Qarmatians) argued that Muhammad's life was just his own life, particular to his historical context, and should not be taken to be normative, other voices—louder voices—disagreed. Under the Abbasids, this was taken to the extreme. They "heard only the androcentric voice of Islam, and they interpreted the religion as intending to institute androcentric laws and an androcentric vision in all Muslim societies throughout time."[286]

And these are the interpretations and regulations that have prevailed until today, underlying the many horrific traditions still rampant in the Muslim world, such as female genital mutilation, "virginity tests" and wife-beatings. Not only are these perpetrated, they are accepted, oftentimes codified in law. Misogyny is endemic. As Nawal El Saadawi wrote back in 1977, "Arab women are sacrificed on the altars of God and Money from the moment of birth to the hour of death."[287] Or, as Mona Eltahawy succinctly put it in 2012: "They [men] hate us."[288] In much of the Arab/Muslim world,[289] women are not viewed as spiritual and moral equals, able and welcome in the battlefield, but instead as primarily sexual, reproductive beings—people to be saved by men and things from which men need to be saved. It was only in July of 2018, after all, that Saudi Arabia allowed women to drive. Had Nusayba lived another two hundred or so years, she would have seen the faith she'd been drawn to—the one in which it was clear that God saw men and women equally—turned into an institution that is strictly segregationist and deeply misogynistic. She would have been more than disappointed. She would have been ashamed.

⋜⋝

Though shame has been much maligned in recent years, it still serves an important purpose. Often, it is an acknowledgement of responsibility, a recognition of collusion or culpability, and this can then "help us meet our own expectations and live up to our values," as Joseph Burgo puts it.[290] An evolutionary necessity for social cohesion, "our feelings of shame tell us we've disappointed reasonable expectations we hold for ourselves or violated our own self-chosen values. Shame might help us to grow and become better people." Shame is the appropriate response, then, to one's unintentional complicity in systemic racism and classism: my shame about these is a necessary, discomfiting and unpleasant acceptance of my role in these systems of oppression,[291] and with this unpleasantness is a tacit promise to change. It is more appropriate than guilt, which seeks absolution and forgiveness from someone else. Instead, shame is aimed entirely at the self: a negative self-evaluation. You have seen yourself, and what you have done, and judged yourself wanting. Thus I, like Nusayba,[292] feel shame about the Arab/Muslim world's treatment of women. I feel ashamed that we haven't established many of the liberties and securities enjoyed by women in the West, and in most Judeo-Christian communities. I feel ashamed that Mona Eltahawy feels safer in America than she does in Egypt.

And I feel ashamed, also, of the ways in which Islam has been used to make the world less safe for people in general. Although I am aware that, as Margaretha A. van Es writes, "the pressure exerted on Muslims to explicitly condemn violent extremism reflects the unequal power relations between Muslim minorities and the dominant majority, while simultaneously reinforcing these unequal power relations,"[293] I still feel ashamed, terribly so, about the atrocities committed in the religion's name. It's true that the constant expectation that I or other Muslims/Arabs denounce Islamic terrorism is problematic, that "members of the dominant majority are never asked to denounce violent crimes committed by people with similar beliefs or a similar cultural background,"[294] and that it's wrong that Muslims are collectively held accountable for crimes committed by a very small number of Muslims. But there is nonetheless a bigger part of me that somehow feels responsible simply by association. I am Arab, I am Muslim, and so I feel connected in some ephemeral way to other members of these communities, implicated when they are vile, tarnished as a result. So when a colleague at Oxford tells me that her mother was killed by the Muslim terrorist attack in Mumbai over a decade ago, it isn't rage that I feel, but a deep and unspeakable shame.

This then seeps, like a watercolor, into a more general sense of unease about Islam and Arabness. In writing these essays, I have acquired a large number of books with the word "Islam" in the title, as well as many books in Arabic. Unlike my numerous English novels—Penguin classics, Picador proofs, Folio editions—which I always showcase rather proudly, as a sort of assertion of my identity as a "reader," as "bookish," I am unsure (nervous, even) about putting these Arabic and Muslim titles on show, all too aware that, though "few people would argue that all Muslims are terrorists, the underlying assumption seems to be that all Muslims are susceptible to radicalization."[295] When I, at one point, frustrated with myself, defiantly included them on the bookshelves of our living room in my shared house in Oxford, my roommate joked that people might get the wrong idea. "I see we've got ISIS over here," another roommate riffed, thumb jerking towards my book on the caliphates. Though this was in jest, they had unknowingly tapped into my own insecurity, and since then I've reverted to my more nervous ways. (No one commented on my roommate's books on Christian mystics, I noticed.)

During Zoom calls, I fastidiously move these research books—which are piled high on the desk and the table, ready to be dipped into at any moment—out of the camera's view. When researching Islam or Nusayba on the internet, I am extraordinarily cautious, always scared of keying in a search term or opening a website that might get me flagged. The evidence needed for Prevent to designate that a Muslim is "preparing for terrorism" is, after all, scarily wispy: documents read, internet search histories.[296] I don't want people—not to mention hostile governments—to, as my roommate put it, "get the wrong idea." As van Es says: "Muslims are increasingly put under surveillance—not only literally, in the sense of being monitored by intelligence services, but also in the sense that they are continually viewed and talked about in terms of how dangerous they are." Suppose someone sees these books and take from them that I am Muslim and Arab—not only in the soft, white ways that I am privileged enough be able to present, but in the harsh, fanatical, unalterably Othering ways as well? *I'm not the kind of Muslim you're thinking of!* I want to preemptively reassure them. *I'm the good kind, I swear!*

This isn't the right response to anti-Islamism, I know. I should be all the more assertive about my Muslimness and my Arabness in the face of people's racism, especially since many Muslims and Arabs are immediately Othered by virtue of a headscarf or darker skin, unable to scoot these things conveniently out of view. Often, my name or my nationality do the same. But there is something particular to being *interested* in Islam and Arabhood that I sense raises eyebrows and sends colleagues to the Prevent website, something suspicious in my exploring this particular culture and religion. (Some of the signs to watch out for, according to Prevent,[297] include "searching for answers to questions about identity, faith and belonging"; in other words, the thesis of this essay collection. Uh oh.)[298] So I don't trust that I will continue to be seen at all, in the context of these books or search histories; I worry that in their shadow I will be cast as Jihadi Jane or someone else on the verge of being indoctrinated by an apparently terrifying and terrorising religion.

Already, just by talking of my connection to Nusayba, I can be placed into this camp, as I discovered at a celebratory dinner with friends several years ago. A few of us had gathered at a tapas restaurant in central London to celebrate both my birthday and my having just, only a few hours earlier, signed with a literary agent. Overwhelmed, a bit anxious, but still buzzing from the excitement, I breathlessly ordered prosecco for the table and then tried to get to know the plus-ones I'd never met before. Inclining my body over dishes of padrón peppers and patatas bravas in order to hear better through the din of the restaurant, I asked my friend's brother about his work and his life. We chatted amiably for a while, squinting and smiling at each other in our struggle to talk over the other people also speaking loudly, and then my friend brought up my new agent, and the book I was planning on writing. What's it about? the brother asked, smiling encouragingly.

It's a collection of essays, I said. You probably don't want to hear about it, it's really quite boring, honestly, don't feel like you need to, you know, I mean, it's a pretty niche topic …

Oh, shut up, my friend said. Tell us!

OK, well, I said, buoyed by my friend's expression and the thought that I now was, in theory at least, a Real Writer. It's loosely about my ancestor, who was this badass warrior woman in, like, seventh-century Arabia. She was called Nusayba, which is where we get our last name from, and was one of the first converts to Islam, like, a really early follower of Muhammad's.

Oh yeah? the brother said coolly, his smile gone. He took a sip of prosecco and adopted an expression of detached interest. That's not unusual for Muslims, right? Doesn't that ISIS leader, the executioner guy, Abu Bakr, also say he's descended from Muhammad? That's common with terrorists, is it?

I felt myself flush.

Uhm, I finally managed through a closed throat. Yah? I'm not sure, actually, I haven't looked into Abu Bakr. But, um, ha, I hope most people won't think of ISIS when they pick up the collection? I tried to force out a laugh, though my body had gone cold.

Hmm, the brother answered, his face still stony.

I looked down at the padrón peppers, my face still hot, while a different friend made a joke about subway trains.

⌀

It is easy for this shame, which begins as a true barometer of moral responsibility, to turn into something acrid. That negative self-evaluation, when made in the context of long-term, unequal power dynamics, can be corrosive, can easily turn into a more generalized self-loathing, formed not only of one's own self-assessment, but of the negative views held by the more-powerful group. The Western discourse that portrays Islam as violent, oppressive, backwards, barbaric; that propagates Arabs as uncivilized, lascivious, immoral—that labels *me personally* as violent, oppressive, backwards, barbaric, uncivilized, lascivious, immoral—can be absorbed not only by white Christian Brits, but by the Arabs and Muslims who are framed by it as well. I feel it in my pores, even as I try to scrub it out; this brutish alter ego. I watch for its appearance in my reflections. "It is a peculiar sensation, this double-consciousness," W.E.B. Du Bois wrote in 1897. "This sense of always looking at one's self through the eyes of others, of measuring one's soul by the tape of a world that looks on in amused contempt and pity."[299]

Although Du Bois was describing the particular situation by which racism was being internalized by Black Americans in the late nineteenth century (and perhaps continues to be today), the same logic is applicable to the Arab/Muslim world, and Arab/Muslim culture, on a large scale. It is difficult, I think, to avoid an internalized oppression, in the context of two hundred years of European imperialism. Already the language of the Crusades had set the scene (Muslims were bloodthirsty, alienated from God); Orientalist explorers followed soon after to create an image of the Arab/Muslim as exotic, fetishist, dirty and dangerous (long-nailed men in harems, leering at veiled belly dancers).[300] Since then, the West's discursive and military influence has only grown, while the picture of the Arab/Muslim has stayed mainly unchanged.

Palestinians in particular are susceptible to a doubled consciousness, having been first colonized and then subsequently occupied—an ongoing situation. Today, we are seen as greedy, Jew-hating, land-grabbing fanatics,[301] but even long before we became synonymous with terrorism, the Arabs in Palestine were already seen as undeveloped, not even recognizable as people: as Ian Black has pointed out, it is, in part, the lack of so-called civilized inhabitants in Palestine that meant the territory was read as "empty" by the Europeans, and consequently conquerable[302] (in the same way that Africa was portrayed as a virgin territory "ready for waves of pioneers," or that America, for that matter, was a "new world" rather than, simply, the other half of this one). If we existed at all, it was as animals: "We who live abroad are accustomed to believing that the Arabs are all wild desert people who, like donkeys, neither see nor understand what is happening around them,"[303] wrote Asher Ginzburg, better known as Ahad Ha'am, the founder of Cultural Zionism, in 1891.[304] Less than thirty years later, the British signed the Balfour Declaration, by which, as Arthur Koestler puts it, "one nation solemnly promised to a second nation the country of a third."[305]

Britain's involvement in imperialism generally, and in the Palestinian-Israeli situation in particular, is another, less complicated source of shame for me. It always strikes me as odd that the conflict is perceived by so many people in Britain as something incomprehensibly far away and foreign ("a brown people problem," as one friend once put it). Often when I tell a person in England that I'm Palestinian, the reaction is one of almost heart-breaking panic. *Crap*, I can almost hear them thinking, *what does that mean again?* (Like the protagonist in the opening scene of Lisa Owen's *Not Working*, who answers the door to a man whose neck is "grey with dirt" wearing a "Free Palestine" badge; she needs to buy herself a minute to "remind myself which side of the Israel-Palestine conflict I am on." The reader never finds out which.) The bold among them will just ask whether my being Palestinian means I am Jewish or "the other thing." The whole situation seems, for many, distant and confused. I've no dog in the race, a friend once told me, in reference to the plight of the Palestinians, wanting this to be taken kindly as a mark of neutrality. Nothing to do with me, is what she meant.

But—like many legacies of British imperialism—geographic distance does not mean that we, as Brits, are not implicated. Had Britain not taken Palestine from the Ottomans at the end of the First World War, partly by promising the Arabs they would have their own nation, but then instead settled into the territory like it was a comfortable pair of someone else's slippers, there would have been no conflict. The establishment of British Mandatory Palestine (a Palestine that was part of the British Empire, in other words) and Britain's subsequent decision to hand the Palestinian-inhabited territory over to a European Jewish population looking for a place to escape European antisemitism—epitomized by Lord Balfour's declaration that Palestine was to be "a national home for the Jewish people"[306]—casually and causally set the scene for decades of dispossession and despair in the region. The knotted, toxic mess created by these decisions remains, apparently, intractable.

As someone half-British, I feel historically and directly connected to this mess. The same sense of shame by association I struggle with when it comes to Arab/Muslim misogyny and violence exists here, too. And it doesn't help matters that Britain used Mandatory Palestine as a type of testing ground for the violent tactics used in the rest of its colonies, tactics such as "night raids on suspect communities, oil-soaked sand stuffed down native throats, open-air cages for holding villagers, mass demolitions of houses"[307]—many of which are used by the occupation forces still. As Sunil Khilnani puts it: "Palestine was the Empire's leading atelier of coercive repression."[308] And this, in many ways, continues. Though the US, of course, provides the heftiest amounts of financial, military and political backing to Israel, Britain is still heavily involved in the occupation, generously providing the Israeli state with impunity. It continues to train its own military with Israel, often in the occupied territories,[309] as well as supply many millions of pounds in military equipment to the country[310]—despite having a policy that supposedly does not endorse actions by Israel deemed illegal under international law. The British not only have a dog in the race, they—we—set up the whole game.

And Britain's colonization of the country has had profound effects on our view of ourselves. A human confusion that equates power with excellence meant that the British, by being our colonizers, became in some ways our superiors as well. To be part of the elite, as Nesrine Malik puts it, "required learning English, adopting Christian values, aligning oneself more and more closely with Britain, maybe even being educated there. In creating this hierarchy, Britain created a center of gravity, both cultural and political, that still has a powerful draw."[311] As in many colonial territories, the well-off urban families in British Mandatory Palestine were educated (as my grandfather was) in English-speaking schools, and often went on to elite English universities (as he did) to study, and then came back British-ized. (Meanwhile, my other great-grandfather found himself exiled to the Seychelles, and his house bombed, by the British, in response to his involvement in the anti-colonial Arab Revolt of the 1930s.) The equivalent was happening in the countries colonized by the French, such as Lebanon, Morocco, Tunisia and Algeria, all across the Arab world. A situation was created in which the educated elite were associated with the colonial—not just in terms of their language or education, but also in terms of their ideas.

The famous nineteenth-century Palestinian feminist and writer May Ziadeh moved from Palestine to Lebanon at the age of fourteen, where she lived on the first floor of a large green-doored mansion in central Beirut. Sitting out on her balcony in the balmy evenings, she would work at her studies in French, eventually devouring the works of European contemporaries such as Shelley and Byron, in addition to the Quran and the poems and other writings of Kahlil Gibran. She was obsessed with reading and learning; in the end she became fluent in nine languages, and this led to a wider passion for women's education.

At the age of twenty-two, she and her family moved to Egypt, which was then, in 1907, still under British rule (and had been, by that point, for almost her whole life).[312] The literary salons that she established while there quickly became famous: held every Tuesday and frequented by men and women alike, the salons brought together Arab and European intelligentsia and artists, becoming a center for debate between the sexes and the cultures. Through these salons and through her writings, Ziadeh became *the* literary voice of Arab feminism. "If you, men of the East, keep the core of slavery in your homes, represented by your wives and daughters, will the children of slaves be free?" she wrote. But, despite her popularity, she was still, as Huwaida Saleh puts it, a "controversial personality" in Egypt; partly, perhaps, because she was "open to Western culture and liberal in a society that was not so."[313]

For Ziadeh's contemporary Arab feminists, like Huda Sha'arawi—suffragette and founder of the Egyptian Feminist Union—the fight for women's rights was tied, from its essence, to the fight for national liberation. Rather than argue, as Ziadeh did, that "women should be open to the ideas of the Occident", Sha'arawi saw Britain's colonial control over Egypt as a major cause of women's suffering and, in 1919, she helped organize the revolution against the British.[314] As Kumari Jayawardena[315] has shown, nationalist ideas, resulting largely from the imperialist exploitation of colonized countries, were very much linked to ideas of women's emancipation across the Global South. So, though eventually distinctive in their foci, both Sha'arawi and Ziadeh's feminisms were, ultimately, informed by the West.

Similarly, Palestinian feminists after Ziadeh have been working within a context of colonization and occupation, one from which their (white) peers in Europe were entirely free. While the women's lib movement in Britain was working to gain the vote in the aftermath of the First World War, women in Palestine were adjusting to the oppressive rule of the Mandate, founding a women's political movement in 1929[316] whose aim was liberation from the British, rather than from men. When feminism reached its second wave peak in the West in the early 1960s (with the publication of such classics as Betty Friedan's *The Feminine Mystique*), and British and American women began pushing for social equality, Palestinian feminists were entering and then reeling from a devastating war with Israel. As Islah Jād describes, "the Palestinian women's movement was shaped to a great extent by the deterioration of the political situation prompted by British colonial policies and the brutality of the Mandate in suppressing the Palestinian revolts, the rise of the Palestinian resistance to the Zionist project, and the consolidation of the Palestinian national movement in the 1920s and 1930s."[317]

Women continued to be involved politically and be integral parts of the national resistance movement in the following decades; my grandmother, for instance, organized and took part in many of the civilian protests against Israeli occupation in the aftermath of the June 1967 war. But, as Jād argues, it was only in the early 1990s, with the promise of political stability thanks to the Oslo Accords, that the Palestinian feminist project could finally focus more explicitly on women within a possible Palestinian nation state. The Palestinian Federation of Women's Action Committees—a Marxist group that believed that women's oppression stemmed from the triple combination of nation, class and gender—was the most famous and successful iteration of the feminist movement at this time. They asserted that "no liberation for the homeland would be possible without women's liberation,"[318] and demanded that women gain equal pay. Unhappily, of course, the promise of the 1990s gave way to the grim reality of continued occupation and worsening apartheid, keeping that nascent women's project locked within the wider struggle for freedom and self-determination. Women were still underneath that powerful trifecta.

The issue was compounded by a lack of intersectionality in mainstream global women's rights movements. Though these (white) feminists espoused a supposed "sisterhood," Palestinian feminism seemed only to be acceptable if completely depoliticized and presented within the framework of the white savior; that is, if the problem was one of Arab/Muslim women being oppressed by Arab/Muslim men. But this, though indeed shameful, has always been rather a moot point. As Nada Elia points out, "Palestinian women's freedom of movement, their right to an education, their right to vote, to work, to live where they want, where they were born, their right to sufficient food, clean water, and medical treatments in their own homeland, are denied them not by their fellow Palestinians, but by the illegal occupying power, Israel"[319]—the oppression of the nation necessarily begetting the oppression of its women.

The ways in which colonizers and occupying powers make use of gender, and gender violence, to maintain their power are well documented. Across the Middle East and South Asia, Western powers often used women as a cover for colonial rule (saving women from child marriage, for instance).[320] In many ways, such as in the military invasion of Afghanistan, they still do.[321] In the context of the ongoing occupation, practices such as sexually assaulting detained Palestinian women and girls, for instance, or threatening sexual violence against wives and daughters during interrogations,[322] are common ways of "extracting information or 'confessions' from [Palestinian] male detainees"[323] and are regularly undertaken by the Israeli authority to maintain the repression of the Palestinian population.[324] As Nawal El Saadawi said, when asked not to bring up the issue of Palestine at the United Nations International Conference on Women in 1985: "How can we speak of liberation for Palestinian women without speaking of their right to have a land on which to live?"[325]

For Palestinians as for other Arabs and Muslims elsewhere, then, the evolution of the feminist movement has been indelibly linked to the forces of conflict and colonization.[326] Patriarchy has throttled women everywhere throughout history, but centuries of colonialism have meant the branching of women's movements into two paths, one of which became entangled with national liberation, internalized oppression, religious parity. A doubled consciousness was formed: the articulation of what it meant to be a free Arab/Muslim woman was not only tied to larger questions about liberty and national identity, but was also made opaque by a fug of anti-Muslim and anti-Arab ideas, particularly of womanhood. For some, an oppositional identity was born, in which asserting an Arabness or a Muslimness in the context of this subjugation became about rejecting the ideals held by colonial powers as much as the colonial powers themselves—leading, in some cases, to the further oppression of women.[327] Which all means that, though feminism over the last two hundred years in the West can be looked at without reference to the East, the same cannot be said the other way around. Feminism in the Arab world was, from its nascence, necessarily *reactive*, and thus unable to be truly of itself.

So, while women's suffrage was achieved one hundred years ago, finally, in Britain, both men and women in Palestine were busy dealing with a British colonial rule that had just promised the country away. The ensuing decades saw the national struggle against Israeli occupation, the disillusionment of the peace process, the consequent growth of fundamentalist Islamist groups and a general regression in women's fortunes. This is not to say that these replaced women's movements—women have been central to the Palestinian struggle, as has their liberation—but rather that, unlike in the West, the feminist project was inevitably and inherently tied to these other projects. In many ways, the colonial powers—even while often claiming to work on behalf on women—poisoned the feminist project in the womb.

But let's be clear: that's not to say that anyone needs "saving." As Lila Abu-Lughod explains, "When you save someone, you imply that you are saving her from something. You are also saving her *to* something. What violences are entailed in this transformation, and what assumptions are being made about the superiority of that to which you are saving her? Projects of saving other women depend on and reinforce a sense of superiority by Westerners, a form of arrogance that deserves to be challenged."[328] Women are women everywhere, no matter their religion or race; they will always need and demand their own liberation. To think that Arab/Muslim women have a unique and inherent desire to be oppressed betrays precisely the kind of racism many women are busy fighting alongside their fight against structural patriarchy.[329]

What is important to understand is that the sense of shame created by the West and its discourse of Islam-and-Arabs-as-misogynistic belies the fact that it is precisely *thanks* to the West that the Arab/Muslim world was not able to develop an uncomplicated feminism of its own. "We the women in Arab countries realize that we are still slaves, still oppressed, not because we belong to the East, not because we are Arab, or members of Islamic societies, but as a result of the patriarchal class system that has dominated the world for thousands of years,"[330] writes Nawal El Saadawi. Yet the legacies of European imperialism and the continuing conflicts and occupations have made it so that Arab and Muslim feminism is always measuring itself by the tape of a world that, as Du Bois said, looks on in pity and contempt.

Perhaps nothing exemplifies the relationship between the Arab world, misogyny and the Western world more neatly than the British slang word "bint." Though commonly used in England as a derogatory term for women, often meaning slut or idiot, the word is, of course, originally Arabic: the word for "girl" or "daughter." (The word is considered so offensive that my publishers refused to use it as the title for this book.) Hence Nusayba's full name—Nusayba *bint* Ka'ab al Khazrajia, as in, Nusayba, *daughter of*. British soldiers in Mandate Palestine and in Egypt picked up the word from the indigenous Arabs whose land they were colonizing and began using it to refer to the women they were "romancing"[331] on the side. "Bint with alluring eyes!" starts one poem from the time. Eventually, the word made its way from these soldiers to the lads back home, and from there the word became common British slang, so much part of the culture that Basil can use it when berating Polly during an episode of *Fawlty Towers*. "Well, whose fault is it, then, you cloth-eared bint?" John Cleese shrieks at her, boggle-eyed. And so an innocuous Arabic word for girl or daughter becomes, in Britain, both misogynistic and entirely alienated from its Arabic roots: stolen and poisoned.

I have often wondered why Nusayba's story has endured and proliferated beyond our family. The tales about her are few, and, as mentioned previously, not particularly well evidenced. What we do know of her was likely written down by men decades, if not centuries, after the fact (men with god-knows-what agendas); and it is possible that she may not have existed at all. I personally suspect she may have been not one woman but multiple women. And yet she remains part of the Muslim consciousness, the namesake of young girls across the Muslim world. She's on YouTube, in Listicles, even in a television show. Reputable scholars invoke her as testament to a type of woman alive during the time of the Prophet, despite the stories about her arising from the "shifting sands"[332] of early Islamic sources.

So why do we keep the warrior woman's legend alive? It is, I suspect, an effort to see ourselves more clearly: to touch a far-off identity, to find a single consciousness, to reach back to a time before all the shame—both the legitimate and the false. Her existence—a female warrior, an eager and willing early adopter of the faith, an assertive mother who questioned the Quran and who existed at the *beginning*—points to an Islam and an Arabness that is natural and also, amazingly, not incompatible with a modern twenty-first-century idea of womanhood. She not only offers a counter-narrative to the Western discourse on women in Islam but also a way of winding back to something more authentic, something untinted by Orientalist lenses. Despite her being more myth than woman, she is powerful as a symbol of our yearning for an organic, unencumbered Muslim and Arab feminism. Perhaps, in fact, we need her, and other figures like her, precisely *for* the myth. As Adeolu Oyekan Oluwaseyi argues in the context of post-colonial states in Africa, "mythmaking, though primordial, plays a significant role that is both constructivist and instrumental in the identity (re)construction process of ethnic groups."[333] If stories are what connect families through time, myths are what remake communities across space. "The sleeping past," as Fatema Mernissi writes, "can animate the present."[334]

Perhaps, for contemporary Arab/Muslim women to find a single consciousness, to articulate an "authentic" feminism for ourselves, we need as many myths of female Arabhood, female Muslimness, as possible. To reclaim an identity denied to us by colonization, we must mine and explore and interrogate our legends, and histories, and the stories that have been passed down from one generation to the next, and find, in these, kernels of our ancestry. Because otherwise, to think about women, feminism, Islam(s) and Arabhood is to enter a deeply dense, dark, tangled, thorny, mucky, muddy part of a forest. In addressing feminist aspirations in the Middle East, you hit the pointy end of a branch that leads back to Orientalist constructions of the Arab "other"; in searching for clarity on Islamic practice, you are snagged by the sharp edge of patriarchy. Nationalism, feminism, colonialism, freedom. Too often, I find myself underneath it all, my own experiences—those of just one secular Muslim British-Palestinian woman—obscured by the muck and mud and branches. Only Nusayba can show me the way out, Arab woman to Arab woman. Bint to bint.

ENDNOTES

All websites were accessed on April 30, 2023.

INTRODUCTION

1   She is also known as Um Umara, Um Amara and Nusaybah bint Ka'b Al-Ansariyah.

2   I use the words "anti-Islamism" or "anti-Islamic bigotry" in place of "Islamophobia" because, as Aubrey Gordon has noted in the context of anti-fatness, "calling it a 'fear' legitimates the bias" and "oppressive behavior is not the same as a phobia. Phobias are real mental illnesses, and conflating them with oppressive attitudes and behaviors invites greater misunderstandings of mental illnesses." Gordon, A. (2021) "I'm a Fat Activist. I Don't Use the Word *Fatphobia*. Here's Why." Available at: https://www.self.com/story/fat-activist-fatphobia.

3   Manzoor-Khan, S. (2022) *Tangled in Terror: Uprooting Islamophobia*. London: Pluto Press.

4   Al-Azmeh, A. and Fokas, E. (2007) I*slam in Europe: Diversity, Identity and Influence*. Cambridge: Cambridge University Press.

5   See, for instance, Rebecca Solnit and Melissa Febos, two writers who beautifully integrate their religious cultural heritage without being labeled as "religious."

6 As Eleanor Abdella Doumato points out, "the Hadith literature as representation of actual events, sayings, doings, and social attitudes of the seventh century has been called into serious question." Weak hadith—that is, hadith with weak chains of transmission—such as in the case of many of the stories around Nusayba, are arguably even more suspect. Doumato, E.A. (2009) "Hearing Other Voices: Christian Women and the Coming of Islam," *International Journal of Middle East Studies*, 23(2), pp. 177–99. Available at: https://doi.org/10.1017/s0020743800056038.

7 Williams, M.E. (2022) "Author Elaine Castillo talks about empathy, Jane Austen adaptations, and 'How to Read Now,'" Salon, August 4. Available at: https://www.salon.com/2022/08/04/elaine-castillo-how-to-read-now/.

8 Agarwal, P. (2022) *(M)otherhood: On the Choices of Being a Woman.* Edinburgh: Canongate Books.

9 Masalha, N. (2018) *Palestine: A Four Thousand Year History*. London: Zed.

10 Zaphiriou-Zarifi, H. (2021) "History, the orphan of our time, or the timeless stories that make up history." In S. Carta & E. Kiehl (Eds.), *Political Passions and Jungian Psychology*. Routledge.

11 Hershberger, S. (2020) "Humans Are All More Closely Related Than We Commonly Think," *Scientific American*, October 5. Available at: https://www.scientificamerican.com/article/humans-are-all-more-closely-related-than-we-commonly-think/.

12 Quoted in Hershberger, "Humans Are All More Closely Related Than We Commonly Think."

BETTINJAN

13 Kane, A. (2014) "How food writing humanizes the Palestinian struggle: Laila El-Haddad on 'The Gaza Kitchen,'" *Mondoweiss*, June 26. Available at: https://mondoweiss.net/2014/06/humanizes-palestinian-struggle/.

14 Kiple, K.F. and Coneè Ornelas, K. (2000) *The Cambridge World History of Food*. Cambridge, UK/New York, US: Cambridge University Press.

15 I use the name "Muhammad" to refer to the Prophet throughout the text. For some Muslim communities, this is unusual, but I mean no disrespect and hope the choice does not cause pain or offence to any readers. I did not take the decision lightly. For me, the Prophet's humanity is one of the most unique and powerful aspects of Islam. It is also important, since I am trying to evoke and imagine Nusayba's life and experiences (many of them devoted to the Prophet), to bring him to life in some way; using the name "Muhammad" feels crucial for this.

16 Ibn Kathir, Imam. (2019) *The Life of the Prophet Muhammad (Saw)—Volume 2—as Seerah an Nabawiyya—السيرة النبوية*. Dar Ul Thaqafah.

17 Kiple, K.F. and Coneè Ornelas, K. *The Cambridge World History of Food*.

18 Armanios, F. (2018) *Halal Food: A History*. Oxford: Oxford University Press.

19 Al-Munajjid, S. (2015) "Virtues of fasting on Ashura," Arab News, October 23. Available at: https://www.arabnews.com/islam-perspective/news/824281.

20 Katsh, A.I. (1979) *Judaism in Islam: Biblical and Talmudic Backgrounds of the Koran and Its Commentaries*. New York: Sepher Hermon Press.

21 Goitein, S.D. (2009) *Studies in Islamic History and Institutions*. Leiden: Brill.

22 Ibn Sa'd, M. (1995) *The Women of Madina*. London: Ta-Ha Publishers.

23 Gable, B. (2014) "Eating Disorders: Prevalence, Perceptions, and Treatments in Jordan," Independent Study Project (ISP) Collection, 1804; Dolan, B. and Ford, K. (1991) "Binge eating and dietary restraint: a cross-cultural analysis," *International Journal of Eating Disorders*, 10(3), pp. 345—53. Available at: https://onlinelibrary.wiley.com/doi/10.1002/1098-108X(199105)10:3%3C345::AID-EAT2260100310%3E3.0.CO;2-9. Also: Al Sabbah, H. et al. (2009) "Weight control behaviors among overweight, normal weight and underweight adolescents in Palestine: findings from the national study of Palestinian schoolchildren (HBSC-WBG2004)," *International Journal of Eating Disorders*, 43(4). Available at: https://doi.org/10.1002/eat.20698.

24 Curran, J.R. (2002) "Jerome, Asceticism, and the Roman Aristocracy, AD 340–410" in *Pagan City and Christian Capital: Rome in the Fourth Century*.

Oxford: Oxford University Press, pp. 260–320. Available at: https://doi.org/10.1093/acprof:oso/9780199254200.003.0007.

25 **An Egyptian sociologist and social researcher.**

26 Nasser, M. (2005) "Dying to Live: Eating Disorders and Self-Harm Behaviour in a Cultural Context." In Levitt, J.L, Sansone, R.A. and Cohn, L. (2005) *Self-Harm Behavior and Eating Disorders*. Abingdon: Routledge.

27 Hornbacher, M. (2009) *Wasted*. London: HarperCollins.

28 Flynn, G. (2012) *Gone Girl*. New York: Random House.

29 Bartky, S.L. (1982) "Narcissism, Femininity and Alienation," *Social Theory and Practice*, 8(2), pp. 127–43. Available at: https://www.pdcnet.org/soctheorpract/content/soctheorpract_1982_0008_0002_0127_0144.

30 Hong Kingston, M. (1989) *The Woman Warrior: Memoirs of a Girlhood Among Ghosts*. New York: Alfred A. Knopf.

31 Jovanovski, N. (2017) *Digesting Femininities: The Feminist Politics of Contemporary Food Culture*. London: Palgrave Macmillan.

32 Miller, C.C. (2020) "Young Men Embrace Gender Equality, but They Still Don't Vacuum," *The New York Times*, February 11. Available at: https://www.nytimes.com/2020/02/11/upshot/gender-roles-housework.html.

33 IMEU (2006) "Palestinian Cuisine." Available at: https://imeu.org/article/palestinian-cuisine.

34 Zaphiriou-Zarifi, H. (2021) "History, the orphan of our time, or the timeless stories that make up history" in Carta, S. and Kiehl, E.K. (eds) (2020) *Political Passions and Jungian Psychology: Social and Political Activism in Analysis*. Abingdon: Routledge. Available at: https://doi.org/10.4324/9780429291845.

WARRIOR, WORRIER

35 أمينة عمر الخراط. 1998. *أم عمارة نسيبة بنت كعب: الصحابية المجاهدة*. دار القلم

36   أمينة عمر الخراط. 1998. أم عمارة نسيبة بنت كعب: *الصحابية المجاهدة*. دار القلم

37   Krishna Kumar, N.P. (2020) "'Art in the Age of Anxiety': Curator Omar Kholeif spells out ambitions," *Arab Weekly*, March 1. Available at: https://thearabweekly.com/art-age-anxiety-curator-omar-kholeif-spells-out-ambitions.

38   *Nadiya: Anxiety and Me,* BBC One, May 15, 2019. Available at: https://www.bbc.co.uk/programmes/m00053fy.

39   Marie, M., SaadAdeen, S. and Battat, M. (2020) "Anxiety disorders and PTSD in Palestine: a literature review," *BMC Psychiatry*, 20, 509. Available at: https://doi.org/10.1186/s12888-020-02911-7.

40   Sudjic, O. (2018) *Exposure*. London: Peninsula Press.

41   Hussein Rassool, G. (2018) *Evil Eye, Jinn Possession, and Mental Health Issues: An Islamic Perspective*. Abingdon: Routledge.

42   Al Busaidi Z. Q. (2010) "The Concept of Somatisation: A Cross-cultural Perspective" in *Sultan Qaboos University Medical Journal*, 10(2), 180–186.

43   van der Kolk, B. (2014) *The Body Keeps the Score: Mind, Brain and Body in the Transformation of Trauma*. London: Penguin Books.

44   Manzoor-Khan, S. *Tangled in Terror.*

45   Sarno, J.E. (2019) *Healing Back Pain: The Mind-Body Connection*. New York: Grand Central Publishing.

46   Belluz, J. (2018) "America's most famous back pain doctor said pain is in your head. Thousands think he's right," Vox, July 23. Available at: https://www.vox.com/science-and-health/2017/10/2/16338094/dr-john-sarno-healing-back-pain.

47   Goldman, B. (2018) "Scientists find fear, courage switches in brain," Stanford Medicine News Center, May 2. Available at: https://med.stanford.edu/news/all-news/2018/05/scientists-find-fear-courage-switches-in-brain.html.

48   أمينة عمر الخراط. 1998. *أم عمارة نسيبة بنت كعب: الصحابية المجاهدة*. دار القلم

49   Khan, M. (2019) *It's Not About the Burqa: Muslim Women on Faith, Feminism, Sexuality and Race*. London: Picador.

50   Ali, K. and Leaman, O. (2007) *Islam: The Key Concepts*. Abingdon: Routledge.

51   Aima, R. (2020) "Artists in Isolation: Wafaa Bilal's 'Domestic Tension,'" *Momus*, April 14. Available at: https://momus.ca/artists-in-isolation-wafaa-bilals-domestic-tension/.

52   American Committee for the Weizmann Institute of Science (2010) "Brave Brains: Neural Mechanisms of Courage," June 1. Available at: https://www.weizmann-usa.org/news-media/in-the-news/brave-brains-neural-mechanisms-of-courage/.

HOUSE GUESTS

53   **In comparison to Palestinians more generally, that is, who are known to be extremely generous and hospitable.**

54   Mernissi, F. (1975) *Beyond the Veil: Male-Female Dynamics in Muslim Society*. Cambridge, Mass.: Schenkman Publishing Company.

55   Aslan, R. (2012) *No god but God: The Origins, Evolution and Future of Islam*. New York: Random House.

56   Slininger, S. (2014) "Veiled Women: Hijab, Religion, and Cultural Practice," *Historia*, 23, pp. 68–78. Available at: https://www.eiu.edu/historia/2014issue.php.

57   Mernissi, F. *Beyond the Veil*.

58   Sadeghi, F. (2020) "Women in the Sasanian Zoroastrianism" in *The Sin of the Woman*. Berlin: De Gruyter, pp. 37–62. Available at: https://doi.org/10.1515/9783112209424-004.

59   Aslan, R. *No god but God*.

60 Stillman, Y. (2003) *Arab Dress: A Short History: From the Dawn of Islam to Modern Times*. Leiden: Brill. Available at: https://brill.com/edcollbook/ title/8742?language=en.

61 Winfrey, O. (2021) "Oprah Explains Why Learning the Power of Intention Can Be 'Life-Altering and Life-Enhancing,'" Oprah Daily, April 4. Available at: https://www.oprahdaily.com/life/a36013378/ oprah-intention-message-oprah-insiders/.

62 Bernstein, E. (January 7, 2013) "Setting Boundaries With Family Members." *Wall Street Journal*. https://www.wsj.com/articles/SB10001424127887323482504578227613937854612.

63 Jawer, M. (2019) "Where Are Your Boundaries?" *Scientific American*, June 18. Available at: https://blogs.scientific american.com/observations/ where-are-your-boundaries/.

64 Lewis, N. (2003) *A Dragon Apparent: Travels in Cambodia, Laos and Vietnam*. London: Eland.

65 Kahf, M. (2008) "Spare Me the Sermon on Muslim Women," *Washington Post*, October 5. Available at: https://www.washingtonpost.com/wp-dyn/content/ article/2008/10/03/AR2008100301968.html.

THE SEDER

66 Chabad.org. (April 7, 2008). *English Haggadah Text with Instructional Guide*. @Chabad. https://www.chabad.org/holidays/passover/pesach_cdo/aid/661624/jewish/ English-Haggadah-Text.htm.

67 Guillaume, A. (trans.) (1967) *The Life of Muhammad: A Translation of Isḥāq's Sīrat Rasūl Allāh*. Karachi: Oxford University Press.

68 Aslan, R. *No god but God*.

69 Aslan, R. *No god but God*.

70 Hossein Nasr, S. (2004) *The Heart of Islam: Enduring Values for Humanity*. New York: HarperCollins.

71   Kashani-Sabet, F. and Wenger, B. (2014) *Gender in Judaism and Islam: Common Lives, Uncommon Heritage*. New York: New York University Press.

72   Kashani-Sabet, F. and Wenger, B. *Gender in Judaism and Islam*.

73   Ames, C. (2020) "Christian Violence against Heretics, Jews and Muslims" in Gordon, M., Kaeuper, R.W. and Zurndorfer, H. (eds) *The Cambridge World History of Violence: Volume II 500–1500 ce*. Cambridge: Cambridge University Press, pp. 470–91.

74   **Because Israel took control of the land militarily, the Fourth Geneva Convention, which makes it clear that annexation of occupied territory is illegal, applies. The United Nations Economic and Social Commission for Western Asia (UNESCWA) has a clear document that explains this further:** *Palestine, the Occupation and the Fourth Geneva Convention: Facts and Figures* (2014). Available at: https://www.unescwa.org/sites/default/files/pubs/pdf/palestine-occupation-fourth-geneva-convention-facts-figures-english.pdf.

75   B'Tselem (2019) "East Jerusalem," January 27. Available at: https://www.btselem.org/topic/jerusalem.

76   Gottesman, E. (2018) "East Jerusalem: A Window on West Bank Annexation," Israel Policy Forum, October 31. Available at: https://israelpolicyforum.org/2018/10/31/east-jerusalem-a-window-on-west-bank-annexation/.

77   Human Rights Watch (2017) "Israel: Jerusalem Palestinians Stripped of Status," August 8. Available at: https://www.hrw.org/news/2017/08/08/israel-jerusalem-palestinians-stripped-status.

78   Middle East Children's Alliance (2012) "Statement on Demolition in Silwan from Madaa Silwan Creative Center," February 15. Available at: https://www.mecaforpeace.org/statement-on-demolition-in-silwan-from-madaa-silwan-creative-center/; and B'Tselem "East Jerusalem."

79   Reeves, B. (2019) "Jerusalem Municipal Data Reveals Stark Israeli-Palestinian Discrepancy in Construction Permits in Jerusalem," Peace Now, September 12. Available at: https://peacenow.org.il/en/jerusalem-municipal-data-reveals-stark-israeli-palestinian-discrepancy-in-construction-permits-in-jerusalem.

80 United Nations Office for the Coordination of Humanitarian Affairs (2019) "Record number of demolitions, including self-demolitions, in East Jerusalem in April 2019," May 14. Available at: https://www.ochaopt.org/content/record-number-demolitions-including-self-demolitions-east-jerusalem-april-2019.

81 Ir Amim (no date) "Settlements and National Parks." Available at: https://www.ir-amim.org.il/en/issue/settlements-and-national-parks.

82 The Office of the European Union Representative (West Bank and Gaza Strip, UNRWA) (2022) "2021 report on Israeli settlements in the occupied West Bank, including East Jerusalem," July 20. Available at: https://www.eeas.europa.eu/sites/default/files/documents/EU%20Settlement%20Report%202021.pdf.

83 **In the last five years, Israel reversed this policy and began to invest significantly in East Jerusalem's infrastructure. While this may sound like a welcome and long-overdue change, there is insidious intent behind it: as the International Crisis Group puts it in a 2019 report, "the real goal is to assert Israeli sovereignty" and "entrench its de facto annexation . . . of Occupied East Jerusalem."** See: International Crisis Group (2019) "Reversing Israel's Deepening Annexation of Occupied East Jerusalem," June 12. Available at: https://www.crisisgroup.org/middle-east-north-africa/eastern-mediterranean/israelpalestine/202-reversing-israels-deepening-annexation-occupied-east-jerusalem.

84 B'Tselem, "East Jerusalem."

85 Schejtman, M. (2016) "Meretz Jerusalem Views about the Future of the City," Palestine-Israel Journal of Politics, Economics and Culture, 21(4). Available at: https://www.pij.org/articles/1707/meretz-jerusalem-views-about-the-future-of-the-city.

86 Siniora, H. (2001) "The Declining Economy of East Jerusalem," Palestine-Israel Journal of Politics, Economics and Culture, 8(1). Available at: https://pij.org/articles/179/the-declining-economy-of-east-jerusalem.

87 **B'Tselem is the Israeli Information Center for Human Rights in the Occupied Territories.**

88 Guarnieri, M. (2012) "East Jerusalemites appeal to UN for help with garbage collection," *+972* Magazine, March 4. Available at: https://www.972mag.com/east-jerusalemites-appeal-to-un-for-help-with-garbage/.

89   B'Tselem. "East Jerusalem."

90   Amnesty International (2022) "Israel's Apartheid against Palestinians,"
     February 1. Available at: https://www.amnesty.org/en/latest/campaigns/2022/02/
     israels-system-of-apartheid/.

91   Palestinian Academic Society for the Study of International Affairs (PASSIA)
     (no date) "Historical Facts & Figures." Available at: http://passia.org/media/
     filer_public/42/39/42395981-77c2-4e7a-a6d4-4ea2566345dd/factsheet_jerusalem.pdf.

92   PASSIA. "Historical Facts & Figures."

93   Amnesty International. "Israel's Apartheid against Palestinians."

94   Lecker, M. (2021) "The Jews of Northern Arabia in Early Islam" in
     Lieberman, P. (ed.) *The Cambridge History of Judaism: Volume 5, Jews in the
     Medieval Islamic World.* Cambridge: Cambridge University Press, pp. 255–93.

95   Bogle, E.C. (1998) *Islam: Origin and Belief.* Austin: University of Texas Press.

96   Yildirim, Y. (2009) "The Medina Charter: A Historical Case of Conflict
     Resolution," *Islam and Christian—Muslim Relations*, 20(4), pp. 439–50.

97   Islamic History (2020) "The Constitution of Medina: Islam's
     First Legislative Treaty." Available at: https://historiaislamica.com/en/
     the-constitution-of-medina-islams-first-legislative-treaty/

98   Lecker, M. "The Jews of Northern Arabia in Early Islam."

99   **Not all scholars agree on this. Several historians have argued that the sources
     for this story are suspect at best, and that it's more likely that the killings and
     expulsions never happened.** See for example: Arafat, W.N. (1976) "New Light
     on the Story of Banū Qurayza and the Jews of Medina," *The Journal of the
     Royal Asiatic Society of Great Britain and Ireland*, 2, pp. 100–07.

100 Margalit, A. (2002) *The Ethics of Memory.* Cambridge, Mass.: Harvard
     University Press.

101 Thrall, N. (2021) "A Day in the Life of Abed Salama," *The New York Review*, March 19. Available at: https://www.nybooks.com/online/2021/03/19/a-day-in-the-life-of-abed-salama/.

102 Raz, A. (2021) "Classified Docs Reveal Massacres of Palestinians in '48—and What Israeli Leaders Knew," *Haaretz*, December 9. Available at: https://www.haaretz.com/israel-news/2021-12-09/ty-article-magazine/.highlight/classified-docs-reveal-deir-yassin-massacre-wasnt-the-only-one-perpetrated-by-isra/0000017f-e496-d7b2-a77f-e79772340000?_ga=2.258764494.512648414.1674724281-1190505939.1674656479.

103 Jacques Derrida was an Algerian-French philosopher.

104 Rahimi, S. (2021) *The Hauntology of Everyday Life*. Cham, Switzerland: Palgrave Macmillan.

105 Some use the Nuseibeh family's supposed descendance from Nusayba as proof that all Palestinians are "Arab colonizers" who arrived in the seventh century (it was a whole thing on Twitter). It's important to point out that this position is ahistorical: the Nabateans and Ghassanids (both Arab peoples) ruled over the Levant for many centuries before the Muslim conquests. Moreover, the country has a rich, complex, intersectional history of many peoples (including the Jewish peoples); as Nur Masalha and others have shown, the Muslim and Arab conquerors added to the natives, rather than replacing them. In any case, regardless of who came to the country how in the seventh century, the fact remains that, in the twenty-first century, ethnic cleansing is considered immoral and illegal.

106 Konrad, E. (2017) "How the world missed a week of Palestinian civil disobedience," *+972* Magazine, July 24. Available at: https://www.972mag.com/why-the-world-missed-a-week-of-palestinian-civil-disobedience/.

107 BBC News (2021) "Israeli strikes on Gaza high-rises may be war crimes—Human Rights Watch," August 23. Available at: https://www.bbc.co.uk/news/world-middle-east-58305586.

108 Émile Durkheim was a French sociologist.

109 Durkheim, É. (1912) *The Elementary Forms of the Religious Life*. Oxford: Oxford University Press.

110 That year, "a country and its people disappeared from maps and dictionaries," writes Elias Sanbar. "'The Palestinian people does not exist,' said the new masters, and henceforth the Palestinians would be referred to by general, conveniently vague terms as either 'refugees,' or in the case of a small minority that had managed to escape the generalized expulsion, 'Israeli Arabs,' a long absence was beginning." Sanbar, E. (2001) "Out of Place, Out of Time," *Mediterranean Historical Review*, 16(1), pp. 87–94. Available at: https://doi.org/10.1080/714004568.

111 Massoud, A. (2022) "UN adopts landmark resolution marking Palestinian 'Nakba Day,'" *The National*, November 30. Available at: https://www.thenationalnews.com/world/us-news/2022/11/30/un-adopts-landmark-resolution-marking-palestinian-nakba-day/.

112 Raz, A. "Classified Docs Reveal Massacres of Palestinians in '48–and What Israeli Leaders Knew."

113 McKernan, B. (2022) "Israel condemns Netflix film showing murder of Palestinian family in 1948 war," *The Guardian*, December 1. Available at: https://www.theguardian.com/world/2022/nov/30/farha-israel-condemns-new-netflix-film-for-showing-palestinian.

114 Masalha, N. (2008) "Remembering the Palestinian Nakba: Commemoration, Oral History and Narratives of Memory," *Holy Land Studies*, 7(2), pp. 123–56. Available at: https://doi.org/10.3366/e147494750800019x.

115 Masalha, N. "Remembering the Palestinian Nakba: Commemoration, Oral History and Narratives of Memory."

116 Sa'di, A.H. (2002) "Catastrophe, Memory and Identity: Al-Nakbah as a Component of Palestinian Identity," *Israel Studies*, 7(2), pp. 175–98. Available at: https://doi.org/10.2979/isr.2002.7.2.175.

117 Masalha, N. (2012) *The Palestine Nakba: decolonising history, narrating the subaltern, reclaiming memory*. Zed Books.

118 As the Israeli Jewish journalist Ariel David puts it, "The Passover narrative is one of the greatest stories ever told. More than any other biblical account, the escape of the enslaved Hebrews from Egypt is the foundational story of the Jewish faith and identity, one that all Jews are commanded to pass on from generation to generation. Also, it never happened. For decades now, most researchers have agreed that there is no evidence to suggest that the Exodus narrative reflects a specific historical event." David, A. (2019) "For You Were (Not) Slaves in Egypt: The Ancient Memories Behind the Exodus Myth," *Haaretz*, April 19. Available at: https://www.haaretz.com/archaeology/2019-04-19/ty-article-magazine/.premium/for-you-were-not-slaves-in-egypt-the-memories-behind-the-exodus-myth/0000017f-f246-da6f-a77f-fa4ef8220000.

UMMAH/MA

119 أمينة عمر الخراط. 1998. *أم عمارة نسيبة بنت كعب: الصحابية المجاهدة*. دار القلم

120 Pettus, A. (2006) "Prenatal Competition?" *Harvard Magazine*, September–October. Available at: https://www.harvardmagazine.com/2006/09/prenatal-competition.html.

121 Sadedin, S. (2014) "War in the Womb," *Aeon*, August 4. Available at: https://aeon.co/essays/why-pregnancy-is-a-biological-war-between-mother-and-baby.

122 Tanner, W., Krasniqi, F. and Blagden, J. (2021) "Age of Alienation: Young People Are Facing a Loneliness Epidemic," Onward, July 8. Available at: https://www.ukonward.com/reports/age-of-alienation-loneliness-young-people/?nocache=1678064461.

123 **I'm from the Nuseibeh house/family.**

124 Gawdat, M. (2022) "Alya Mooro—How to Free Yourself from Shame as a Woman and Rebrand Love and Sex," *Slo Mo: A Podcast with Mo Gawdat*, June 8. Available at: https://www.mogawdat.com/podcast/episode/78f8ea99/alya-mooro-how-to-free-yourself-from-shame-as-a-woman-and-rebrand-love-and-sex.

125 Said, E.W. (2000) *Out of Place: A Memoir*. London: Granta.

126 BBC News (2021) "Racial Impostor Syndrome: When you're made to feel like a fake," February 3. Available at: https://www.bbc.co.uk/news/stories-55909105.

127 Appiah, K.A. (2018) *The Lies That Bind: Rethinking Identity*. London: Profile Books.

128 **And a full or pure Englishness has worryingly racist connotations.**

129 Cusk, R. (2019) *A Life's Work*. London: Faber & Faber.

130 Offill, J. (2015) *Dept. of Speculation*. London: Granta.

131 Yoder, R. (2021) *Nightbitch*. London: Harvill Secker.

132 Agarwal, P. (2022) *(M)otherhood: On the Choices of Being a Woman*. Edinburgh: Canongate Books.

133 Brooks, K. (2016) "A Portrait of the Artist as a Young Mom," *The Cut*, April 12. Available at: https://www.thecut.com/2016/04/portrait-motherhood-creativity-c-v-r.html.

134 Patterson, Y.A. (1990) "Simone de Beauvoir and the Demystification of Motherhood," Simone de Beauvoir Studies, 7, pp. 61–4. Available at: https://doi.org/10.1163/25897616-00701009.

135 Ali, K. and Leaman, O. *Islam*.

136 Rich, A. (2021) "Anger and Tenderness" in A. O'Reilly (Ed.), *Maternal Theory: Essential Readings*, The 2nd Edition. Demeter Press.

137 Pasternak, C. (2010) "Palestinian Versus Western Mothering: Reconsidering Dichotomies in Media Representation," *Journal of the Motherhood Initiative for Research and Community Involvement*, 1(1).

138 Morrell, V. (2014) "Why Do Animals Sometimes Kill Their Babies?," *National Geographic*, March 28. Available at: https://www.nationalgeographic.com/science/article/140328-sloth-bear-zoo-infanticide-chimps-bonobos-animals.

139 Agarwal, P. *(M)otherhood*.

140 *Frente Sandinista de Liberación Nacional* (Sandinista National Liberation Front).

141 Norat, G. (2010) "Up in Arms! A Brief Women's History of Militancy in Latin America," *Journal of the Motherhood Initiative for Research and Community Involvement*, 1(1).

142 Norat, G. "Up in Arms! A Brief Women's History of Militancy in Latin America."

143 Hill Collins, P. (1994) "Shifting the Center: Race, Class, and Feminist Theorizing about Motherhood" in Glenn, E.N., Chang, G. and Forcey, L.R (eds) Mothering: Ideology, Experience, and Agency. Abingdon: Routledge.

144 Shibli, A. (2017) "The Making of Bad Palestinian Mothers During the Second Intifada" in Yaqub, N. and Quawas, R. (eds) *Bad Girls of the Arab World*. Austin: University of Texas Press, pp. 92–111. Available at: https://doi.org/10.7560/313350-010.

145 Pathak, M. (2021) "Warrior Mothers: Narratives of Women from the United Liberation Front of Assam (ULFA)," *Journal of International Women's Studies*, 22(9), pp. 271–84.

146 **In the country as a whole, from the river to the sea, the Jewish Israeli population has always been a minority, currently standing at 48 percent—a problem for a nation with Israel's particular exclusivist aims.**

147 Khawaja, N. (2018) "The Politics of Demography in the Israeli-Palestinian Conflict," *Journal of International Affairs*, April 27. Available at: https://jia.sipa.columbia.edu/online-articles/politics-demography-israeli-palestinian-conflict.

148 Abu-Duhou, J. (2003) "Motherhood as 'an Act of Defiance': Palestinian women's reproductive experience," *Development*, 46(2), pp. 85–9. Available at: https://doi.org/10.1057/palgrave.development.1110452.

149 Munayyer, Y. (2011) "Palestine's Hidden History of Non-violence," May 18. Available at: https://foreignpolicy.com/2011/05/18/palestines-hidden-history-of-nonviolence-2/.

150 Heti, S. (2018) *Motherhood*. Henry Holt and Company.

151 Levy, G. (2021) "A Brief History of Killing Children," *Haaretz*, November 20. Available at: https://www.haaretz.com/opinion/2021-11-20/ty-article/. premium/a-brief-history-of-killing-children/0000017f-ee07-d639-af7f-efd7eede0000.

152 Al Omoush, K.S. et al. (2012) "The impact of Arab cultural values on online social networking: The case of Facebook," *Computers in Human Behavior*, 28(6), pp. 2387—99. Available at: https://doi.org/10.1016/j.chb.2012.07.010.

153 Alsahi, H. (2019) "The Twitter Campaign to End the Male Guardianship System in Saudi Arabia," *Journal of Arabian Studies*, 8(2), pp. 298—318. Available at: https://doi.org/10.1080/21534764.2018.1556871.

154 Mohamed, E., Douai, A. and Iskandar, A. (2019) "Media, identity, and online communities in a changing Arab world," *New Media & Society*, 21(5), pp. 1035—42. Available at: https://doi.org/10.1177/1461444818821360.

155 Yee, V. and El-Naggar, M. (2021) "'Social Media Is the Mass Protest': Solidarity with Palestinians Grows Online," *The New York Times*, May 18. Available at: https://www.nytimes.com/2021/05/18/world/middleeast/palestinians-social-media.html.

156 Alhamdan, N. and Campbell, E. (2021) "How social media is failing Palestinians," *Middle East Institute*, October 25. Available at: https://www.mei.edu/publications/how-social-media-failing-palestinians.

157 Human Rights Watch (2021) "Israel/Palestine: Facebook Censors Discussion of Rights Issues," October 8. Available at: https://www.hrw.org/news/2021/10/08/israel/palestine-facebook-censors-discussion-rights-issues.

158 Ronson, J. (2015) *So You've Been Publicly Shamed*. London: Picador.

159 Al-Azmeh, A. (1993) *Islams and Modernities*. London/New York: Verso Books.

160 Agarwal, P. (2022) *(M)Otherhood: On the Choices of Being a Woman*. Edinburgh: Canongate Books.

THE ROAD TO DAMASCUS

161 Gruber, C. and Chatterjee, P. (2020) "Hagia Sophia has been converted back into a mosque, but the veiling of its figural icons is not a Muslim tradition," *The Conversation*, August 18. Available at: https://theconversation.com/hagia-sophia-has-been-converted-back-into-a-mosque-but-the-veiling-of-its-figural-icons-is-not-a-muslim-tradition-144042.

162 Sariyuce, I. and Reynolds, E. (2020) "Turkey's Erdogan orders the conversion of Hagia Sophia back into a mosque," CNN, July 26. Available at: https://edition.cnn.com/2020/07/10/europe/hagia-sophia-mosque-turkey-intl/index.html.

163 Causevic, S. (2020) "Hagia Sophia: turning this Turkish treasure into a mosque is at odds with its UNESCO status," *The Conversation*, July 29. Available at: https://theconversation.com/hagia-sophia-turning-this-turkish-treasure-into-a-mosque-is-at-odds-with-its-unesco-status-143372.

164 Bordewich, F.M. (2008) "A monumental struggle to preserve Hagia Sophia," *Smithsonian Magazine*, December. Available at: https://www.smithsonianmag.com/travel/a-monumental-struggle-to-preserve-hagia-sophia-92038218/.

165 Wooden, C. (2020) "Pope Francis: Pandemic is prime time for conversion," *America: The Jesuit Review*, April 8. Available at: https://www.americamagazine.org/faith/2020/04/08/pope-francis-pandemic-prime-time-conversion.

166 Guillaume, A. *The Life of Muhammad*.

167 Al Jazeera (2011) "Boom in UK converts to Islam," January 5. Available at: https://www.aljazeera.com/news/2011/1/5/boom-in-uk-converts-to-islam.

168 **Tony Blair's sister-in-law.**

169 Seddon, M. (2010) "How Tony Blair's sister-in-law converted to Islam," *The National*, October 29. Available at: https://www.thenationalnews.com/world/europe/how-tony-blair-s-sister-in-law-converted-to-islam-1.519446.

170 The Prevent program is the UK government's controversial counter-extremism policy, which aims to identify people "at risk of committing terrorist acts" and "intervene."

171 Webster, J. (2003) "With the immediacy of yesterday," *The Guardian*, February 22. Available at: https://www.theguardian.com/books/2003/feb/22/featuresreviews.guardianreview5.

172 BBC News (2019) "The British Victorians who became Muslims," May 19. Available at: https://www.bbc.com/news/uk-england-48069763.

173 It is only here, in the UK, that I feel aware of my Muslimness as a form of otherness that I am expected to represent.

174 Gilliat-Ray, S. (1999) "Rediscovering Islam: A Muslim Journey of Faith" in (eds) Lamb, C. and Darrol Bryant, M. (1999) *Religious Conversion: Contemporary Practices and Controversies*. London/New York: Cassell.

175 Garman, E. (2019) "Feminize Your Canon: Isabelle Eberhardt," *The Paris Review*, February 11. Available at: https://www.theparisreview.org/blog/2019/02/11/feminize-your-canon-isabelle-eberhardt/.

176 Kershaw, E. (ed.) (2003) *The Nomad: The Diaries of Isabelle Eberhardt*. Northampton, Mass.: Interlink Books.

177 Eberhardt, I. (2003) *In the Shadow of Islam*. La Vergne: Peter Owen Publishers.

178 James, J. (2016) "The Many Faces of Isabelle Eberhardt" in *The Glamour of Strangeness*. New York: Farrar, Straus and Giroux. Available at: https://fsgworkinprogress.com/2016/08/25/the-many-faces-of-isabelle-eberhardt/.

179 *The Guardian* (2020) "Hagia Sophia's conversion into a museum—archive, 1935," July 29. Available at: https://www.theguardian.com/world/from-the-archive-blog/2020/jul/29/hagia-sophia-conversion-into-museum-archive-1935.

180 Al-Azmeh, A. and Fokas, E. *Islam in Europe*.

181 Hern, A. (2020) "'Eat out to help out' may have caused sixth of Covid clusters over summer," *The Guardian*, October 30. Available at: https://www.theguardian.com/business/2020/oct/30/ treasury-rejects-theory-eat-out-to-help-out-caused-rise-in-covid.

182 El Cheikh, N.M. (2015) *Women, Islam, and Abbasid Identity*. Cambridge, Mass.: Harvard University Press.

183 **He wore a sack cloth and "stayed away from women on their periods," so maybe she wouldn't have been that close to him.**

184 Rambo, L.R. and Farhadian, C.E. (eds) (2014) *The Oxford Handbook of Religious Conversion*. New York: Oxford University Press.

185 Ahmed, L. (1992) *Women and Gender in Islam: Historical Roots of a Modern Debate*. New Haven: Yale University Press.

186 Lamb, C. and Darrol Bryant, M. *Religious Conversion*.

187 **As in "Islamist tries to kill white European woman!"**

188 Pitel, L. (July 10, 2020) "Erdogan orders Istanbul's Hagia Sophia to revert to being a mosque." *Financial Times*. https://www.ft.com/content/ bd0c89be-0b8b-4a63-954a-50caa36549bb.

189 Ali, K. and Leaman, O. *Islam*.

GOOD GIRLS, NASTY WOMEN

190 Guillaume, A. *The Life of Muhammad*.

191 El Cheikh, N.M. *Women, Islam, and Abbasid Identity*.

192 Sontag, S. (1967) "The Pornographic Imagination," *Partisan Review*.

193 Prince for Vanity 6. "Nasty Girl" (1982) Available at: https://genius.com/ Vanity-6-nasty-girl-lyrics.

194 Seneca, whose full name was Lucius Annaeus Seneca the Younger, was a Stoic philosopher of Ancient Rome.

195 Seneca believed anger was a form of temporary insanity that should never be acted on. More on that here: https://aeon.co/ideas/anger-is-temporary-madness-heres-how-to-avoid-the-triggers.

196 Ibn Saʻd, *Tabaqat*, 8:236–237.

197 Zuckerman, J.R. (2019) "Nasty Women: Toward a New Narrative on Female Aggression," *Contemporary Psychoanalysis*, 55(3), pp. 214–51. Available at: https://doi.org/10.1080/00107530.2019.1637392.

198 Jaggar, A. (1989) "Love and knowledge: Emotion in feminist epistemology," *Inquiry*, 32(2), pp. 151–76.

199 Phillips, W. (2020) "Whose Anger Counts?" *Boston Review*, August 28. Available at: https://www.bostonreview.net/articles/whitney-phillips-tk/.

200 Fuster, J. (2017) "Ashley Judd to Trump Supporters in Her Family: 'You Voted for a P—y Grabber,'" *The Wrap*, January 21. Available at: https://www.thewrap.com/ashley-judd-womens-march-speech-video/.

201 Though she is, arguably, aggressive and nasty in her politics.

202 Eltahawy, M. (2019) *The Seven Necessary Sins for Women and Girls*. Boston: Beacon Press.

203 Traister, R. (2018) *Good and Mad: The Revolutionary Power of Women's Anger*. New York: Simon and Schuster.

204 Lorde, A. (1981) "The Uses of Anger," *Women's Studies Quarterly*, 9(3). Available at: https://academicworks.cuny.edu/cgi/viewcontent.cgi?article=1654&context=wsq.

205 Sir Peter Frederick Strawson was an English philosopher.

206 Callard, A. (2020) *On Anger*. Boston: Boston Review.

207 The aim of the Birthright program is to connect Jews in the diaspora to Israel, a country whose native inhabitants have been expelled and occupied. While Jews from the diaspora—with previously no connection to the land—are encouraged to return to their "birthright," Palestinians driven out during the Nakba cannot, and resident Palestinians are denied many rights and freedoms.

208 El Cheikh, N.M. (2015) *Women, Islam, and Abbasid Identity*. Cambridge, Mass.: Harvard University Press.

209 Griffin, R.A. (2012) "I AM an Angry Black Woman: Black Feminist Autoethnography, Voice, and Resistance," *Women's Studies in Communication*, 35(2), pp. 138–57. Available at: https://doi.org/10.1080/07491409.2012.724524.

210 **Martha Nussbaum is an American moral philosopher.**

211 de Gorog, R. (1976) "The Etymology of Nasty," *American Speech*, 51(3/4), pp. 276–8. Available at: https://doi.org/10.2307/454978.

212 Herman, B. (2020) "What's Past Is Prologue," *Boston Review*, April 17. Available at: https://www.bostonreview.net/forum_response/barbara-herman-whats-past-prologue/.

213 Callard, A. *On Anger*.

214 Arruzza, C., Bhattacharya, T. and Fraser, N. (2019) *Feminism for the 99%: A Manifesto*. London/New York: Verso.

215 Phipps, A. (2020) *Me Not You: The Trouble with Mainstream Feminism*. Manchester: Manchester University Press.

216 El Cheikh, N.M. (2015) *Women, Islam, and Abbasid Identity*. Cambridge, Mass.: Harvard University Press.

217 محمد مرتضى الحسيني الزبادي. 1989. *تاج العروس من جواهر القاموس*. دار صادر

218 Lorde, A. (1981) "The Uses of Anger: Women Responding to Racism" in *Women's Studies Quarterly*.

219 Butler, J. (2020) *The Force of Non-Violence: An Ethico-Political Bind.* London/ New York: Verso.

TIED TONGUES

220 al-Udhari, A. (2017) *Classical Poems by Arab Women.* Saqi Books.

221 **It has recently been reborn in modern-day form in Saudi Arabia as a market and festival, complete with literacy competitions and prizes, as in days of yore.**

222 **Mahmoud Darwish was a famous Palestinian poet.**

223 Darwish, M. (2007) "In Jerusalem" in Joudah, F. (trans.) *The Butterfly's Burden.* Hexham: Bloodaxe Books.

224 Sagan, C. (1985) *Cosmos.* Ballantine Books.

225 Haeri, N. (2003) *Sacred Language, Ordinary People: Dilemmas of Culture.* New York: Palgrave Macmillan.

226 Abouzahr, H. (2021) "How Arabs Have Failed Their Language," *New Lines Magazine*, July 13. Available at: https://newlinesmag.com/argument/how-arabs-have-failed-their-language/.

227 Haeri, N. *Sacred Language, Ordinary People.*

228 Romdhani, N. (2019) "The Arab world needs literacy programmes more than ever," *Arab Weekly*, June 16. Available at: https://thearabweekly.com/arab-world-needs-literacy-programmes-more-ever.

229 Haeri, N. *Sacred Language, Ordinary People.*

230 Quoted in Forbes, M. (2015) "Iraqi writer Sinan Antoon on his novels about his embattled homeland," *The National*, May 14. Available at: https://www.thenationalnews.com/arts/iraqi-writer-sinan-antoon-on-his-novels-about-his-embattled-homeland-1.116492.

231 UNESCO Silk Roads Programme (no date) "Did you know?: The evolution of the Arabic language in the Silk Roads." Available at: https://en.unesco.org/silkroad/content/did-you-know-evolution-arabic-language-silk-roads.

232 Nehmé, L. (2010) "A glimpse of the development of the Nabataean script into Arabic based on old and new epigraphic material" in Macdonald, M.C.A. (ed.) "The development of Arabic as a written language," *Proceedings of the Seminar for Arabian Studies*, 40, pp. 47–88; Benmamoun, E. and Bassiouney, R. (2020) *Routledge Handbook of Arabic Linguistics*. Abingdon: Routledge; "The Nabataean script: a bridge between the Aramaic and the Arabic alphabets." Available at: https://www.pathsofjordan.net/some-facts-about-the-nabataeans/the-nabataean-script-a-bridge-between-the-aramaic-and-the-arabic-alphabets.

233 Macdonald, M.C.A. (2008) "Ancient North Arabian" in Woodard, R.D. (ed.) *The Ancient Languages of Syria-Palestine and Arabia*. Cambridge: Cambridge University Press, pp. 179—224.

234 Stein, P. (2009) "Literacy in Pre-Islamic Arabia: An Analysis of the Epigraphic Evidence" in Neuwirth, A., Sinai, N. and Marx, M. (eds) (2009) *The Qur'ān in Context: Historical and Literary Investigations into the Qur'ānnic Milieu*. Leiden: Brill.

235 Stein, P., "Literacy in Pre-Islamic Arabia: An Analysis of the Epigraphic Evidence."

236 Coope, J.A. (2017) "The Umayyads" in T*he Most Noble of People: Religious, Ethnic, and Gender Identity in Muslim Spain*. Ann Arbor: University of Michigan Press, pp. 20–37.

237 Al Suwaiyan, L.A. (2018) "Diglossia in the Arabic Language," *International Journal of Language and Linguistics*, 5(3), pp. 228–38. Available at: https://doi.org/10.30845/ijll.v5n3p22.

238 Aslan, R. *No god but God.*

239 Aslan, R. *No god but God.*

240 Nasr, S.H. (2004) *The Heart of Islam: Enduring Values for Humanity*. New York: HarperCollins.

241 Bakhtin, M.M. (1982) *The Dialogic Imagination*. Austin: University of Texas Press.

242 Forsyth, M. (2016) *The Etymologicon: A Circular Stroll Through the Hidden Connections of the English Language*. London: Icon Books.

243 Shehadeh, R. (2015) *Language of War, Language of Peace: Palestine, Israel and the Search for Justice*. London: Profile Books.

244 Hamid, R. and Morris, A. (2021) "Media Reporting on Palestine," Centre for Media Monitoring, May. Available at: https://cfmm.org.uk/wp-content/uploads/2021/05/MediaReportingOnPalestine-Report-and-Toolkit-Final.pdf.

245 Ghalayini, B. (ed.) (2022) *Palestine +100: Stories from a Century after the Nakba*. Dallas: Deep Vellum Publishing.

246 Willingham, D.T. (2018) "Is Listening to a Book the Same Thing as Reading It?," *The New York Times*, December 8. Available at: https://www.nytimes.com/2018/12/08/opinion/sunday/audiobooks-reading-cheating-listening.html.

247 The Scientific World (2021) "What Happens to Your Brain When You Read?," February 7. Available at: https://www.scientificworldinfo.com/2021/02/how-does-reading-affect-your-brain.html.

248 Darwish, M. "In Jerusalem."

SUPERWOMAN

249 Lepore, J. (2014) "Wonder Woman's Secret Past," *The New Yorker*, September 15. Available at: https://www.newyorker.com/magazine/2014/09/22/last-amazon.

250 Worth, R. (2021) *The Creators of Batman: Bob, Bill & the Dark Knight*. Barnsley: White Owl Books.

251 Yueh, L. (2014) "Superheroes and the billion dollar global box office," BBC News, May 30. Available at: https://www.bbc.co.uk/news/business-27637292.

252 **She exists only in the comic books, rather than in the film franchise.**

253 Baldanzi, J. and Rashid, H. (2020) *Ms. Marvel's America: No Normal.* Jackson: University Press of Mississippi.

254 Woerner, M. (2017) "Why I Cried Through the Fight Scenes in *Wonder Woman*," *Los Angeles Times*, June 5. Available at: https://www.latimes.com/ entertainment/herocomplex/la-et-hc-wonder-woman-crying-20170605-htmlstory.html.

255 **With admittedly conservative results, of course.**

256 Thomas, N. (2018) "Superheroes and villains: Who's more violent might surprise you," CNN, November 2. Available at: https://edition.cnn.com/ 2018/11/02/health/superhero-movie-violence-study/index.html.

257 Philips, M. (2021) "Violence in the American Imaginary: Gender, Race, and the Politics of Superheroes," *American Political Science Review*, 116(3), pp. 470–83. Available at: https://doi.org/10.1017/s0003055421000952.

258 Quoted in Shaheen, J. (2012) "How the Media Created the Muslim Monster Myth," *The Nation*, June 14.

259 Kramer, M. (2006) "Islam's Coming Crusade," The Washington Institute for Near East Policy, March 20. Available at: https://www.washingtoninstitute.org/ policy-analysis/islams-coming-crusade.

260 Lyons, J. (2014) *Islam Through Western Eyes: From the Crusades to the War on Terrorism.* New York: Columbia University Press.

261 Beydoun, K.A. (2016) "America banned Muslims long before Donald Trump," *Washington Post*, August 18. Available at: https://www.washingtonpost. com/opinions/trumps-anti-muslim-stance-echoes-a-us-law-from-the-1700s/2016/08/18/6da7b486-6585-11e6-8b27-bb8ba39497a2_story.html.

262 John Ashcroft was the attorney general of the United States in September 2001.

263 Quoted in Esch, J. (2010) "'Legitimizing the "War on Terror': Political Myth in Official-Level Rhetoric," *Political Psychology*, 31(3), pp. 357–91. Available at: https://doi.org/10.1111/j.1467-9221.2010.00762.x.

264 Friedman, T. (2001) "There Is a Long, Long War Ahead," *The New York Times*, September 13.

265 Lyons, J. *Islam Through Western Eyes.*

266 Al-Azmeh, A. and Fokas, E. *Islam in Europe.*

267 Goody, J. (2004) *Islam in Europe.* Cambridge, UK/Malden, MA: Polity Press.

268 Kundnani, A. (2015) "Violence comes home: an interview with Arun Kundnani," *OpenDemocracy*, November 22. Available at: https://www.opendemocracy.net/en/violence-comes-home-interview-with-arun-kundnani/.

269 Aslan, R. *No god but God.*

270 Berlatsky, N. (2015) "What 'Ms. Marvel' Gets Right about Comic Book Violence," CBR, January 2. Available at: https://www.cbr.com/what-ms-marvel-gets-right-about-comic-book-violence/.

271 **And this is true even though she is a teenage girl, thus signaling two types of vulnerability (childhood and femaleness).**

272 **See my essays on worry and anger.**

273 Butler, J. *The Force of Non-Violence.*

274 Butler, J. (2020) "Judith Butler on the Case for Nonviolence," *Literary Hub*, February 18. Available at: https://lithub.com/judith-butler-on-the-case-for-nonviolence/.

275 Lee, S. (November 17, 2013) "Stan Lee on what is a superhero." OUPblog. https://blog.oup.com/2013/11/stan-lee-on-what-is-a-superhero/.

BINT

276 Bouhdiba, A. (2008) *Sexuality in Islam*. Abingdon: Routledge.

277 Sahih al-Bukhari, Book 67, Hadith 125.

278 Doumato, E.A. "Hearing Other Voices: Christian Women and the Coming of Islam."

279 Ahmed, L. *Women and Gender in Islam*.

280 Among these are Amina Wadud, Leila Ahmed, Fatema Mernissi, Riffat Hassan and Asma Barlas.

281 Keddie, N.R. (2006) *Women in the Middle East: Past and Present*. Princeton: Princeton University Press.

282 **Not unlike the federal system in the US, which means, for instance, that women now have the right to an abortion in New York, but not Alabama.**

283 Ahmed, L. *Women and Gender in Islam*.

284 Droß-Krüpe, K. and Fink, S. (2021) *Powerful Women in the Ancient World: Perception and (Self)Presentation. Proceedings of the 8th Melammu Workshop, Kassel, January 30–February 1, 2019*. Münster: Zaphon.

285 **Not all scholars agree that Aisha was a child; however, the mainstream view is that she was quite young.**

286 Ahmed, L. *Women and Gender in Islam*.

287 El Saadawi, N. (2007) *The Hidden Face of Eve: Women in the Arab World*. London: Zed Books.

288 Eltahawy, M. (2012) "Why Do They Hate Us?" *Foreign Policy*, April 23. Available at: https://foreignpolicy.com/2012/04/23/why-do-they-hate-us/

289 **Obviously, not all Muslims are Arab and not all Arabs are Muslims! However, since I sit at the intersection of these two identities, it is the**

combination of the two, both culturally and personally, on which I focus in this essay.

290 Burgo, J. (2019) "Why shame is good," *Vox*, April 18. Available at: https://www.vox.com/first-person/2019/4/18/18308346/shame-toxic-productive.

291 As someone who benefits, with my white skin, from the white supremacist structures that affect our world, but also as someone who does not suffer the anti-Blackness and classism within both Palestinian society and Muslim society more generally.

292 I imagine she felt this way, of course.

293 van Es, M.A. (2018) "Muslims Denouncing Violent Extremism," *Journal of Muslims in Europe*, 7(2), pp. 146–66. Available at: https://doi.org/10.1163/22117954-12341374.

294 van Es, M.A. "Muslims Denouncing Violent Extremism."

295 van Es, M.A. "Muslims Denouncing Violent Extremism."

296 Manzoor-Khan, S. *Tangled in Terror.*

297 Suhaiymah Manzoor-Khan also discusses a 2017 Prevent presentation given to university staff which included a list of views to be monitored: among these were "support for Palestine."

298 Manzoor-Khan, S. *Tangled in Terror.*

299 Du Bois, W.E.B. (1903) *The Souls of Black Folk: Essays and Sketches.* Chicago: A.C. McClurg & Co.

300 Said, E.W. (1978) *Orientalism.* New York: Pantheon Books.

301 Whitehead, J. (2008) "Why I Hate the Palestinians," *Zionism Now*, January 6. Available at: http://zionism-now.blogspot.com/2008/01/why-i-hate-palestinians.html.

302 Black, I. (2018) *Enemies and Neighbours: Arabs and Jews in Palestine and Israel, 1917–2017.* London: Penguin Books.

303 Jewish Virtual Library (no date) "Ahad Ha'am." Available at: https://www.jewishvirtuallibrary.org/ahad-ha-rsquo-am.

304 **He also presciently wrote that "for now, they [the Arabs] do not consider our actions as presenting a future danger to them . . . But, if the time comes that our people's life in Eretz Israel will develop to a point where we are taking their place, either slightly or significantly, the natives are not going to just step aside so easily."**

305 Koestler, A. (1949) *Promise and Fulfilment: Palestine 1919–1949*. London: Macmillan.

306 The Editors of Encyclopaedia Britannica (2023) "Balfour Declaration" in *Encyclopaedia Britannica*. Available at: https://www.britannica.com/event/Balfour-Declaration.

307 Khilnani, S. (2022) "The British Empire Was Much Worse Than You Realize," *The New Yorker*, March 25. Available at: https://www.newyorker.com/magazine/2022/04/04/the-british-empire-was-much-worse-than-you-realize-caroline-elkinss-legacy-of-violence?utm_source=NYR_REG_GATE.

308 Khilnani, S. "The British Empire Was Much Worse Than You Realize."

309 Curtis, M. (2021) "How the UK Military Supports Israel's Combat Operations against Palestinians," Declassified UK, May 15. Available at: https://declassifieduk.org/how-the-uk-military-supports-israels-combat-operations-against-palestinians/.

310 Campaign Against Arms Trade (2021) "Israel: Country Profile," November 18. Available at: https://caat.org.uk/data/countries/israel/.

311 Malik, N. (September 27, 2021) "Badenoch's empire comments speak to the enduring mentality of colonialism." *The Guardian*. https://www.theguardian.com/commentisfree/2021/sep/27/badenoch-empire-comments-enduring-mentality-colonialism-britain.

312 Al Jazeera (2018) "May Ziade: The Life of an Arab Feminist Writer," March 21. Available at: https://www.aljazeera.com/program/al-jazeera-world/2018/3/21/may-ziade-the-life-of-an-arab-feminist-writer.

313 Al Jazeera video (2018) "May Ziade: The Life of an Arab Feminist Writer." Available at: https://www.youtube.com/watch?v=Z4oAf7HivKg.

314 Jaffer, J. (no date) "Huda Sharawi" in *Encyclopaedia Britannica*. Available at: https://www.britannica.com/biography/Huda-Sharawi.

315 Author of *Feminism and Nationalism in the Third World*.

316 Fleischmann, E.L. (2000) "The Emergence of the Palestinian Women's Movement, 1929–39," *Journal of Palestine Studies*, 29(3), pp. 16–32. Available at: https://doi.org/10.1525/jps.2000.29.3.02p0054x.

317 Jād, I. (2018) *Palestinian Women's Activism: Nationalism, Secularism, Islamism*. Syracuse, New York: Syracuse University Press.

318 Jād, I. *Palestinian Women's Activism: Nationalism, Secularism, Islamism*.

319 Elia, N. (2017) "Justice is indivisible: Palestine as a feminist issue," *Decolonization: Indigeneity, Education & Society*, 6(1), pp. 45—63.

320 Abu-Lughod, L. (2015) *Do Muslim Women Really Need Saving?* Cambridge, Mass.: Harvard University Press.

321 **Laura Bush famously said, "Because of our recent military gains in much of Afghanistan, women are no longer imprisoned in their homes. They can listen to music and teach their daughters without fear of punishment . . . The fight against terrorism is also a fight for the rights and dignity of women."** https://www.washingtonpost.com/wp-srv/nation/specials/attacked/transcripts/laurabushtext_111701.html

322 Strickland, P. (2014) "Israeli interrogator threatens sexual assault, home demolition, says Palestinian child," *The Electronic Intifada*, March 21. Available at: https://electronicintifada.net/blogs/patrick-strickland/israeli-interrogator-threatens-sexual-assault-home-demolition-says.

323 Jād, I. *Palestinian Women's Activism: Nationalism, Secularism, Islamism*.

324 Al Issa, F.A.-R. and Beck, E. (2020) "Sexual Violence as a War Weapon in Conflict Zones: Palestinian Women's Experience Visiting Loved Ones

in Prisons and Jails," *Affilia*, 36(2), pp. 167–81. Available at: https://doi.org/10.1177/088 6109920978618.

325 Quoted in Awad, S. and Bean, B. (eds) (2020) *Palestine: A Socialist Introduction*. Chicago: Haymarket Books.

326 Jād, I. *Palestinian Women's Activism: Nationalism, Secularism, Islamism.*

327 **For some, this has meant that a more "authentically" Arab or Muslim feminism had to be found elsewhere, such as, as Jād has shown, in a fundamental, political Islam.**

328 Abu-Lughod, L. *Do Muslim Women Really Need Saving?*

329 And racism, and classism, and homophobia.

330 El Saadawi, N. *The Hidden Face of Eve.*

331 Murphy, M. (2018) "The 'Hole-y' City: British Soldiers' Perceptions of Jerusalem during Its Occupation, 1917–1920" in Clarke, J. and Horne, J. (eds) *Militarized Cultural Encounters in the Long Nineteenth Century*. London: Palgrave Macmillan, pp. 343–63. Available at: https://doi.org/10.1007/978-3-319-78229-4_15.

332 Bashear, S. (2004) *Studies in Early Islamic Tradition*. Jerusalem: Hebrew University, Max Schloessinger Memorial Foundation.

333 Oluwaseyi, O.A. (2020) "Mythmaking, Identity Formation and Ethnic Nationalism in Post-colonial Nigeria Through the Lens of Yoruba and Igbo Nationalism" *Politikon*, 48(1), pp. 74–97. Available at: https://doi.org/10.1080/02589346.2020.1861510.

334 Mernissi, F. (1991) *Women and Islam: An Historical and Theological Enquiry*. Hoboken, NJ: Wiley-Blackwell.

FURTHER READING

SELECTED PRIMARY TEXTS

Al-Sīrah al-Nabawiyyah (السيرة النبوية) **Muhammad Ibn Ishaq**

There exist multiple versions and translations of this early Islamic text, reconstructed a century or so after the Prophet's death; the most famous of these is the 1955 translation by Alfred Guillaume, *The Life of Muhammad: A Translation of Ishaq's Sirat Rasul Allah* (Oxford University Press, 1955).

Kitab At-Tabaqat Al-Kabir (كتاب الطبقات الكبير) **Muhammad Ibn Sa'd**

This multi-volume collection of short biographies of early Islamic personalities, written by Ibn Sa'd (d. 845), includes a volume titled *The Women of Medina*, which refers to Nusayba. The most readily available English-language version of this collection is published by Ta-Ha publishers and translated by Aisha Bewley.

Tarikh al-Tabari (تاريخ الطبري) **Abu Ja'far Al-Tabari**

This other great tome of early Islamic history was written in the tenth century and includes much more than just the life of the Prophet. Again, multiple versions and translations exist; one of them, edited by Ehsan Yarshater and published by SUNY Press, consists of forty volumes!

Sahih al-Bukhari (صحيح البخاري) **Muhammad al-Bukhari**

This multi-volume collection of hadiths (the sayings and teachings of the Prophet Muhammad and his companions), put together by the Uzbek Muslim scholar Muhammad al-Bukhari, is considered one of the most authentic of the hadith compendiums. Multiple versions and translations exist; there are even electronic versions available online.

SELECTED SECONDARY TEXTS

Ahmed, Leila. (1992) *Women and Gender in Islam: Historical Roots of a Modern Debate*. New Haven; London: Yale University Press.

Ali, Kecia and Leaman, Oliver. (2007) *Islam: The Key Concepts*. Abingdon: Routledge.

Aslan, Reza. (2012) *No God but God: The Origins and Evolution of Islam*. New York: Ember.

Bashīr, Sulaymān. (2004) *Studies in Early Islamic Tradition*. Jerusalem: Max Schloessinger Memorial Foundation, The Hebrew University of Jerusalem.

Bouhdiba, Abdelwahab. (2013) *Sexuality in Islam*. Abingdon: Routledge.

Donner, Fred McGraw. (2012) *Muhammad and the Believers: at the origins of Islam*. Harvard: Harvard University Press.

Hazleton, Lesley. (2014) *The First Muslim: the story of Muhammad*. New York: Riverhead Books.

Hourani, Albert Habib. (2013) *A History of the Arab Peoples*. London: Faber.

Hoyland, Robert G. (2001) *Arabia and the Arabs: From the Bronze Age to the Coming of Islam*. Abingdon: Routledge.

Kashani-Sabet, Firoozeh. (2015) *Gender in Judaism and Islam: Common Lives, Uncommon Heritage*. New York: New York University Press.

Mackintosh-Smith, Tim. (2019) *Arabs: A 3,000-year History of Peoples, Tribes and Empires*. Yale: Yale University Press.

Maria, Nadia. (2015) *Women, Islam, and Abbasid Identity*. Harvard: Harvard University Press.

Masalha, Nour. (2018) *Palestine: A Four Thousand Year History*. London: Zed.

Mernissi, Fatima. (2004) *Women and Islam: An Historical and Theological Enquiry*. New Delhi: Women Unlimited.

Mernissi, Fatima. (1975) *Beyond the Veil*. Cambridge, Mass: Schenkman Publ. Co.; New York: Wiley.

Nasr, Seyyed Hossein. (2004) *The Heart of Islam: Enduring Values for Humanity*. New York: Harpercollins.

Neuwirth, Angelika, Sinai, Nikolai and Michael Marx (eds). (2010) *The Qur'ān in Context: Historical and Literary Investigations into the Qur'ānic Milieu*. Leiden: Brill.

Peters, F.E. (2017) *The Arabs and Arabia on the Eve of Islam*. Abingdon: Routledge.

Sadawi, Nawal. (2015) *The Hidden Face of Eve: Women in the Arab World.* London: Zed Books.

Udhari, Abdullah. (2017) *Classical Poems by Arab Women.* London: Saqi Books.

Wadud, Amina. (1999) *Qur'an and Woman.* Oxford: Oxford University Press.

PERMISSION CREDITS

ACKNOWLEDGEMENTS

I am incredibly grateful to my agent, Clare Alexander, without whom I would not have had the self-belief to put a proposal together, let alone a whole manuscript. I am equally grateful to my editor at Canongate, Ellah Wakatama, who then saw something in the proposal and took a big chance on it. Thank you. Between the pandemic and my health falling off a cliff, this book was, in the end, written in less-than-ideal circumstances, but it is thanks to you both that it exists at all. I still can't quite believe it does.

Having worked in publishing for a little while, I am more aware than most how much time (often unpaid!), effort (often under-recognized!) and energy (often in place of all other activities!) goes into the making of a book by every single member of a publishing team. So, thank you, I am so grateful to you all and am sorry I can only name a few here: Rali Chorbadzhiyska, thank you for doing all the crucial editorial assistant work with which I am very familiar; Leila Cruickshank, thank you for managing complicated timelines and being so understanding of my complex health needs; Alice Shortland, thank you for your creativity and hard work in getting the book to readers; Rafi Romaya, thank you for dealing with my endlessly annoying feedback and creating the eye-catching cover; Alison Eagle Eyes Rae, thank you for your close reading, kind words and tireless work sorting through variations in transliteration; Lorraine McCann, thank you for your incredibly thorough close reading; Jenny Fry, thank you for all your confidence, compassion and support; and Anna Frame, thank you for being such a generous and thoughtful publicist—I don't know how you juggle so much work and still manage be so kind and great at your job. I aspire to be like you!

My thanks also go to the brilliant U.S. team at Interlink: thank you to my wonderful editor Michel S. Moushabeck for the warmth and encouragement, and to David Klein for the perceptive copy-edits.

I am indebted to the Royal Society of Literature and the judges of the 2021 St Aubyn Award—Homi K. Bhabha, Fiona St Aubyn and Violet Moller—who, in choosing me as a recipient, provided me with the means to keep going with my writing. I remain extremely surprised at having been chosen, but forever grateful.

I have been extremely fortunate to have had kind and gracious friends and readers who helped shape the manuscript. A huge and special thank-you to Patrick Nathan, your sharp edits transformed the entire collection and gave me much-needed confidence; Noor Hemani, your insights and comments were absolutely vital, I cannot thank you enough; a giant thank-you also to Rachel Kincaid, without your brilliant feedback I would have never taken the time to think about Nusayba more deeply, or played the scenes against each other. I hope I ultimately managed that triangulation you explained! Thank you to my fellow comrades-in-arms, Erica Berry and Octavia Bright, I can't believe I get to regularly message such brilliant writers. I'm so grateful for your time, feedback and encouragement. I am so grateful, also, to all the members of the Creative Non-Fiction group; I was a late addition, and so didn't get your sharp eyes over as much of the book as I would have liked, but the small part I was able to share was ten *thousand* times improved by your generous and insightful comments.

Writing this book was, at times, almost impossible, because holding a laptop was impossible, and thinking in sentences was impossible, because that's what being incredibly unwell does to a body: it makes day-to-day living close to impossible. But I am getting through it, thanks in large part to the friendships both young and old that have made these years of illness bearable, so: thank you, all. I am especially grateful to members of the Yoga for Life Project, as well as to the wonderful women in my life who bring me joy and thought-provoking chats and make me feel OK about not doing so well at the whole writing thing: Ansa, Emma, Catherine, Sigrid, Sasha, Nads, Katy. You are all so inspiringly talented and brilliant, you make me feel cool by as-sociation. An endless thank-you to my lifelines, Hannah and Mairi. Without you and your incredible generosity and warmth, I would be utterly lost. And thank you, of course, to R, for all that you've done.

It feels like an unmanageable task, trying to capture the love and grati-tude I have for my family in a paragraph. They have been kind enough to let me bring them, as characters, into this book and out into the world, but even before that they were kind enough to always support me, to be my constant protectors and providers. Big brothers are often idolized just because they're big brothers, but mine really are special. I'm more grateful than the three of you know—for all that you give me, but also, just to get to be your sister. Thank you especially to Jamal: without your support these last few years, there would definitely have been no book, but there would also possibly have been no *me*.

And the biggest thank-you to my inspiringly hardworking, endlessly giving parents. You are the most impressive people I know. Thank you not only for reading and helping with this book, but for everything that you do—I'll never be able to express the extent of my gratitude and love. I'm so lucky to be your daughter.

Principal de los Libros le agradece la atención dedicada a *Secretos en la oscuridad*, de Robert Bryndza. Esperamos que haya disfrutado de la lectura y le invitamos a visitarnos en www.principaldeloslibros.com, donde encontrará más información sobre nuestras publicaciones.

Si lo desea, también puede seguirnos a través de Facebook, Twitter o Instagram utilizando su teléfono móvil para leer los siguientes códigos QR: